GOD'S ECONOMY, ISRAEL

AND THE NATIONS

— DISCOVERING GOD'S ANCIENT
KINGDOM PRINCIPLES OF BUSINESS —

by

Morris E. Ruddick

ALSO AVAILABLE BY MORRIS RUDDICK

THE JOSEPH-DANIEL CALLING: Facilitating the Release
of the Wealth of the Wicked

TABLE OF CONTENTS

DEDICATION

Dedicating a book is a very personal matter. I've been uniquely blessed by the friends and family the Lord has surrounded me with. Many names have come to mind as I've prayed about this dedication. First, to the man whose name I bear, my father. He was unequivocally the most incredible person I've ever known. Businessman, leader and politician, his love for others, along with the virtues of honor, integrity and excellence were always a model and standard for me.

Then, to my mother, Marguerite Ruddick, who taught my grade school Sunday School classes that introduced me to God's Word. Her love, encouragement and generous spirit have time and again made the difference in me staying the course in the paths I've followed.

And of course, to my dear wife Carol, who is a mighty woman of God with extraordinary talents. I will always be grateful for the wonderfully engaging way she touches the lives of those around her. I treasure her friendship and her faithfulness in sticking with me through my unorthodox journeys in my quest to follow God's will.

Then, to Jill Mitchell. Jill has been not only an encourager of my role in praying into and articulating this Joseph-Daniel calling and the reemergence of these Kingdom principles of business and wealth, but she has unselfishly championed my efforts within many different spheres within the Body.

I also want to note three special friends who made a difference that only God knows. Dave Cerullo, a ministry executive and Gene Nichols, an entrepreneur/prayer warrior, each found time in their busy schedules to call me daily to pray and encourage me during some very dark days many years ago. Bill Biggs, a forerunner and model among Kingdom entrepreneurs, stepped to the plate to make a significant impact on God's plan for my life. Most of us will never know when our obedience is the only thread that holds fast the vision, for those to whom we reach out.

Finally, I want to mention Peter Wagner, Cindy Jacobs, Mike Jacobs and Barbara Wentroble. They have served as forerunners and facilitators in this move of God in the marketplace. Without them, the unfolding timetable of this paradigm shift would not be where it is today.

ACKNOWLEDGEMENTS

D ale Neill, Kingdom entrepreneur, business-owner and president of the International Christian Chamber of Commerce has been a friend and co-laborer in our mutual calling whose input and sensitivity to the Lord have been of inestimable value in both the timing and wholeness represented by the message of this book.

Dr. Bill Bolton's keen insights and experience as a Christian leader and world-class strategist in entrepreneurship have been a priceless source of input as I have sought to define the biblical dynamics of God's economy.

Brad Herman's inside knowledge of the publishing business has been an invaluable asset to both the setup and positioning of this effort.

Irene Thomas' professional editing capabilities, coupled with her own elegant style of writing, have added much to the flow and continuity of this book. Barbara Fox's perceptive and anointed input has resulted in greater clarity, focus and continuity of key points tied to my message.

I also want to acknowledge those who have invested their time on my behalf in interceding for me and for the fulfillment of God's purposes in my life. I'm deeply humbled by this type of sacrifice coming from a long list of dear friends, family and co-laborers in the Lord.

PREFACE

In eras past those who reigned and conquered were those who wielded the military might. Then there was a time when the seats of power rested with those controlling the organizational religious establishments. Most recent centuries have seen rule and authority controlled by national governments defined by geographic boundaries. But during the last decade or so, global rule and power is tilting toward those with economic power.

The realities awakened from 9/11, along with the shift in global seats of power are a part of the reemergence of the clash of all ages, which has frightening parallels to the Nazi rise to power in the late thirties. Despite this radical change in the course of world events, there is a subtle realignment of God's Kingdom rule: with God's economy, Israel and a new breed of Kingdom leaders at the forefront. Kingdom leaders who will build communities and impact nations.

This realignment will release the greatest move of redemption and restoration the world has ever seen. It will usher in the power shift of all ages. God's sovereignty over His creation is being restored, His covenant confirmed and His covenant people becoming the head and not the tail.

The parachurch model that arose in the sixties is giving way to models more suited to the strategic, critical and practical needs of this era: models incorporating not only the spiritual, but the community and economic dimensions of God's riches. They will birth a mix of both micro and macro-level entrepreneurial initiatives designed to build God's Kingdom.

These models will operate on the basis of God's economy, and be driven by cooperative, community and inter-organizational efforts. The restoration of God's economic model will exemplify the scriptural principle of the "power to get wealth that He might establish His covenant."

In addition to sharing an array of personal experiences as I sought to understand and embrace a non-traditional call of God to interlink business and ministry, this effort outlines the significance and timeliness of what has become a significant move of God.

Ancient biblical foundations for this calling, along with biblical principles of entrepreneurship, business and Kingdom wealth are among the topics addressed. Models of Kingdom ventures bypassing regional economic downturns and fulfilling God's purposes in the face of reversals, persecution, disasters and political strife illustrate how God's economy defies the odds. Insights into the times and seasons explain the significance and purpose for this strategic call of God.

God's call on my life, shaped by a Word the Lord spoke to me in the mid-seventies, took me into uncharted waters. Having left a military career in mid-stream to prepare myself in biblical studies for service for the Lord, I was puzzled as the Lord clearly led me into the business world.

Then almost a decade after entering the business world, I took a couple of weeks to get alone with the Lord to fast and pray. Spiritually-speaking, I was a bit battered and confused. First, I had experienced the folding of a once very successful business I knew the Lord had led me to start. Then, despite all my efforts to seek first His Kingdom and His righteousness – the position in the corporate world that had opened after shutting down my business had also seemingly cratered.

High on my priorities of issues brought before the Lord during this time alone with Him was "what am I doing and where is this all going?" And the Lord in His faithfulness spoke a word to me that gave me understanding for that time. But that word, over the years, has also progressively served to provide release and understanding, not only for my own calling, but also for that of others who have been called as I have. What the Lord told me was that I would be serving Him in:

"An interlinking between secular enterprises with overriding ministry objectives."

Then more than another decade later, I had occasion to speak at the big mission conference held every three years known as the GCOWE conference. The Global Conference on World Evangelization attracts between 5,000 to 6,000 mission strategists and practitioners from over 150 nations around the globe.

It was a message that had been burning in my heart since the Lord spoke to me in the mid-seventies about my role in making an impact on kings, rulers and leaders. It was a talk based on the proto-type I had been gleaning from the life of Joseph over the years. I simply called it "The Joseph Calling." The unusual life of this patri-arch seemed to provide clues to the unorthodox steps I was being so strongly drawn to take as I sought God's higher plan for my own life.

The presence of the Lord I sensed as I presented this talk at the Business Executives venue at GCOWE was very strong. But I never expected the type of reception I received after the talk. A number shared that I had defined how God had been leading them for the last ten to twenty years. One man said he thought he had been all alone in being called in this way. Another just grabbed me and hugged me as he repeated the words *thank you* over and over.

For each who came up after my talk, it appeared the message was a release for them. My own calling as a Joseph and a Daniel for this day was one shared by a number of other marketplace believers from around the world. These are ones who had been led and prepared in some very similar ways. It was a calling that would serve a number of strategic community and nation-building func-tions. It was a defining moment for me as I realized my call into uncharted waters was a part of a move of God, designed to counter-act the turbulence of the times we have entered.

Alongside my calling into the business arena, the Lord has molded me as an intercessor. In the mid-nineties, I helped to launch and became the director of an email-based intercession ministry known as the Strategic Intercession Global Network (SIGN). The ministry of SIGN has as its charge "addressing strategic-level issues impacting the Body globally. As I would ask the Lord for wisdom and revelation into these issues there came a clear focus on issues such as Israel, Jewish revival, the persecuted church, Kingdom initiatives to reach the nations and God's economy.

As such this book combines insights I've drawn from my time in God's presence with experiences I've had in implementing these Kingdom initiatives. It includes practical biblical insights into the dynamics comprising this reemergence of His ancient principles of business and wealth.

Strategically, this move of God which is penetrating seats of power in business and government is one I believe will parallel and exceed in impact the rise of the parachurch ministry movement of the late fifties. It is a move of God designed to build communities and impact nations.

It is for these men and women of God – called as God's ambassadors into the spheres of business and government, that this book has been primarily prepared. And to each one, I salute you in the Name of the Lord. May the words of this book provide the release you need to fulfill what the Lord has called you to for this hour.

CHAPTER 1

THE CALLING

This story was not planned. It has simply unfolded. Its foundations really began when I told the Lord that whatever He wanted me to do, wherever He wanted me to go — I was available. What followed has become the journey of one who simply sought to follow and please the Lord.

The calling reflected in this story has been shaped by a Word the Lord spoke to me in the mid-seventies, early in my walk with Him:

> *Just as in the days of Joseph and Daniel, God will bring out mighty works at your hand. As you are led into the midst of the world, kings, leaders and rulers will be converted and humbled. You will work beside them and be given authority; and your counsel will be heeded for their good.*

My hunger to know Him resulted in an insatiable desire to spend time praying and reading the Word of God. As I did, I found myself drawn to reading and re-reading the biblical accounts of Joseph and Daniel. I had cut short a career in the US Marine Corps to pursue biblical studies at a Christian university and seek what I sensed was God's plan for my life — although at that point it was largely undefined, and something akin to the obedience and pilgrimage reflected by Abraham's life. God's unfolding plan for my life became the outgrowth of a mix in commitment, obedience and the time I spent with Him.

It was during this initial time in the re-tooling of this professional combat veteran that the Lord began speaking to me about business. But, business was NOT my background, specialty — or even my desire. So, as one who left a military career with the expectation of joining the pioneering efforts of a para-church operation, I was somewhat taken aback at God's leading and guidance to enter the secular business world as a consultant. It was also becoming apparent that my journey with the Lord was not going to be a traditional one.

The doors opened for a position in a consulting operation with clientele from around the world. This position became the training ground where the Lord honed my expertise and abilities associated with identifying central issues, conducting research into markets and economies, and developing plans and strategies for senior levels of management within Fortune 500 and multi-national corporations.

Yet, despite being convinced of God's "leading" at the point of decisions, I struggled and questioned whether this was really His plan. Hadn't I placed a sterling military career on the altar to make myself available for His purposes for my life? I simply didn't really grasp it, because the traditional mind-set was that if you were REALLY committed, you would be either in the pulpit, a missionary, or working for a para-church ministry.

Then the Lord spoke a very clear Word to me: that I was to start my own consulting business. Now that rattled me. While I had become a pretty good consultant, starting and operating an independent business was outside my comfort zone. However, I received strong words of confirmation and encouragement. So, I took the step.

Stepping Out in Faith

That first year in business was terrible. I mortgaged my home for operating capital. I spent a lot of early morning hours in prayer. I was able to sell one project during that whole first year. I remember my banker admonishing me because he felt my pricing on that project should have been four times what I had charged. At the end of that first year in business; very humbled, out of money, with no projects on the horizon, the Lord showed Himself faithful and strong. In one week, I got requests for six assignments. Half of them started right away. And little by little, things began coming together.

Even at that point, while I knew I was following His leading into the business world, I still really didn't understand. While my primary clientele consisted of Fortune 500 firms, I worked hard at selling my work to ministry organizations. I knew I could help and did. But frankly, despite the strong guidance I had consistently been getting from my time with the Lord, I still didn't completely understand the role of someone completely sold-out to Him — in the world of business.

My consulting firm grew and grew. I took on partners. We had offices in Tulsa, Houston, Chicago and New York. But as we got bigger, instead of simply following His plan, I began looking to use what was developing as a means to please Him. This is not an unusual response from a truly committed believer in business. But in that subtle process of paving new ground, what began as His plan, became my own plan. It was a good plan, but the paradigm had shifted from where this journey had started. And rough waters came.

Challenges

The major markets in which we specialized began drying up. We entered a period of having to shut down offices and let people go. Finally, out of desperation and the need to support my family, we shut this wonderful God-initiated venture down. We shut it down honorably and I moved into the only door that opened — one that opened wide into a position as senior vice president of a $1.4 billion corporation.

The position was challenging and the opportunity was very much of the Lord. Yet, one morning a few months later, as I sat alone in my executive suite, I asked the Lord, "Why?" My original company was very much a God venture. And my heart was greatly saddened that I had somehow missed the Lord's intention for it. The Lord then said to me, "Morris, My purpose for that company was for what I was doing in you."

That response again challenged my "mind-set" of what serving Him with a "full commitment" was all about. Then it was during that time in the corporate world that I began getting simple impressions during my prayer-times concerning "re-possessing the land." I began to consider that $1.4 billion organization, along with its staff and its resources, as belonging to the Lord. That thought and approach — which became reflected in the marketing and planning strategies I had charge over — did not go unchallenged.

I found myself faced with key people hidden in the infrastructure of that organization who belonged to a coven of witches and warlocks. And they considered that organization as "a seat of **their** power." At that juncture in my walk with the Lord, I considered myself as having a fairly robust anointing as a prayer warrior — but the spiritual backlash I began encountering definitely challenged and humbled me.

Yet, I continued to follow God's leading to use my position to begin mobilizing the believers in the organization. I founded and led a Bible study that gained much attention because I had acquired permission to hold it in a seldom-used extra office belonging to the Chairman of the Board. Then, because of a mix between my senior position and my boldness, other Bible studies and prayer groups began springing up, as other believers in turn became bolder and started exercising their God-given authority.

At a point when it appeared everything was about to move into high gear, my time at this organization abruptly came to an end. The man who hired me (the president) held a position sought by others at my peer level — and through craft and deceit, he was terminated. Since I was one of the king's men, my exit followed soon thereafter.

As I went through a painfully slow time of getting resituated, I took a couple of weeks to be alone with the Lord to fast and pray. Spiritually speaking, I was a bit battered and confused. First, my own business folds. Then, all my efforts to seek first His Kingdom and His righteousness in the corporate world also seemingly cratered.

Understanding the Context

High on my priorities of issues brought before the Lord during this time alone with Him was "What am I doing and where is this all going?" And the Lord, in His faithfulness, spoke a Word to me that gave me understanding for that time. That Word, with time, has progressively provided release and understanding not only for me, but for others who have been called as I have. What the Lord told me was that I would be serving Him in:

> *"An interlinking between secular enterprises with overriding ministry objectives."*

In a way that only a Word from God can do, this Word brought peace to my heart. But initially, I frankly didn't know what to do with it.

Since that time, my consulting practice was reestablished, albeit on a much smaller and more flexible basis. Simultaneously, the Lord began giving me more understanding as He progressively refined and defined my function as an intercessor. Then, during the mid-nineties, the Lord began imparting greater insights into that original Word He spoke to me of "Just as in the days of Joseph and Daniel, God will bring out mighty works at your hand – as you are led into the midst of the world." And with the understanding have come opportunities.

So, what has evolved has been forged and tempered as, over the years, I have sought to follow His call into the world of business and enterprise as a Joseph-Daniel: as a businessman called as an instrument of God's purpose. But on another dimension, this calling is the result of a progression of steps of obedience, drawn from the guidance received during my time with Him.

Again, it was during the mid-nineties, when after years of ups and downs and waiting for what I had long been sensing the Lord telling me about my calling, things began to click. It was a time I have to admit when I was very weary in waiting on what I was hearing the Lord tell me. And at times, questioning whether I was really hearing from Him — in the pivotal, life-impacting decisions and steps I had been making, in my pursuit of this plan and purpose which I sensed He was calling me to.

But while there was a weariness in waiting for the manifestation of His promises, there were hours upon hours being spent with Him. Pressing in. Times with Him. Times very precious to me.

They were not only precious times, they were awesome. Times spent just worshiping. Times hashing through things. Times pondering issues. Times just listening. Time just being with Him. There is nothing this world has to offer that can even begin to compare with His presence. With time spent with Him.

Perspective and Release

Then very early one morning, as I found myself sitting in His presence, I realized something very significant. As I did, I told the Lord, that if He NEVER had anything further for me than what He had blessed me with during these times with Him — I wanted Him to know that I would consider it more than enough. And it seems from that point, things began accelerating and dovetailing together.

From that point, the Lord began showing me agendas to target in intercession. He began giving me perspectives and insights into His purposes for penetrating the marketplace with emissaries and ambassadors who would serve on a number of levels — like the Biblical Joseph and Daniel. I began realizing that this unique calling of mine into the marketplace was also the calling of many other committed men and women of God.

It was soon thereafter, through a series of unusual events, that I found myself a part of birthing a very simple Internet ministry designed to address strategic-level issues impacting the Body on a global basis. This humble ministry grew. Primarily by word of mouth, it grew to include intercessors, pastors and heads of prayer ministries from around the world. It grew to have a focus of targeting the revelations I was bringing out of my time with Him.

It was also around this time that opportunities to get involved with what I called **Joseph-type projects** starting emerging. Projects that combined aspects from both business and ministry. As the intercession ministry and Joseph projects crystallized, it became increasingly clearer not only for what the Lord had been preparing me, but the context of what He was doing within the marketplace.

It was at that juncture that the doors began opening to speak about this "interlinking of business and ministry" calling which I had been bantering about for so many years. This began in Pretoria, South Africa, as I addressed a group of missions-minded business executives at the largest gathering of mission strategists and practitioners in the world. Other speaking opportunities followed — each of which has thrust me further into this arena encompassed by this move of God into the marketplace.

CHAPTER 2

THE INTERLINKING OF BUSINESS AND MINISTRY

There is nothing particularly earth-shattering about committed believers operating in the marketplace. **What IS a step beyond the ordinary in all this is when seats of power — in business and in government — are genuinely harnessed to achieve God-ordained purposes** designed to directly advance the Kingdom of God.

Serving the Lord through business was definitely not what I had in mind as I left an exciting and challenging military career. Early in my walk with the Lord, almost mid-stream in my military career, I was captivated by a phrase in a booklet I came across. That phrase stated that "God has a perfect plan for your life." My military career was a good plan for my life; but the Spirit of the Lord seemed to be offering something a great deal more, if I would but trust Him. And I did.

The first steps involved resigning my Marine Corps officer commission and returning to school — to immerse myself in Biblical studies, and then on to get a master's degree. During this time in school, I was intrigued with the pioneering efforts underway within the parachurch arena. I was very impressed by the potential that many of these ministries had to extend the reach of the Church to the unchurched. Probably because of the years I had spent overseas in the Marine Corps, I quickly realized that the Lord was giving me a missions heart.

Yet, upon finishing my graduate studies, God clearly led me into the business arena. I thought perhaps this was just a stepping stone. The position the Lord opened thrust me into a fast-paced role in the consulting business that had me working with senior executives in Fortune 500 and multinational operations. I was definitely operating outside my comfort zone. But the Lord gave me both favor and wisdom to perform the assignments with which I was being tasked.

Traditional Mind-Sets

Still, I continued to struggle with the mind-set that equated a "sold-out" commitment to the Lord with those in pastoral, evangelistic, missionary or parachurch endeavors. Despite a genuine gift of being able to grasp the dynamics of the big picture in my business planning and forecasting consulting activities, I somehow was slow in grasping the significance of what the Lord was developing relative to the uniqueness of my own calling.

Even after launching my own firm, and arriving at a place to where the biggest challenge was in keeping up with growth, I was not completely content. There was something more to the equation of operating a Christian-owned business than what I was able to grasp. I was active in my church. I taught a series of adult classes there and then started and led the first of several home prayer groups for this fellowship. I was on the local board of a Full Gospel Businessmen's Fellowship chapter. As time went on, my wife Carol and I also sponsored a Junior Achievement company at the local Christian high school — which fostered entrepreneurialism from a Christian perspective among the students participating.

But something was missing. And then the primary market our firm served took a radical nosedive. We had grown to almost $1 million in annual revenues with offices in four major cities. But no amount of downsizing seemed to work and we eventually shut down. I already related the transition from a family-owned business to the corporate world, where I found myself on the wrong side politically and out of work after playing a key role in putting this

$1.4 billion corporation back in touch with the marketplace. I was convinced I had missed God and simply wanted to get back on track.

It was at that juncture in my life — out of work and scrambling with intermittent, interim consulting assignments — that I took an extended time to get alone with the Lord and pray. During that time of seeking Him, He spoke a phrase to my heart that has become pivotal in everything I have done since. What the Lord told me was that I would be involved in an "**interlinking between secular business enterprises with overriding ministry objectives.**"

New Mind-Sets

A Word from the Lord will often bring an understanding that initially is grasped more by our spirits than our intellects. However, I was not alone in puzzling over how this worked. The equation of business and ministry — business and missions — or simply the concept of Kingdom businesses — has long both challenged and puzzled those in ministry, those in missions and those in business. Mission strategists have pondered whether you take a missionary and teach him business; or whether you take a businessman and train him in missions.

The answer is neither. It is a calling. It was at that juncture that the Lord began showing me models of some who were forerunners in this arena.

It was soon thereafter that Bill Biggs came into my life. Bill is the CEO and principal stockholder of a firm that manufactures agricultural instrumentation equipment. His firm's unique high-tech equipment is serving to greatly improve the agricultural output wherever it is used. His clientele extends to many nations around the globe. This uncompromising, high-principled yet humble and generous man of God seeks, by his firm's continuing research and development efforts, to provide only the very best innovation to his clientele. Bill's stance in serving the Lord is wisely and non-offensively shared with those he serves. His firm's profits have been reinvested into the development and support of many church community projects impacting numerous nations.

Bill's operation was modeled after that of another Christian entrepreneurial pioneer with whom he was acquainted. While operating my own business, I had always considered the Lord my senior partner. I likewise had sought Him on decisions being made. But Bill's firm and his *modus operandi* demonstrated to me a new dimension in how an interlinking of secular enterprises with overriding ministry objectives could operate.

Despite an income that could support a lavish lifestyle, Bill chose a very simple one. His success in business has long since established for him a handsome personal net worth. Yet, he has chosen to live in tasteful simplicity. His priority and passion were not in the houses or cars he owned, but in the King and His Kingdom he so faithfully served.

Bill also introduced me to a book authored by Stanley Tam, the Christian businessman who had strongly influenced him. His book is titled, "God Owns My Business." (Stanley Tam, God Owns My Business, Horizon House Publishers, Alberta, 1969)

Stanley Tam has become a modern-day model of the principle that "you can't out-give God." He began his entrepreneurial pursuits by building a plastics manufacturing company. As his company grew and matured, he began giving increasingly greater ratios of the firm's profits to support mission outreaches. Primary ownership of his firm eventually was transferred into a foundation, with 96 percent of the profits of his family-owned business going into ministry outreaches.

Precedence for the Business-Ministry Model

It was also during this time of professional transition that I came across an article that spoke of the emergence of business activities within the missions arena — being tagged as tentmaking. Until the Apostle Paul was imprisoned, he was financially supported by his own skills as a tentmaker. I began networking to find out more about this particular form of missionary strategy. I learned that at that time in the mid-eighties, over one-third of the world's population was under the control of totalitarian governments, with either closed or very controlled freedom of worship. That ratio of limited access and closed access nations was growing and one of the means to penetrate these barriers was through business enterprises.

During this search to learn more about tentmaking, I became

acquainted with Ralph Winter and his efforts with the US Center for World Mission. Dr. Ralph Winter is known and respected globally within mission circles as a dean among mission strategists. His books and missions "Perspectives" courses have had an incredible impact on the effectiveness and awareness of modern-day missions. Ralph invited me out to California to discuss the possibility of my heading up a valiant fund-raising effort to acquire the campus facilities his missions coalition group was occupying. That visit revealed to me that the opportunity was not in keeping with God's next step for me.

While visiting with Ralph, he advised me that missionaries who attempted to operate businesses were only diluting the efforts that brought them to the mission field. However, he said that historically there were some models that I might find interesting and with that, he gave me a copy of a pertinent out-of-print book by William Danker. This classic, titled, "Profit for the Lord", (William J. Danker, Profit for the Lord, William Eerdmans Publishing, Grand Rapids, 1971) suggests that the Church's outreach must include ministry to man's economic needs. "*In this nationalistic age, each church must find its own particular economic structure, not adopt one that is dictated by the tradition of other countries.*" Danker points out that we must move beyond the collection plate economy and look to the models developed by "*missionary pioneers like the Moravians and the Basel Mission Trading Company.*"

These models reflected community based businesses that supported the start-up of other strategically located businesses run by believers who used their businesses and associated community relationships as platforms to share the Good News of Jesus. Their operations grew and prospered, both economically and in terms of their ministry. They indeed reflected a genuine "interlinking of secular business enterprises with overriding ministry objectives."

It was also during this time that I became acquainted with Wyn Fountain, a wonderful Christian businessman from New Zealand. Wyn wrote a very compelling book titled "The Other Hundred Hours." His entire premise is based on the fact that there are 168 hours in a given week. Typically, most committed Christians will spend about 12 hours a week in church activity. They'll spend roughly 56 hours sleeping. His book addresses the question facing every believer in business: "What about the other hundred hours?" Wyn writes:

> *These OTHER HUNDRED HOURS are where we live the most important part of our lives. They are the hours where our creativity is channelled into our careers and family life. These are the hours that mainly make us what we are. These hours are important to God. When Jesus taught us to pray*
> > *"Thy Kingdom come, Thy will be done, on earth ...."*
> *He was referring to those other 100 hours more than the 12 we may spend in church activity. This is our great hour of opportunity, as believers in the gospel of Jesus, but unless the church can give a much clearer lead for life in the other hundred hours, that opportunity will be lost. The answer is not just in mere evangelism. Post evangelism instruction must penetrate the fabric of society, where society lives."*

Wyn's book makes repeated reference to "the whole of life." (Fountain, Wyn; *The Other Hundred Hours,* 1984, WIG Fountain Publishing) God's purposes for His people, have always been in the totality of their lives. The book of Deuteronomy is a repository of wisdom on communications, relationships, how to operate a business enterprise, and principles for community and national government. My friend Wyn Fountain understood this principle the Lord was revealing to me step by step about an "interlinking between business and ministry."

The input from Ralph and Wyn proved to be invaluable. During this time, I received a job offer, which was not only a good opportunity professionally, but also seemed to hold potential for the business-ministry goals I was beginning to understand.

CHAPTER 3

CASTING DOWN CROWNS

I became Chief Operating Officer for a group of three interrelated, family-owned businesses. The owner was a believer and had left the helm of these businesses to pursue a fourth, more lucrative opportunity. As such, these operations were somewhat without direction and very much in the red. My can-do Marine Corps background, coupled with my successful experience in developing the marketplace strategy for a large corporate turnaround situation enabled me, with God's help, to bring things into the black for the entire group of firms within four months of joining this operation.

Simultaneously, God had brought my wife Carol and me to a dynamite fellowship known as Happy Church. It combined a strong local church with a first-class worldwide television teaching ministry. A real model for its time, balancing the local church and parachurch functions. Two individual ministries operating autonomously, yet in complete support of one another — combining a local thrust with an impactful worldwide outreach. This prayer-centered fellowship's husband-wife team combined the operation of the church, led by Pastor Wally Hickey, with some of the strongest, soundest Biblical teaching available through his wife Marilyn.

Not only did I have a unique organizational model that combined the two very essential functions between the local church and parachurch functions, but I had in my pastor an example of one whose heart is fully sold-out to God's agendas. As a bonus, this

Spirit-led man of God had a special burden for encouraging business leaders into the fullness of their calling.

Professionally, I knew I had been called into the business world. I knew, like Joseph the Patriarch, that God had a purpose for this calling. I also knew that God's purpose in my business pursuits was for more, much more than simply being a witness for Him in the marketplace. I do not mean in any way to demean or degrade the importance of being a witness, especially in arenas like the marketplace where His light traditionally is quite dim. I also knew that while I had some good natural talents and abilities, my role in the business world — as an instrument of God's purpose — would require me to tackle challenges that I was incapable of doing in the natural.

Balance and Preparation

God's handiwork in molding me for what He was leading me toward involved bringing me to a place of balance between my own talents and abilities, my relationship with Him, and the recognition that I can do all things in Him. However, in being able to do "all things," my dependency is totally and completely upon Him.

It was soon after I moved into this new position and new location that I became acquainted with Gilman Hill. Gil owns a small oil operating company and like my friend Bill Biggs, has set his operation up to be used for God's purposes. Here was still another Christian-owned business model, that had as its purpose utilizing a business as a means to accomplish God's purposes. There was another dimension to Gil's operation — to harness resources with God's agendas in mind.

During this time, I was invited to attend a gathering of the Fellowship of Companies for Christ. This unique organization targets a membership from among the ranks of CEOs and COOs of entrepreneurial to large corporate enterprises. Members of this organization indeed were believers at the helm of organizations who were looking for "something more" in their roles as Christians serving as CEOs and COOs.

Spiritually, this proved to be a rich time. The Biblical teachings I was getting from my fellowship gave focus to the importance of continually immersing ourselves in the truths of God's Word. Of committing God's Word to memory. And of prayer. Time spent with the Lord on a regular basis. Understanding and operating through the ministry of the Holy Spirit. None of this was new; but it was a place of genuine nourishment and growth. I was soon asked to teach adult classes on intercession and missions. In addition, I again became increasingly involved in leading small groups in which I was called upon, not only to teach, but to lead the prayers offered for the members of the groups. As I found opportunity to pray regularly for others, I began to notice something. People were coming back — frequently — with reports of what the Lord had done in answer to a particular prayer.

At work, the challenges of bringing my group of companies back into profitability were accomplished; and now we were starting to grow. I began implementing strategies — involving wholesome value-based corporate images — that I had tested and found to have a very positive impact while working in my previous role in the large corporation. Both the owner and clients seemed pleased. I was again in a position in which I could approach the firm I was working for, along with its influence and resources, as belonging to the Lord. After all, it was owned by a Christian.

Setbacks, Challenges and Change

This again proved naïve on my part. I again ran into a **seat of power,** led by an employee who had been with the firm for several years, and was threatened by the steps I was taking and policies I was establishing. Through craft and deceit, and the employee's long-term relationship with the owner, I was accused of unfounded improprieties with a client. Without the opportunity to answer the accusations, I was abruptly told I had an hour to clean out my desk. This group of three firms subsequently folded eighteen months later, and the employee who had brought the accusations against me walked away with their clientele. As for me, I was again out of work. I couldn't help wondering if the Lord simply wanted me in a place where I could operate independently and be available to do His bidding.

I began seeking the Lord in prayer about the situation and what He had in store next. Things soon began happening — and quickly. Within a week I received a phone call from a man by the name of

John Craigen. John was back in the U.S. for a visit. He was founder and Managing Director of a unique management consulting firm operating within mainland China. The staff was a joint venture between a group of Western consultants and a group of Chinese professionals serving as their counterparts. Each member of the Western team was an expert in his or her own field. Each had at least a master's degree, with most possessing doctorates. But the distinctive of the Westerners with this firm, was that they were all believers, who upon being invited to join this operation, raised their own support for the privilege of serving with this group. While conducting a diversity of management consulting assignments for Chinese enterprises and government entities, these Western professionals established relationships in Chinese professional and governmental circles and held discreet Bible studies for those they found spiritually hungry. John and I had a number of phone conversations and I was then invited to join this group. It would be necessary for me to raise funds to support my family in China and to provide for such essentials as transportation and moving overseas.

Raising our own support was a new paradigm for me. But there was no question in my mind that the Lord was in this. If He had brought us this far, then raising the needed support would be a small matter. I was encouraged by my pastor and many others. I didn't know the first thing about what missionaries call "itinerating" — or how missionaries are supposed to raise the funds for their support. But we prayed, and began to take steps toward this move. There were a couple of other hurdles — like the unsold home at our previous location; and the moderate amount of debt I had taken on while getting resituated from the transition after losing my position in the large corporation. But, since God had opened this unusual opportunity to join this unique group in China, there was no doubt in my mind that He had an answer to taking care of each of these hurdles.

Everything about this move was coming together in such unusual ways at that point, that it seemed almost like we were walking on the water. Then during the midst of an incredible array of developments in these step by step preparations, the bottom fell out. My pastor came to me and solemnly told me that he felt something was wrong and that we needed to cancel our plans. While we still had several weeks before our scheduled time of leaving, no one seemed to know where our support was going to come from, plus there was the issue of this unsold house.

In retrospect, two separate groups of business owners I knew were putting together both funding and commitments to enable us to participate in this venture. But we didn't know it at the time. Nor did those in our church leadership, who no doubt had decided against our move because they felt they were providing wise guidance. I was crushed, more than I'd ever been crushed in my life. I genuinely thought I knew what Joseph must have felt after having correctly interpreted the dream of Pharaoh's chief butler — who undoubtedly had the means to bring about Joseph's release — only to be ignored for two more years.

I was out of work. We had just given away our second car, plus a wide array of our household belongings. I simply didn't understand. It seemed the more I pressed into the Lord and the more I got involved in this interlinking of business and ministry, the more serious our problems became.

Yet, I knew beyond any shadow of a doubt of God's goodness. I knew that His plans for us are for good and not for evil, to give us a hope and a future. I knew of His faithfulness. Despite that knowledge, at that juncture, more than any other in my life, I struggled with despair. Yet, in the midst of what had become almost a whirlwind of chaos and disillusionment — I kept praying and seeking the Lord. Even then, the darkness seemed to keep encroaching at our door. My wonderful, faithful wife, Carol was understandably fed up with me at that point. But despite her own disillusionment, she hung in there with me, although as I look back, I suspect only by a thread.

New Horizons

Shortly thereafter, an unusual thing took place, which may simply have been the Lord's way of helping to begin restoring my shattered confidence. Our church office called to tell me I had been provided with a fully paid ticket for a group trip to China. I suspect the funding for that trip came from one of the businessmen, who had been planning on supporting our move to China.

The trip was a time of renewal and restoration for me. Our group served as couriers in making several crossings into mainland China with Bibles destined for the persecuted believers in the underground church. Some of our people were caught with the Bibles as they went through customs and had them confiscated. I led a team that, by the grace of God, got everything we carried on each trip through the border.

This trek to China took place only a couple of months before the Tienanmin Square incident. The spiritual hunger in that nation was fueled by the spiritual vacuum created when Mao expelled all the missionaries and imprisoned or martyred the Chinese church leadership during the cultural revolution. Despite the persecution, the underground church in China was alive and it was growing. Our simple efforts of carrying a couple of heavy bags laden with Chinese Bibles were helping. At that time, there were believers with only a single Bible being shared among a whole community. I will never forget the exhilaration the first time I successfully crossed the border — with all the Bibles intact — knowing how much they were needed. I simultaneously wanted to weep and to shout for joy. That trip established relationships and restored a fresh zeal in my heart for what the Lord might have ahead for us.

Yet, whereas we witnessed things coming together with incredible speed and precision as we had been taking steps to join the Christian-owned consulting operation in China, the time of recovery was very different. We faced closed doors and stone walls. My efforts to get resituated were slow and arduous and at times seemed like crawling from the bottom of a deep pit. I looked for job opportunities, but nothing materialized. The only thing that seemed to come to mind as I prayed was what the Lord had told to me several years prior.

It was after I had left the security of a military career. The summer after completing Biblical studies, prior to entering a secular university to get a master's degree, I was in prayer. During that time some incredible developments had taken place toward this venture of finding God's perfect plan for my life. I had established some life-long relationships. I was befriended and mentored by two very powerful men of prayer from the faculty. Men whose lives exemplified the scripture in Romans that "as many as are led by the

Spirit of God, they are the sons of God." (Romans 8:14) Men of faith, who like Abraham knew what it meant to believe God — *"to call those things that are not as though they are."* (Romans 4:17)

The Cost of the Calling

Yet, we had also faced a level of spiritual backlash during that time of Biblical studies that sought to both derail and destroy us. Carol had given birth to a long-awaited, beautiful baby girl. We named her Rebekah. Tragically, Rebekah died three weeks later. I remember Carol crying and crying as we lay in bed at night. It was hard to understand. We had placed the security of a fast-paced military career on the altar to follow God's leading — now this.

I had recently been reading and reflecting on the Biblical story of Job. Job's response when calamity befell him was to turn to God. The scripture in Job 1:20 says that after Job received a series of devastating reports regarding his business and his family, *"Job fell to the ground and worshipped."* It also says (v 22) that *"through all this Job did not sin nor did he blame God."* We didn't understand. But, the scripture was clear. We sent out announcements to friends and family that quoted Job. It said, *"The Lord gave and the Lord has taken away. Blessed be the name of the Lord."*

The heaviness of losing a child was compounded by our unpaid medical bills. Our Christian community surrounded us with their love and prayers. Yet, there were some who suggested that perhaps this time of returning to school to seek God's will had become foolhardy. Maybe it was time to simply leave and reenter the work force. However, despite the setbacks and the challenges, we continued toward the goal of what the Lord had guided us to do.

In an unusual set of circumstances, the Lord opened the doors for me to start a motor-home rental business. Due to the gasoline shortage in the early '70s, I had been unable to sell our motor home when we returned to school. So we simply parked it alongside our home. Then one day, there was a knock on the door. A couple who lived two blocks away asked if we would consider renting it to them. They went so far as to advise us of what the going rate was, AND to bring us a copy of a rental contract they had used a year prior. That simple business arrangement enabled us to continue.

Faith, Perseverance and Wisdom

Several months after losing our daughter Rebekah, after I had finished my Biblical studies and was preparing to enter graduate school, I was in prayer and asked the Lord, "where is this all going?" The Lord almost immediately spoke to my heart as clearly as I had ever heard Him. He said simply, "You're going to be a consultant." Hearing from Him that day brought such a level of peace to my heart, that I never thought to ask any "hows" or "for-whats". But without ever seeking to fulfill that Word myself, the only door that opened for me after completing my master's program was with an international consulting firm.

So now as I was trying to get my bearings and get settled after the reversals of our attempted venture to China, I was desperately trying to hear what the Lord had by way of direction. The only thing that came to mind consistently as I prayed was the recollection of that time the Lord spoke to me and said, "You're going to be a consultant." So that was the course I took. It didn't happen overnight. Getting reestablished seemed to come slower and harder than anything I had ever done before.

During the midst of this difficult time, I also had an unusual thought occur to me. If we had been planning to go to China to reach out to our Asian counterparts through home Bible studies, why couldn't we just reach out to our local unsaved international community in the same way — right where we were?

Faithfulness and Opportunity

We teamed up with another couple who served as our assistants. Mary Langan played a key and faithful role in what developed. Mary is a Filipina national. She is a faithful and powerful intercessor and had many contacts within the international community. We came up with a format that seemed to break the mold of any home groups in which I had been involved to date. And we had been in some good ones!

Carol and I were products of the Charismatic renewal/Jesus movement of the late '60s and early '70s. Believers got together in those days regularly and often just spontaneously; because we were simply hungry for more of God. These home gatherings had a variety of formats. Some were centered around a study of Scripture. Some were simply times of sharing and praying and fellowship. But in all of them, there was a vitality and aliveness that prevailed. A vitality reflected by **God operating in our midst**. There was a spark that each day brought, because at the forefront of everything else going on was the wonderment of seeing God answer prayer in the everyday situations of our lives. And these gatherings — for prayer, for fellowship and to study the Word — were very important facilitators in what we were seeing God do in our midst.

Indeed we had been a part of some very exciting and effective home groups. But we modeled this international outreach group to fit the purpose we sought. We held it on a Saturday evening. It was centered around a potluck dinner. Leaders arrived early for typically thirty minutes to an hour of prayer prior to the meeting. The first hour combined some lively uplifting songs of worship with a simple and straight-forward practical teaching from Scripture, followed by a time of prayer for the individual needs shared by those present. Then we broke for the very informal potluck dinner and fellowship.

The believers who attended included Americans who had lived and traveled overseas and some from the international community. This core of believers was encouraged to bring their unsaved international friends, which they did. God began answering prayers. We also found the informal time of fellowship, standing around in small groups nibbling the exotic international dishes, gave much opportunity to share the Lord and to continue praying for those who may not have mentioned their needs during the first hour of the gathering. As much and sometimes more was happening spiritually over these meals than in the Bible study/prayer times themselves. God was indeed operating in our midst. The number of those attending each week was averaging between 15 and 20 people.

The requests for prayer were practical and real. One week an unsaved man from the Middle East came who had been out of work for almost a year. The report the next week was that a call had come to him two days after he had been prayed for and he was now happily re-employed.

A New Dimension

Then one week, as I was conducting the Bible teaching, I began having strange physical sensations. Something distracting. Something amiss that I was almost physically "feeling." Finally, I stopped my teaching and simply asked, "Is there anyone here who is in pain?" Six hands shot up. The Asian lady sitting next to me had a migraine headache. An African brother had a growth that had appeared on his neck. We simply stopped and prayed. Suddenly, four of the six people became quite excited. The problem they had walked in with was no longer there. Word of this got out. The next week, over forty came. From then on, our average attendance was between 40 and 50, and sometimes more. The non-believers who came began increasing. One particular month, of those being baptized at our church — 16 were among those who had been brought to the Lord during our simple Saturday evening gatherings.

In this process of the Lord acquainting us with these new paradigms of both business and ministry, He was giving us strategic insights into effective models needed in the marketplace — both business and ministry models. In many ways I was starting to realize that what I had been called to do represented some breaking of old molds and a paving of new ground.

Despite the missteps surrounding our botched attempts to join the Christian management consulting group in China, the Lord was still with us. He was not only still with us, He was not by any means finished with us.

So, step-by-step, we began recovering from our painful setbacks and began moving forward.

CHAPTER 4

EMBRACING HIS HEART

It was not long until I transitioned back into the consulting arena. My consulting practice grew and stabilized, yet at that juncture, it never took on the dimensions of my original firm. But the ministry dynamic in my calling was coming to the forefront. My activities at church and within the mission arena grew and prospered. I moved into serving as a district home fellowship group leader with oversight of several home groups. Our groups represented well over 200 of the people in our church. I was teaching classes on how to run an effective home group. I was also active in our fellowship's prayer and missions activities. In addition, I was leading a small group of businessmen. It was at that time I was asked to serve on the board of our combined church-ministry, which included a respected worldwide television ministry, a Bible-school and a K-12 Christian school.

Significant changes were underway during the early '90's. Changes impacting my approach to business. PCs were gaining in application. With all my ministry activities, our income was adequate, but left things a bit cramped when it came to something like computerizing my business.

Richard Mull and his wonderful wife Eva had been part of a home group I led. Although this dynamic couple had moved in order to further the opportunities before them with their outreach to the Korean community, we had stayed in touch. Richard and Eva were people of prayer. Richard called me one day and told me the Lord had spoken to him to send me a rather large check — that was to be applied to the purchase of a computer.

Richard's act of generosity and obedience was timely and strategic. It made the goal of computerizing my business pertinent and possible. I took the leap and transitioned into putting my client reports together via my new 486 personal computer. The changes that came from that cannot be calculated. The Lord was providing the first steps toward developing my consulting practice into being increasingly flexible and mobile.

Around that same time I began feeling there was something more the Lord wanted from my time with Him. As I prayed about what that might be, I found myself telling the Lord that "if He wanted to awaken me in the middle of the night to intercede in prayer for specific agendas of His — I would be available." I learned years ago, when I told the Lord that "wherever He wanted me to go, whatever He wanted me to do, that I was available" — not to make commitments like that lightly — the Lord will indeed take them very seriously.

My Call to Intercession

My call to intercession had actually come several years prior to that. Right after completing my master's degree program, I was on my first business trip in my new position with the international consulting firm I had joined. I had just checked into my hotel. I opened the door to my room and noticed an open Bible on the table across the room. A distinct thought occurred to me as I glanced across the room at that Bible, that *maybe the Lord had a message for me on the open page.* I went over to the Bible. It was opened to Jeremiah 51:20. My eyes fell to the verses that read, *You are my battle axe and weapon of war, with you I will break nations in pieces, with you I will destroy kingdoms.* I wondered what that might mean for me – and dropped my bags and headed out to a meeting. That evening, after dinner, I sat down and pulled out my Bible. It fell open to that very same verse. The next day, in my devotions I again opened my Bible to Jeremiah 51:20!

By that time, I KNEW the Lord had a message for me in that

verse. After returning home, my wife Carol and I got together with Paul and Connie McClendon to pray. Paul had been a professor of mine. He and Connie had become close friends during my Biblical and mission strategy studies at Oral Roberts University. His friendship had grown from a strong mentoring relationship to one in which we had become regular prayer partners. Paul, was a man with a strategic, global perspective and a keen insight into new paradigms for building the Kingdom of God. Paul and Connie were world-class intercessors. We got together regularly in each other's homes — mostly for the purpose of praying together. I shared with them the unusual experience with the Jeremiah 51 scripture.

Connie's response was almost immediate. She said, "Maybe the Lord is calling Morris into a special ministry of intercession." I replied, "I know, but it is something more than that." My time with Him was already a high priority for me; but I was being challenged to reach toward something more. And I did. Indeed that did prove to be my actual call into intercession; but "the something more than that" began unfolding many years later and would prove to be an important part of this interlinking of business and ministry calling.

Strategic Steps

So, almost two decades later, another key step in this call as an intercessor took place when I told the Lord I was willing to allow Him to awaken me in the middle of the night to intercede. The result was the Lord would periodically awaken me at 3:00 A.M. to pray specifically for something or someone. Then there would be times I'd be awakened at 2:00 A.M. and sometimes at 1:30 A.M. Coupled with the agendas the Lord would impress me to be praying for during these times was a dimension to my fellowship with Him unlike anything I had ever previously experienced. There were times that I can only describe as though I was actually with Him in His Throne Room. His presence with me was that strong. It was during these times in His awesome presence, that as I prayed, I KNEW I was experiencing His heart on the matters for which I was interceding.

In the business arena, I began to recognize a strategic dimension to the assignments being sent my way. A man I had known several years prior while serving on the board of a Full Gospel Businessman

Fellowship gave me a call to tell me about a new firm he was forming.

Bill Bartlett had previously been the CEO of the largest manufacturer of flares, incinerators, burners and kilns for the petrochemical industry. He had served faithfully at the helm of that firm. His role in directing 15 years of its growth resulted in the company enjoying the business of clientele from around the world.

When the owners wanted to cash in on their investment, Bill brought in the new owners. After the takeover, the new owners thanked him for his contribution to the firm's successful growth and position in the marketplace — but they wanted their own man in the top position. After an interim time of various consulting activities, Bill called to tell me that he had found an investment partner, a Fortune 500 company to help him build a competitor to his old firm.

Bill is a first-class team builder, and he put together an incredible team of world-class experts in this field for his new operation. I was contracted to conduct the first market strategy evaluation when this firm was launching its first few months of business. The report I prepared proved pivotal, and became the first of several such evaluations I conducted for Bill and his firm. His success with this operation is a tribute not only to his hard work and wisdom, but to God's hand on this man of God. Bill's firm grew to $70 million (US) in annual revenues in seven years.

Spiritual Dimensions

I also recognized that my consulting services seemed to be called upon at pivotal junctures for a select group of global ministries. I have always sought the Lord in prayer on behalf of each of the assignments I've conducted. While the largest preponderance of my clients has been senior executives with Fortune 500 and multinational firms, it has always been a distinct and special blessing to me when I have been called in to serve ministries that have been making an impact in building God's Kingdom.

I've never quite fit the mold of most ministry consultants. No doubt there are numerous good ones. But not unlike the consultants that specialize in the Washington-based defense industries, known as the beltway bandits; there are similar ministry specialists who keenly understand the ropes and hot buttons needed to gain entrance and exploit the inner circles of their target clients. At issue is expediency and making recommendations that dovetail with the pet agendas of the movers and shakers within client organizations.

Making an Impact

In positioning myself to clients over the years, I have made the statement to large corporations as well as to ministries that I tell the truth. That well may be why I seem to be brought in at pivotal junctures — to address matters and come up with plans and recommendations that will bring change, innovation and results rather than more of the same. Don't misunderstand me. I'm not talking about being crass or indiscrete, but to simply allow truth and wisdom to prevail for the client's long term benefit.

In 1980 I began a series of assignments for Xerox Corporation. They were designed to evaluate trends and come up with a forecast of what the "office of the 1990s" was going to require. My assignment followed Xerox's loss of the low-end of the copier market to the Japanese. Until that time they had dominated the copier market and the erosion of this important segment of their business had jolted them. Our results "that there would be a major paradigm shift from a hardware orientation to a software orientation" came nose-to-nose with a major blind-spot that was adversely impacting not only Xerox, but other major high-tech suppliers of that day.

The momentum of Xerox's success had stifled their innovation and ability to realistically respond to the fast-change taking place in the office environment. Xerox had been seriously losing market share to competitors who were in touch with the marketplace and able to respond to the change underway.

Our assignments with Xerox took place during the time of the inception of PCs. Xerox had the technology, but they were out of touch and were misapplying the advantages they had. When we entered the picture they had already "bombed out" in their attempts to promote an executive work-station they developed called the "Star." But then not long afterward, due to the transmigration of key personnel, the design of the "Star" became the foundation for what is now the Macintosh computer line.

My recommendations to Xerox included entering the facsimile

business — because in the minds of potential customers Xerox had great credibility with anything that made a "copy." Their move into this line of equipment became one of their most profitable divisions before arthritic institutional policies again separated them from the market they sought to serve.

In the entrepreneurial sphere, I've conducted a number of assignments in support of Israel's Technology Incubator Program. Over the years, new immigrants to Israel have included inventors of numerous world-class technologies. This comprehensive business incubator program serves to commercialize these technologies. It is one of the most successful technological innovation programs operating in the world.

In ministry circles I've been told that my appeal is my innovation and flexibility, and that I bring the credibility of having the experience and skills required in serving large global corporate clientele.

Specialty in Addressing Change

In almost every instance, my consulting services have been addressing organizations or markets undergoing significant change. That has especially been the case with the assignments I have periodically been called to conduct for CBN. CBN has been and is a pacesetter because they have refused to allow their past successes to define their current course and thrust. My recommendation in an assignment for CBN established what has become a standard among ministry organizations to call their clients to thank them for their support and ask if they could pray for them — without any appeal for funds. Later, I helped position the format of their flagship television program to appeal more to the unchurched, while still attracting those believers who supported their premiere TV show.

But in returning to the transitions that were taking place in my own *modus operandi* in the early '90s — in the balance reflected in my business versus ministry activities — I was being guided by the truth in Matthew 6:33. *"Seek ye first God's Kingdom and His righteousness, and all these other things will be added unto you."*

In getting up to pray in the middle of the night, I was indeed putting my time with Him before my desire for sleep. Meanwhile, the time requirements for my growing ministry activities were encroaching on the time I spent with my business. Simultaneously it seemed that I now had to fight for each step of success in the business arena. While it was evident that I was moving more deeply into this "interlinking of business and ministry," I also at times felt as though the Lord had me on a leash. While there was the thought that short-term sacrifices are required for the higher-level answers to my willingness to follow the Lord on this venture of my calling, I was experiencing frustration.

There simply wasn't the fullness and business success I was expecting. Based on what I knew I was able to accomplish, my revenues from business never seemed to allow me to get beyond the level of just juggling our finances. There was very little by way of savings, and nothing to speak of being put away for retirement.

My Own Transitions

So, I began bringing these issues to the Lord in prayer. Was I missing something? Were there blind spots I needed to recognize and adjust in what I was doing? Was I hearing Him correctly regarding this balancing act between business and ministry that I kept doggedly pursuing? Was I to make a move into "full-time ministry?" Little did I realize, but at the time I was on the brink of a number of very important transitions in my calling. Neither did I realize at the time that there was a pioneering dimension to my calling — a paving of new ground. With that there were costs to pay in staying the course. My calling was one that fit outside the box of the ministry models to which I had been exposed.

The way the Lord answered these specific inquiries is something I'll carry with me through the rest of my days here on earth. It was one of those VERY early morning hours. The rest of my household was asleep and I was in the family room just basking in His presence. Although I had been pondering the issues of what appeared as constraints to more of a fullness on the business side of things, I realized that there was nothing that could compare with these times spent with Him.

With that came an awareness. Although my focus on business activity was very much something to which God had opened the doors, guided me into, and given me the wisdom in which to excel, I realized that in this interlinking of business and ministry calling on my life — I had chosen the "better portion (Luke 10:42)." As this awareness came upon me, it was then that I told the Lord, that if I never took another step beyond the level I was operating in with my business, because of these times spent in His presence, I would consider it more than enough.

From that point, things began to change. I already had had more than a couple of clients who referred to me as a strategic thinker, one gifted in being able to identify central issues. It seemed that my perspective was broadening, and a number of things began to accelerate and dovetail together. Among them were new relationships and activities that were to thrust me into a new realm of God's opportunity and purpose.

CHAPTER 5

CHANGE AND TRANSITIONS

Change was happening on a number of levels. Fast change. Change that would broaden my horizons. One significant area of that change began when I first started connecting to the Internet. I was fascinated. I marveled at the ease of communicating between distant parts of the globe. I discovered web sites from all around the world. As I investigated more, I had a keen, growing interest in learning what Christians were doing on the Internet. I couldn't help comparing the parallel to the early days of television and earnestly prayed that Christians would recognize and seize the opportunity to use this growing medium for God's purposes.

Far too many Christians in the early days of television viewed the medium as evil, when in fact it was neutral. Television would become the product of those who paved the way in its development, those who recognized and seized the opportunities to use it — for God's purposes. Unfortunately, despite some very forward-thinking Christians, far too many Christians were much too slow in discerning and capitalizing on the opportunities for utilizing this medium for God's agendas. In the mid-nineties the Internet was clearly at the same juncture as TV was back in the early '50s.

As I began to visit some of the early Christian web sites, I found myself with a growing desire to learn if there was a place or group operating via the Internet — where Christians were able to address in intercession strategic-level issues impacting the Body of Christ globally. As I would visit what appeared to be pertinent web sites, I'd shoot off an email to the sponsoring organization, asking if they or some group they knew were targeting intercessory efforts toward strategic-level issues impacting the Body.

Of the many emails I sent off I did not get one affirmative answer to my inquiry. However, I did get two replies indicating that 'no,' they were not aware of any such activity – BUT that they were very interested in what I was suggesting: interceding for strategic-level issues impacting the Body on a global basis.

One of the answers came from a pastor with his own web site. The other came from a former engineering consultant, who had set up a server to host Christian discussion groups. The goal he was working toward was to build a ministry that — via the Internet — connected and enabled communications between members of the Body of Christ. He was already hosting special interest groups and forums on worship, cell groups, the prophetic and another that involved discussions and testimonies from the renewal movement. The interesting thing about the two replies was that these two men, and one other had recently begun talking to one another.

Michael Enos, the hydro-engineer, was in the early stages of developing Global Resources Ministries Inc. (GRMI) which has had a vision of networking believers through interest-specific email discussion groups. Rich Carey, the pastor, was already writing some very penetrating newsletter columns that he was posting on his own web site. Rohn Price was the third person. He was at the forefront of activities involving a significant move of God within Messianic Judaism. Not long thereafter, the Strategic Intercession Global Network — SIGN — was birthed.

God-Birthed Opportunity

Everyone agreed that my description of "addressing in intercession strategic-level issues impacting the Body on a global basis" was to be the core purpose of this new email-member-based ministry. Web-site notices, as well as notices on the other discussion groups hosted by GRMI began identifying those intercessors interested in participating in this new Internet ministry.

Then the issue came down to what needed to be sent out to the growing number of intercessors joining the SIGN team. As I prayed, a number of key points seemed to come together; and I put together a draft and sent it to Rich, Michael and Rohn to review. They each felt that I had not only hit on the key issues, but also on the format to be sent out to the member intercessors. The others in the group felt I had both the vision and anointing to lead this unique Internet intercession group. Thus, I assumed the helm of the Strategic Intercession Global Network.

Simultaneously, in my quest to learn more about what Christians were doing on the Internet, I began communicating and meeting with a growing number of mission-oriented strategists and practitioners. One key relationship which resulted from these meetings was with Pete Holzmann. This humble man of God has probably done more than any single individual to bring technology to the forefront — to connect and facilitate communications between those involved in global missions. Pete is one of those forward thinkers who operates behind the scenes getting the job done — without any desire for recognition or credit. A former business owner from Silicon Valley, Pete is very much at the forefront of this move of God in the marketplace.

I didn't realize it at the time, but Pete would later make a simple suggestion that would prove to be a pivotal step forward in my marketplace calling. Yet, even at this point, I wondered if the Lord had not kept me in this business-ministry harness all these years — just to release me into these new paradigms of ministry starting to emerge, as the Body started communicating and strategizing on a more in-depth and spontaneous basis.

Expanding and Defining

I began giving more and more focus to my role with the Strategic Intercession Global Network (SIGN). Yet, I realized, for all my talents in the area of being a strategic thinker and defining central issues, that I didn't know where to begin in defining and targeting "strategic-level issues impacting the Body." So I simply started to take these inquiries to the Lord. As a result, step by step, I began to recognize and discern key issues to target in intercession. Global issues impacting the Body.

Around that same time, the Lord began impressing me with a particular truth found in Psalm 15. This psalm speaks of one *walking with integrity and working righteousness, and speaking truth in his heart ... of swearing to his own hurt and not changing.* **Speaking truth in your own heart**. What this means is that defense mechanisms, self-justification, deceptive perceptions and anything else that causes us to fall short in our own thought-lives need to be brought before the Lord and adjusted.

Scripture tells us that our God is a consuming fire. The closer we draw to Him, the hotter the fire — His holiness — and with that, the more essential is this requirement of speaking truth in our own hearts. Our level of intimacy with Him is contingent on our willingness to be genuinely real in prayer — AND to allow Him the latitude to take us beyond our issues. Pressing into the Lord in this way is always a joy. But at times, it can be humbling and even painful. It certainly goes against the grain of our natural, self-protective "human nature." However, it's a cost with incalculable rewards.

This pressing into the Lord with honesty was needed for my venture into the SIGN ministry — if I expected these efforts to bear fruit and to result in those Words I so long to hear at the end of this life: *"well done, good and faithful servant."* With the costs of this ministry was coming a remarkable unfolding of insights and keys into mysteries. Keys into the mysteries of God's Kingdom.

Meanwhile, Michael and Rohn invited me to become the third partner in the incorporation of GRMI. I accepted. Rohn is a man of prayer with an unusual prophetic gifting. Michael is a brilliant visionary, with a fervent devotion to the Lord. The primary GRMI vision to provide the framework for connecting key groups within the Body via the Internet was, in my mind, a worthy objective. Our first board meeting followed the 1996 annual Messiah Conference hosted by the Messianic Jewish Alliance of America (MJAA). This proved to be my introduction into Messianic Judaism and an awakening into one of the most significant, yet subtle moves of God underway in our day.

Introduction to Messianic Judaism

At the foundation of Messianic Judaism is its mission strategy that respects the integrity of the culture of the people being reached with the Good News of the Messiah Jesus. Despite the fact that the Church founded by the Apostle Peter was essentially a Jewish Church, modern-day outreach to the Jews has, for the most part, served to assimilate them into a culturally Gentile Church. Yet, the Gentile Church has so much to learn about the Hebraic roots of our faith.

The modern-day Messianic Jewish movement is attracting a growing number of Jewish believers in Jesus who hunger to reach other Jews with the good news of Messiah Jesus, and they are dramatically doing so by rightfully retaining their Jewish identity. More Jews have come to the Lord since the Israeli Six-Day War in 1967 than in all the time since our Lord walked the face of the earth. During the '50s, there were only a handful of Messianic Jewish synagogues in the US. Today there are more than 400.

One of the pivotal pioneers in this movement is a man, now with the Lord, by the name of Martin Chernoff. The mantle that was on this mighty man of God has fallen to his two sons, Joel and David. David is the rabbi/pastor of the Messianic Jewish synagogue started by his father. Joel heads up the Messianic Jewish Alliance of America (MJAA). The MJAA's annual conference is the largest gathering of Messianic Jewish believers in the world.

I felt right at home at the Messiah conference. As a bonus, I finally met Rohn Price and his wife Wendy face to face! I not only soaked in the worship and the talks, but I began meeting people who would later become lifelong friends. Some were a part of the Strategic Intercession Global Network I was leading. Others were involved in the popular "New Wine" email forum hosted by GRMI. At the core of those I was getting to know were members of David Chernoff's congregation, Beth Yeshua.

Amidst the regular activities of the conference was a special meeting for people interested in a venture that Joel Chernoff believed would prove to be a significant support to Israel as times became more tenuous in the Holy Land. This was my first introduction to the MJAA Joseph Project.

It was at this conference that I was befriended by Bob and Tara Winer. Bob, a pioneer and leader in the Messianic Jewish movement, is a medical practitioner with specialties in neurology, psychophar-macology and psychiatry. Bob operates his medical practice three days a week and spends two days a week with his numerous ministry pursuits. I also really connected with Mitch and Barbara Fox. Mitch and Barbara have been a part of the infrastructure of Beth Yeshua and of the MJAA since the '70s. Barbara is an incredible intercessor and one of the early members of the SIGN ministry team. Jeff Lowenthal, attorney and author, and his wife Dinky exemplify that revival passion that we should each maintain for the Lord. There were many, many others.

The spiritual vitality and presence of the Lord evidenced not only by this conference, but also by the services I later attended at Congregation Beth Yeshua, reminded me of the early days of the Charismatic renewal when Carol and I were brand new, very hungry believers.

This was all yet another part of the equation that the Lord was bringing me into — as I continued to seek Him first, in what seemed to be a very long and extended quest to find His plan and purpose my life. A quest that had precipitated my resigning my commission mid-course in my military career. Over twenty years had passed since turning the reins over to Him. And I still wasn't there. I knew it involved an interlinking of business and ministry. But there was a richness and a purpose to this journey with the Lord that He was placing in my heart. No doubt, I was making an impact as I followed the steps of His leading, but I still felt like there was much more to what was currently unfolding.

CHAPTER 6

BROKENNESS

The SIGN ministry grew. At one point, Rich and I noticed that we had members from 18 nations around the globe. Yet, we also concluded that we weren't after numbers, but quality in the maturity of the intercessors on the team. The email posts that went out began to take on an increasing prophetic quality to them. An increasing importance was being given to Israel, Jewish revival and the persecuted church. We gave much focus to what we called the "Issachar context"— an understanding of the times with a knowing of what to do.

My connections and activities within the mission community were increasing and proving fruitful. GRMI was growing. Meaningful consulting projects were landing at the right time. Whenever I was on the East Coast, I made it a point to swing by and visit my friends at Congregation Beth Yeshua. Not only did they make me feel welcome, but I felt this wonderful group of dynamic believers had adopted me! The number of ministries that had been birthed from this congregation's members astounded me. This group of believers was not just active, but making an incredible impact for the Lord. If there was ever such a thing as an apostolic congregation, this was certainly it.

Tragedy

In August of 1996, our second oldest daughter Trisha came out for a visit. Trish was 30 at the time. She was the administrator for a unique mission organization that trained and mobilized health-care professionals in the disaster response arena. I showed Trish what I had been doing with the SIGN ministry, as well as within the mission realm. The dovetailing of our respective passions in our service to the Lord made this one of the sweetest times we had ever spent together. Carol and I had planned a trip to Durango — which included a scenic ride across the wilderness on an old steam-driven train. We decided that it was a fortuitous opportunity for Carol and Trish — instead of Carol and me — to take this trip together, and have a special time as mother and daughter. It proved to be just that.

Then in late October, we received a phone call. A call after which we would never be the same. Trisha — wife, mother of two, missionary — was found dead. Foul play was suspected. In shock, we caught the first flight out. Amidst tears, Carol and I prayed together as our flight proceeded to its destination — and told the Lord that we forgave whoever was responsible. That was a decision which the Lord honored and one on which we've never turned our backs.

The next few days were a blur. The tragedy didn't seem real. But it was. It was all too real. I contacted our pastor, as well as those I was in ministry with via email. Prayers on our behalf were being offered from around the world. The shock of Trish's death was compounded by the revelation that she had been murdered — brutally murdered.

The events surrounding a funeral have a contagion all of their own. Being surrounded by family. The phone calls. The visits. Reaching out to other family members. Being reached out to. The touching, meaningful things said. The stupid, inane things said. For me, the only thing that brought real relief and comfort was the time I was able to get alone with the Lord. I had been a professional warrior with over two years of front-line and behind-enemy-lines combat experience. But this was more than anything I had ever encountered before. I did the only thing I knew how to do. Pray. I arose very early and poured out my heart to the Lord. I sent email messages to those I knew would pray for us.

I remember pondering the years past — leading up to this time. Knowing beyond any shadow of a doubt that Trisha was with the

Lord, but still not having anything close to all the answers as to what had happened. She was gone — in the prime of her life — that was enough.

I was comforted in knowing of Trish's deep commitment to the Lord. We had raised our children to know Him. And Trish had been on fire for the Lord. She had had one of those defining moments — in which a believer realizes their purpose for being — while she was involved in mission work in India. Her life had truly become hidden with God in Christ.

As I reflected on the memories, so much seemed to have evolved from my own life-changing salvation experience. For a believer, a situation like this is where the rubber meets the road.

Satisfying Spiritual Hunger

I remember a time when I had questioned my own purpose for being. In the early '70s, less than a couple of years after my second year in Vietnam, I found myself hungry spiritually. I wasn't interested in what I then referred to as "churchianity." After more than two years of combat, I wasn't looking for something frilly or superficial — or in "playing church." But I was very interested in "knowing" the Lord. A year prior, not long after returning to the States from my last visit to Vietnam, for the first time in my life, I had met some people who carried their Bibles around with them .... and talked about Jesus like they really "knew" Him. I was a fairly seasoned Marine combat officer, who had traveled the world, lived in other cultures and languages. As one who had the ability to size people up fairly quickly and accurately, I saw something in the lives of some turned-on believers fresh out of the hippie culture. Something that was very, very real.

I had grown up in a little Dutch Reformed Church on the East Coast. It was a fine little church. My mother taught Sunday School. I memorized all the verses along the way that I was supposed to. I was taught to believe in God and that Jesus was the Son of God. But I remember as a teenager, even as a kid, recognizing that there was a gap I simply hadn't bridged. God seemed so distant. I recall praying and I recall that hunger to "know" the Lord. I tried one time to read the Bible. Never got through Genesis. But then, the impact of these former hippies resulted in my starting to read the New Testament. At the time, I headed up a mobile training team that was teaching a three-week training course down in Puerto Rico for Marine recon units. I read the New Testament every free moment I could get, and was praying .... "Lord, I want to know You."

I had read through all of the Gospels and was at the seventh chapter in the book of Acts. Stephen was getting stoned. In light of my own combat experiences, I could relate to what was happening to Stephen. Stephen was indeed dying for what he believed in. I had been in many situations — more than I cared to recall — in which I really thought I was about to die for what I believed in.

Then the question crossed my mind. In what did I believe for which I was willing to die? The answers that came to my mind were very clear. As a professional Marine, I'd been willing to die for my country. For the Marine Corps. And that those I left behind might know that I'd died honorably and bravely — fighting like a Marine.

At that point, with these thoughts going through my head, the Lord spoke to me — for the first time — and very simply asked, "Would you be willing to do that for Me?"

In a moment in time I recognized, despite my good intentions, how empty my priorities had been, because the Lord had not been in them. So I said, "Yes, Lord. Wherever You want me to go, whatever You want me to do, here I am." I experienced the awesome presence and peace of God. It was unlike anything I had ever experienced before. His presence lasted and lasted. My life was never the same after that. My hunger for more of Him was insatiable. Serving Him became my purpose for being.

Change, Challenge and Perspective

A couple of years later, I had left my military career to step out on faith and pursue the preparation I felt I needed to fulfill HIS plan and purpose for my life. Although I already had a college degree, I returned to university life to pursue Biblical studies as a full-time student. Married, three children, and my wife Carol was pregnant. We were out there really walking on the water!

I recalled in the middle of this time at Oral Roberts University when our daughter Rebekah died suddenly. It was after her death that the Lord imparted to me a real heart understanding of Philippians 1:21 — "to live is Christ and to die is gain." Rebekah's passing, and the mountain of hospital bills we faced (along with the devil mocking), seemed to test everything we had stepped out in faith to follow.

After Trish's death, I couldn't help but sense the parallel. Trish was 30. That was the same age as I was when Rebekah died. Some things in this life simply are not designed for answers in the way we know them — but if we allow the Lord, He will connect the dots, where HE deems it important. Trish's death brought me back to that same truth the Lord imparted with our loss of Rebekah.

The perspective in Philippians, "to live is Christ," was the only answer that had *any* relevance. In a word, apart from Him, nothing this life has to offer has any real meaning. Over the years, I've found that scripture to be profoundly applicable in both the good, as well as the challenging times, whether the answers have been clear – or whether we've been going through a time in which the answers allude you. I've had many times in which I've felt "*to live is Christ*" has been the only reason I've had for being here. Times of brokenness. But in the times of brokenness, I found that it is "*no longer I who lives, but Christ who lives in me.*"

We all have areas in our lives that make us happy. Yet, I've come to realize that joy, that is His joy, is much more satisfying and genuine. So far beyond my aversion for "churchianity" that I wanted to sidestep during the time I sought to "know Him." Joy, real joy, comes from walking with Him, being "touched" by Him and allowing ourselves to be a vessel to touch the lives of others. That's why it's been of critical importance to me to truly understand the calling and anointing He has on my life, as well the gifts in which I operate most fluently — so that I can "flow" IN HIM.

The longer I have walked with the Lord, the more I have come to realize that this life we are now living is nothing without Him. This is what Paul refers to as "dying daily." If we truly desire in this life to be instruments of His love, instruments of His power — and instruments of His purpose, then our life truly must be so completely merged with His that the issues of the flesh no longer have any bearing or importance for us. It is the transference of His

Life into our goals, activities, circumstances and relationships —
not as a one-time infusion, but on a daily basis. His Life!

I also recalled that during my time in Vietnam there were the
Marines I called "dress-blues" Marines. The Marine dress blue
uniform is pretty sharp. It's used in parades and ceremonies. It's
worn by Marines serving on White House duty. But there were
some Marines I encountered who I don't think typically lasted long
or got very far. These were ones who liked the glitter of the dress
blues and the parades, but not the mud — or the sacrifices — or the
dangers associated with what Marines are trained for in combat. In
the same way, we have our share of fair-weather, "bless-me club"
Christians. In reflecting on Trish's death and Rebekah's death, I
realized that what this walk with the Lord comes down to is the
cost. The cost of commitment. The cost of total surrender to Him.

Watchman Nee was a man who paid a high cost for his faith
through years of imprisonment in China. He once made the statement
that "it is the crushed flower that exudes the greatest fragrance." I
think Watchman Nee's words really sum it up. It's not the fair
weather types who exude that sweet aroma of Christ, of Messiah
Jesus. 2 Corinthians 2 through 4 really capture this truth: (2:14) *"Now
thanks be to God who always leads us in triumph in Christ, and
through us diffuses the fragrance of His knowledge in every place.
For we are to God the fragrance of Christ among those who are being
saved and among those who are perishing .... to the one we are the
aroma of death to death, and to the other the aroma of Life itself ...
(4:2) Therefore, since we have this ministry, as we have received
mercy, we do not lose heart .... (4:6) for it is God who commands light
to shine out of darkness .... But we have this treasure in earthen
vessels, that the excellence of the power may be of God and not us.
We are hard pressed on every side, yet not crushed; we are perplexed,
but not in despair; persecuted, but not forsaken; struck down, but not
destroyed, always carrying about in our body the dying of the Lord
Jesus, that the Life of Jesus also may be manifested ....*

So, after Trish's death, as I reflected on the "cost." This was not
a time to turn away from the Lord. Trish's death was in no way
God's doing. We needed Him now more than ever.

I remembered something significant the Lord showed me while

serving as a Senior VP in the turnaround of the $1.4 billion corporation. I was reading in Proverbs one morning and came across a verse that gripped me. The 32nd verse of the 16th chapter read: *"He who is slow to anger is better than the mighty, And he who rules his spirit than he who takes a city."* I knew the Lord was preparing me for something. The man who had hired me — the president of the firm — had been released in a very unjust way. On the same day that verse in Proverbs 16 was made to seem so real to me, the Chairman of the firm called me into his office. He explained that his reason for calling me in had nothing to do with how well I had been performing in my job. I was simply one of the former president's men and I also was being released. But I knew that despite the Chairman's intentions, the Lord had His own intentions in the matter, and that He was the one moving me on. So, without any rancor, I told him that. The Chairman, who professed to be a believer, commented before I left his office that day, that he wished he had what I had in my walk with the Lord. *"He who rules his own spirit is mightier than he who takes a city."*

I can't say that I felt much like I was ruling my own spirit as we went through the steps leading to Trish's funeral. But that was the point the Lord had imparted to me years prior with the scripture on *"ruling your own spirit"* — it's not about feelings. And the difference is in making the choice — to rule your own spirit and keep focused on the Lord. I kept praying and God was indeed very real to me during that time.

A Turning Point

The day after the funeral, I was in prayer, and I asked the Lord if He would share with me what was happening in the heavenlies that gave entrance to Trish's death. I knew from my time in prayer during those previous few days, that there are times when we simply can't allow ourselves the latitude to pursue the unanswerable "whys" and "what ifs" and "if onlys." But understanding the dynamics of what was taking place spiritually was something I sought for wisdom about, so that I could alert others to this wisdom via my SIGN intercession ministry.

I didn't realize it then, but that was the first time I had

approached something I was experiencing — in quite that way. It was an act that incorporated the truths of dying to self and ruling your own spirit. It was pushing past my own pain, in order to discern the spiritual dynamics underway — that were impacting others in the Body. That would prove to mark a new means to uncover enemy strategies operating against the Body — a very significant aspect to what I was doing with the SIGN ministry.

CHAPTER 7

THE JOSEPH MODEL

As I began seeking the Lord for an understanding of the dynamics of what was taking place spiritually — surrounding Trish's death — my first impression was of an incredible level of warfare taking place in the heavenlies. The trials of life are a fact of life. As I prayed I became aware that there are times when attacks against committed believers take place, and that these times are the result of one of two things. Either it is a result of spiritual backlash for something that has recently been accomplished for the Kingdom. Or it is designed as a desperate diversion by the evil one to attempt to throw off course something that is about to be accomplished.

As I was praying the morning after Trish's funeral, I recalled that right after the service, a family member shared a vision which an acquaintance with a strong prophetic gifting had had. The vision simply was of the hand of a heavenly being pointing and saying: "You talk too much." This in turn was followed by a related story about a dream someone else had in which there was a fire — a fire set in motion due to loose, misguided tongues.

As I was sitting before the Lord in prayer, I began to realize the consequences resulting from loose tongues of those in ministry. Misguided and loose tongues create open doors of vulnerability among those in the Body to attacks from the enemy. Especially, the loose tongues of those called and anointed for Christian service.

The "impressions" and thoughts were coming fast at that point.

I reflected that the power of the evil one compared to the power of God is nothing. But, if the enemy can entice anointed believers into the soulish realm and direct their efforts according to His purposes, the enemy can not only undermine and sidetrack individuals called by God, but entire ministries and moves of God.

I began to realize that the enemy is after the anointing. He wants to harness and divert for his own purposes the power of God operating in anointed believers. It all came back to the key truths the Lord had been speaking to me during this difficult time of preparing for Trish's funeral. Dying to self — daily. Ruling our own spirits. The spiritual protection which my daughter — who was deeply involved in ministry — should have had, simply was not there.

Loose, misguided tongues from God's anointed give prey to the enemy's intentions, with the result that innocent believers in God's service get hurt and the Lord's agendas are undermined. I began sending out a series of email posts to the SIGN team of intercessors. It was the first of many similar insights to counter strategies being unleashed by Satan.

Realities and Pressures

The time after the funeral was harder on me than the time before it. The gatherings and activities with friends and family help strengthen you during the time immediately after a death. And the amassing of prayers on our behalf were certainly critical. But, after returning home from the funeral, and as I settled back into my work routine, there was simply a heaviness that seemed to accompany me. I remembered the Words Jesus spoke to Peter in Luke 22: *"Simon, Simon, Satan has asked to have all of you, to sift you like wheat. But I have pleaded in prayer for you, Simon, that your faith should not fail."* Jesus' admonition to Peter was that when he had come through the sifting and fully addressed the issues of his heart, he should *"strengthen and build up the brethren."*

I knew that but for the grace of God, Satan's intention was not only to sift us, but to destroy us. Coming through this situation whole and transitioning into the next step God had for us was not something we could do in the natural. We desperately needed more of Him than we had ever had before.

Our pastor's wife, Marilyn Hickey, has a worldwide teaching ministry. It's an incredible ministry making a pivotal impact for the Kingdom around the world. At the core of her teaching is the truth of the importance of each of us spending time daily in God's Word. Marilyn emphasizes that when things get rough, we need even more of God's Word. God's Word is truth and truth will always reign over the circumstances of life. Hebrews 10 took on special relevance to me at that point: *"Do not throw away this confident trust in the Lord, no matter what happens. Remember the great reward it brings you! Patient endurance is what you need now, so you will continue to do God's will. Then you will receive all that he has promised. For in just a little while, the Coming One will come and not delay. And a righteous person will live by faith. But I will have no pleasure in anyone who turns away."*

Adversity and New Horizons

Several years prior, I had put together my own Bible reading program that typically has me in ten chapters within ten different parts of the Bible each day. It has me in Psalms and Proverbs on a daily basis. I'm always in the Gospels, Acts or Revelation. And daily, I'm in three epistles and in four points in the Old Covenant. I knew I needed to immerse myself in God's Word to get past the heaviness associated not just with the loss of Trish, but now with all the revelations coming forth concerning her murder. I tripled and quadrupled my regular Bible reading program — and it indeed strengthened me and my resolve to make a difference in my own calling. A calling that by now I had long been describing as "an interlinking of business and ministry."

A few months after Trish's funeral I was visiting with my friend Pete Holzmann. Pete was in high gear with others in mission planning circles for the big mission conference held every three years known as the GCOWE conference. The Global Conference on World Evangelization attracted between 5,000 to 6,000 mission strategists and practitioners from over 150 nations around the globe. I had a growing sense, as I prayed, that I was to speak at that conference, which was coming up in Pretoria, South Africa in the summer of 1997.

Since early in my walk with the Lord, He has been imparting truths about my own calling into the marketplace. An interlinking between business and ministry. A calling that in many ways has been modeled after the life of Joseph the Patriarch. I told Pete that I felt I had a message for the business-in-missions practitioners at this conference. He encouraged me to contact Gunnar Olson, founder and chairman of the International Christian Chamber of Commerce, who was responsible for the business executives' venue of the GCOWE conference. When I contacted Gunnar he asked for a tape with a sample of what I would be sharing. After listening to the tape, he told me to come prepared to speak. I did just that.

In my prayer closet, I prepared a talk based on the prototype I had been gleaning from the life of Joseph. I entitled my talk "The Joseph Calling."

Since the time I spent at Oral Roberts University, I have been strongly drawn to the life of Joseph. The unusual life of this patriarch seemed to provide clues to the unorthodox steps I so strongly felt drawn to take as I sought God's higher plan for my own life.

Some books about the life of Joseph are written on the premise that he was an arrogant youth who God had to break in order to use. I have never seen the basis for those conclusions. I admit that Joseph undoubtedly must have been very impetuous and immature in his earlier days. He no doubt enjoyed the favor of his father and possibly was indulged. I strongly suspect however, that Joseph may have been the only one of his father's sons who truly understood the spiritual heritage of his family. My conclusions are based on the indiscreet activities of Joseph's brothers, even prior to them quibbling over whether to kill him or sell him into slavery. Joseph's painful journey from slavery to prison to ultimately sitting alongside of Pharaoh was much, much more than a man working his way out of a bad situation because he finally matured so God could use him. I have never had any question that Joseph was called by God. For Joseph to be used for God's redemptive purposes, he first had to be molded into the ways of the Egyptians; while simultaneously developing the spiritual gifts that already were in strong evidence before he was sold into slavery.

The Joseph Favor Factor

As I read and re-read the story of Joseph, I noticed two scripture verses in Genesis 39 which describe an unusual dynamic operating in Joseph's life. They each basically say the following:

The Lord was with Joseph .... and he was a successful man ..... and everyone saw that the Lord was with Joseph and made all that he did to prosper. Genesis: 39: 2-3; 21-23

It is amazing that the first time this scripture was written, Joseph was in slavery. The second time, he was in prison.

In essence, they strongly underscore **the depth of Joseph's character and calling, which were recognized by the people of the world he worked with** long before he was elevated to work alongside of Pharaoh. They reflect a man of integrity and excellence who brought honor to the Lord by the way he lived his life, and by the way he got the job done. For me, this was certainly an incredible example of how a man or woman of God is expected to operate in the midst of the world's system. An incredible balance was reflected in Joseph's wisdom and faithfulness to the Lord as well as to those he was serving.

I saw clues in Joseph's life that can only be explained by the priority he gave to spend time in the presence of the Lord. The visions he was given as a youth — visions which proved to be incredibly accurate. But also, the accuracy he had in interpreting the dreams of the baker and the butler. Indeed, I conclude that the foundational attribute that differentiated Joseph the patriarch, and will differentiate the Josephs of today, is that they give priority to **spending time in the presence of the Lord.** Everything else will flow from that.

Breaking with Religious Tradition

Another key observation I saw in Joseph's life was the religiously unorthodox context in which the Lord chose to place Joseph, in order for him to be used so uniquely as an instrument of God's purpose. **Joseph was totally immersed in the world's**

system! I've got to confess that there were times in my early days in business when I would have been far more comfortable working for a ministry, surrounded by others who believed as I did. But this was not God's plan in my call into the business-ministry arena.

Yet, in the midst of the world's system, Joseph was serving the Lord's purposes for His people. It was a time which required the harnessing of the world's seats of power for God's redemptive purposes. Joseph's role in sitting alongside of Pharaoh was a genuine alliance of secular systems being used for God's purposes.

R. G. LeTourneau was a modern-day Joseph. This committed believer was a man of prayer. Early in his career, he began receiving guidance in his prayer closet on the design of innovative earth-moving machinery. The earth-moving equipment Robert LeTourneau designed has revolutionized the construction, engineering and mining industries. During World War II his company built over 50 percent of the earth-moving equipment used by the Allies. It was reported that with the building of highways like the Alcan and the Ledo Road in Burma, along with the building of airports and installations across the globe, more earth was moved during World War II than during all the combined previous wars in history.

R. G. LeTourneau not only played a significant role with his technological contributions during World War II, but he also built a multi-million dollar corporate empire that has impacted countless thousands of lives. He established a Christian college that bears his name. He is known for the adage that "you can't outgive God." As the LeTourneau empire grew, so did its impact in the area of Christian service. Ninety-five percent of his firm's earnings went into Christian outreach and humanitarian efforts. (R. G. LeTourneau, *Mover of Men and Mountains*, Prentice-Hall, 1967)

The Most Distinguishing Joseph Characteristic

Yet another essential dimension is reflected in the model of Joseph's life. This key dimension differentiated Joseph from others with unique talents and abilities.

Much importance is ascribed to Joseph's insights into Pharaoh's dreams. That was certainly important, but not Joseph's most distinguishing characteristic. More than the fact that he "understood the times" – which he certainly did! It was even more than the fact that he "knew what to do" by mapping out a really great plan of action. No doubt about it. Joseph was a genuine strategic planner. But his most distinguishing characteristic was more than that. Much more!

In Genesis 41:38 Pharaoh first acknowledged that the Lord was with Joseph when he said, *"Can we find a man like this, in whom is a divine spirit?"* That recognition of the Spirit of the Lord operating in Joseph was certainly a pivotal foundation for the accomplishment of God's purposes through Joseph's service to Egypt.

BUT it was when Pharaoh both recognized the Lord being with Joseph – AND in verse 39, when Pharaoh added, *There is no one so discerning and wise as you are."* It was at this point that Joseph was promoted to sit alongside of Pharaoh.

The characteristic that Pharaoh had recognized that caused Joseph to be elevated to sit alongside of Pharaoh was not the interpretation of the dream or the brilliant plan. It was **the recognition of the wisdom operating in Joseph that Pharaoh saw as coming from the Lord**. Otherwise, Pharaoh could have just taken the plan and dismissed Joseph.

Pharaoh discerned the flow of God's wisdom. A Word of wisdom from on high. A prophetic Word of wisdom that unlocks dilemmas that baffle even the most astute kings of this world.

Joseph's most distinguishing characteristic that resulted in him being promoted to sit alongside of Pharaoh was:

> **a prophetically sound impartation of wisdom from on high as an answer to the challenge of the particular situation.**

This characteristic of God's wisdom operating within Joseph dovetails with the characteristic reflected by Joseph's worldview and his *modus operandi*. Joseph's outlook was shaped by the time he spent with the Lord. His perspective on things was never tainted by his own circumstance. Despite his faithfulness when he was a slave, while he was in prison, as when he served Pharaoh, Joseph was always a God-pleaser, rather than a man-pleaser.

These points on the life of Joseph and their applicability to a unique calling of modern-day Josephs were at the core of my talk to the Business Executives at the GCOWE conference in 1997. The presence of the Lord I sensed as I shared was very strong. But I never expected the type of reception I afterwards received from those to whom I had spoken.

A number shared that I had defined how God had been leading them for the last ten to twenty years. One man said he thought he had been all alone in being called in this way. Another just grabbed me and hugged me as he repeated the words, "thank you" over and over. I recalled being in prayer after Trisha's death. The words of Peter were so applicable to me at that time. Jesus had told Peter to strengthen and build up the brethren after Satan had sifted him. For each who came up after my talk, it appeared the message was a release to those whom God had been preparing in this way. It was an encouragement to these modern-day Josephs, who had been called to develop significant Kingdom initiatives in the business arena, that their steps of obedience indeed had a purpose.

For me, this talk I presented at the GCOWE conference was one of those defining moments in which my time of walking by faith and not by sight began having clearer relevance. There was no question that the Lord had used me as a catalyst in releasing those with this unique marketplace calling. I began recognizing that my own calling — the interlinking of business and ministry — was a part of something much bigger that the Lord was quietly preparing. I couldn't get away from the thought reflected by the words of Mordecai to Queen Esther: *"Who knows whether you have come to the kingdom for such a time as this?"*

CHAPTER 8

NEW HORIZONS

I was starting to see that the Words the Lord spoke to me so many years prior had a time factor associated with them.

> *Just as in the days of Joseph and Daniel, God will bring out mighty works at your hand. As you are led into the midst of the world, kings, rulers, leaders will be converted and humbled. You will work beside them and be given authority and your counsel will be heeded for their good.*

My calling as a Joseph and a Daniel for this day is a calling shared by a number of other believers working in the secular world from around the world, those who had been led and prepared in some very similar ways. It is a calling that would serve a number of strategic functions in the business arena. Yet there was a great deal more the Lord was to unfold in my understanding of this mosaic in this unique marketplace calling of the Josephs and Daniels.

The Joseph Calling speaking engagements and the writings produced from my intercession ministry began to connect me to many others involved in this calling into the marketplace. For most, the principles I was sharing served as a confirmation which released them to move forward in their own Joseph-Daniel callings. For many, it has let them know that they are not alone in what they've been pursuing in this unique calling. For others, it has provided an understanding to God's leading that they previously did not have.

The Lord indeed is raising up many, many modern-day Josephs and Daniels. The Josephs and Daniels are certainly not the only ones called into this arena of business and government. But it was what the Lord had been preparing me for in this interlinking of business and ministry — of secular enterprises which had overriding ministry objectives. A calling whereby men and women of God served uniquely and strategically as instruments of God's purpose — in secular positions of influence within the seats of power of this world. Strategically, I believe this move of God in penetrating the world of business and government will come to parallel the rise of the parachurch ministry movement of the early '50s.

Our generation has always had committed believers operating in the marketplace. But unfortunately only a handful have fully understood the calling into the places of business. Far too many Christians called into the secular workplace have viewed their calling as a second-class calling, secondary to those called to "full-time" work as pastors, evangelists and missionaries. Too often pastors have simply not understood this marketplace calling, and have had a mind-set that the businessman's role in the church is for the most part to "pay, pray and get out of the way."

Yet, the Lord did not count the calling of Joseph or Daniel as second-tier callings. If this were so, then the callings of the pioneers and patriarchs such as Abraham, Isaac, Jacob, Moses, Joshua and David would likewise be secondary to those who operated as the priests and prophets of their day. But this was not the case.

God's pattern for His people of old and His principles reflected in the New Covenant address the issue of the totality of life and the balance between the natural and the spiritual. The pattern outlined in the Old Covenant reflects the operational balance between those who were the kings and those who were the priests. God's pattern always began with a focus on enterprises and communities. But before going in to that, I must recount still other new developments the Lord was using to shape my approach to the business-ministry equation.

Business-Ministry Initiatives

In 1998, the Messianic Jewish Alliance (MJAA) launched a very unusual initiative, called The Joseph Project. Operating through the Israeli Messianic Jewish community, it serves to augment the aid needed for the growing number of immigrants coming into Israel. I was involved in the planning, kick-off and early development of the Joseph Project. Organizationally, the Joseph Project is a consortium of organizations — both ministry and business — operating in concert with one another to bless the growing number of Jews fleeing the anti-Semitism in Eastern Europe and the CIS states.

In my mind, what set this effort apart from others is the selfless way it was set up to operate. Spearheaded by Messianic Jewish organizations with Christian groups working alongside, the Joseph Project is a mechanism to bless these immigrants in the Name of the Lord — without there being a single entity which can grab the recognition or take the credit. Some organizations came forward and simply said "our doors are open to help." They were simply willing to be a part in order to get the job done. There were other organizations that were concerned with the politics, the control, the issue of recognition. The dynamic of serving without the need for recognition holds much potential in the days we are entering.

Around this same time, my partner in the Strategic Intercession Global Network (SIGN), Pastor Rich Carey, and I felt we needed to separate SIGN from GRMI. As one of the founding board members of GRMI, I saw much potential in the symbiosis between the various email forums GRMI hosted and SIGN. However, I took issue with GRMI's approach to growth and as a result resigned my position as a board member.

New Global Relationships and Initiatives

Our independent status with SIGN proved to be a significant turning point. The substance and direction of the issues being sent to our Internet -connected group of intercessors began to have a much greater focus on Israel; Jewish revival; the penetration of the marketplace by God's ambassadors; and the role which a select group of modern-day Josephs would play in funding God's emerging agendas.

1999 arrived. A year that extended the foundations of what had previously appeared to be simply isolated acts of obedience as I pursued the interlinking of secular enterprises with overriding ministry objectives. In retrospect, 1999 was an incredible year. It began with my good friend Bob Winer sending me on a mission to Ethiopia. Two months later, I was in Singapore and other points in the Far East. Two months after that I was back in Israel.

The journey to Ethiopia included lay-over visits in the UK and Kenya. My mission was to investigate business opportunities that might assist a community of persecuted Ethiopian Jews. During the two weeks among these wonderful people, I met with government officials, chambers of commerce and business people. A personal highlight was attending a rural church service that had to turn people away when the fenced-in, seated area reached an attendance of 2,800. People walked five to ten miles to attend this dynamic six-hour service. The hunger, fervor, and the expectation they had for more of God shown brightly on their faces throughout the service. I was told that this meeting was but one part of a revival that began when members of the Orthodox church began meeting quietly eight years prior. Over forty fellowships similar to the one I attended have been birthed through this revival.

The result of my myriad of meetings and investigations in Ethiopia was that I recognized the potential of a business model that could help the economically depressed and persecuted ethnic group Bob had a vision to assist. This model could create revenues and at the same time provide employment. I found that Ethiopia, like many other third world nations, has a close-knit infrastructure of those who import goods into their country. But much opportunity exists for those willing to *export* Ethiopian products to other parts of the world. With this in mind, my recommendations targeted a two-step business model. The initial business would be an export business. This business would create the revenues that in turn could be used to establish community-based industries, or "cottage industries" in the communities Bob was reaching out to.

From Ethiopia I went to Kenya. My visit in Kenya provided a very interesting complement to the Ethiopian venture. Peter Michell, an officer with the International Christian Chamber of

Commerce, graciously introduced me to several business associates in Kenya. The meetings that resulted provided incredible insights into both the business and spiritual tempo in eastern and central Africa. The very gracious Kenyans I met with were dedicated, mature Christians, most of whom owned their own businesses or law practices. I learned from these brethren that there is a powerful network of prayer among Christians across the continent of Africa. It is significant that within the boundaries of this one continent are all the natural resources sought by the other segments of the world — resources that in many cases are still virgin and available for development.

My visit to Singapore two months later began on a very unusual note. An International Christian Chamber of Commerce conference was being held there; my new friends in Kenya had just told me about it — and had strongly advised me to attend. Three weeks before that conference, I finally made a decision to go and Carol and I purchased our tickets. Two days later, I received an email from a man I had never met — who had recently received a summary of the talk I had given in South Africa on the Joseph Calling two years prior. This man was from Singapore and we arranged to meet.

The ICCC Singapore conference was a time filled with reports of some very unusual and significant activities being sponsored by the Chamber. There was, of course, much networking. This unique international organization has national chambers in over eighty nations around the world. There were workshops to attend, and I felt uniquely led by the Spirit to attend the finance workshops, being led by Laura Kent, who was ICCC VP and Treasurer at that time. The sessions she ran were stimulating and engaging.

In the middle of her workshops, Laura announced she would be going to Israel in June — for both ICCC business and to begin work on establishing a venture fund designed to be part of her investment business. She invited anyone in her workshop who sensed the Lord speaking to them to accompany her on her upcoming meetings in Israel. I KNEW I was supposed to go on that trip, and was among the handful who indicated they wanted to join her in the activities she was spearheading in Israel. It didn't seem either practical or realistic, with the time I had already spent in Africa and now in Asia over the last two months. But as I spoke to Laura, she indicated she also bore witness that I was to be on that trip. She then assigned me a small consulting assignment that provided the finances to make this trip possible.

Divine Appointments

Apart from the ICCC meetings, I felt it much more than happenstance that the gentleman who had emailed me shortly before this conference just happened to be in Singapore. And he was inquiring about something very close to my own heart — more information on the Joseph calling and the interlinking of business with ministry. It was indeed a high priority for me to take time to get together and meet this man.

I was not disappointed. Bill was a missionary businessman with a most unusual story. He had met the Lord some twenty years prior. At that time he was a geophysicist. God led him into mission work. He relocated from his home in the UK to Singapore.

Bill shared with me that roughly ten years prior, he began having the strongest impression while in prayer that he was to pray that someone would GIVE him a business! He related that he had no interest in business, nor any real background in business. But he was faithful in praying in this rather unusual way. Then, almost a year later he met a Singaporean Christian businessman. As these two men got to know one another, Bill was almost startled to learn that this man had been praying for someone with whom he could establish a business, someone with a Kingdom orientation, AND a willingness to venture out in serving the Lord through the avenue of business.

The business that resulted flourished and grew. With headquarters in the financial district of Singapore, they expanded across the Pacific Rim. All their employees are committed Christians. They provide a first-class service to their clients. Their reputation and demand for their business began extending to closed access nations, that is nations closed to traditional missionary efforts. Their staff of Christian professionals included people with expertise in planting Christian fellowships and supporting the efforts of local believers.

This venue developed to the degree that they began to use

corporate profits to plant community businesses in poor, rural areas.

These community businesses were operated by local Christians. In one instance, the business grew and prospered to the extent that everyone in the village worked for it — AND, because of the difference these people saw in the lives of the believers, the entire village came to the Lord.

Not only is employment being provided for those in an otherwise economically depressed area, but the villagers now have a platform to share the Good News with adjoining villages. A platform based not only on there being something different about the believers, but also on the fact that they have come together economically in such a way that this village has not suffered the economic downturns of that area. This type of enterprise has its foundations in the principles outlined in Deuteronomy and in the approach to business and community represented by the lives of Abraham, Isaac and Jacob.

Bill and I had some very engaging conversations. He then brought another business associate of his into our visits. The result was an alliance between Bill's firm and mine — and a new office for us in Singapore.

June came, and with it the trip to Israel. Laura Kent is an entrepreneur business-owner and money manager. She has an investment Fund she has developed and manages. And she has an unusual calling that is centered around Israel.

Mapping Out, Building Up and Bringing Wealth into Israel

I couldn't help recalling a call I had received from our friend Barbara Fox a year earlier. Barbara related that she had been praying for me and had felt impressed to pray in a very specific way. She said she'd had the distinct impression that she was to release in prayer the mantle of **my role in mapping out, building up, and bringing wealth into Israel.** There was no question of the clear parallel Barbara's word had to the purpose of this trip to Israel. But its implications since that time have far exceeded my expectations.

It was during this trip to Israel, that I learned that Laura also serves on the board of another organization called Enterprise Development. I had met the Chairman of Enterprise Development at the talk I gave on the Joseph Calling at the conference in Pretoria,

South Africa two years prior.

Enterprise Development International provides micro-loans and business training for community-based entrepreneurs in economically distressed areas around the world. This impressive program has launched more than 100,000 entrepreneurs in some fifty nations since 1985. The distinctive for this worldwide program is new business owners meeting weekly for prayer with facilitators brought in to provide guidance and support for the new businesses. Over the years, they have realized full repayment on 96 percent of the loans they've granted. Having spent time working in and with the banking industry, I know that that is a very impressive figure. I was seeing here another model to establish and operate believer-owned businesses.

On this trip to Israel I had a number of strategic meetings with potential business opportunities. I was exposed to the fast-paced venture capital scene in Israel. The dynamic of what is taking place in Israel's venture capital arena is globally second only to that underway in Silicon Valley.

For me, the pivot point of my time in Israel was centered around a meeting with the head of an Israeli consulting firm who worked closely with the leadership of Israel's Technology Incubator program. Our discussions resulted in a personal and professional relationship that has extended from conducting market opportunity evaluations to brokering strategic alliances on behalf of some of Israel's fast-growth technology firms.

This new alliance was not only an important one, but it was for me, another piece in the puzzle of the Lord's interlinking between business and ministry. The business models, the entrepreneurial framework. Now I was playing a small role in one of the most successful business incubator programs anywhere on the globe!

God's Economy

In the work I have been doing over the years with multinationals, I realized that God has His own economy. His economy holds the potential to bypass the economic downturns that come with the aberrations of the world's economy.

The Lord was challenging my mind-sets about the nature and order of business and economics. And He was also giving me a

Kingdom perspective as He was introducing me to the principles of His economy. Principles that undergird the operation of enterprises linked to His agendas.

CHAPTER 9

THE KINGDOM PERSPECTIVE AND NEW WINESKINS

So, to better understand God's economy, I need to describe what I refer to as the Kingdom perspective.

The Kingdom perspective begins with the assumption that there is a Kingdom of God and a kingdom of darkness. When God created man, He gave man dominion over the earth. God created man to be complete, whole and in unity and fellowship with Himself. But Adam relinquished man's dominion through his disobedience to God at the fall. God then began His plan of redemption and restoration through His chosen people Israel, through whom Messiah Jesus would come. Jesus came as the redeemer. He came to reestablish man's relationship with God and to restore his dominion over the earth. Indeed, Jesus announced His earthly ministry with the Words, *"the Kingdom of God is at hand."*

The foundational principles for God's Kingdom rule in business, community, and government were laid out in the Pentateuch — the Torah. The process of the fulfillment of God's redemption and restoration — and the ability to exercise authority in God's Kingdom came through Jesus.

Indeed, the history of God's people has reflected the conflict marked by the redemption of God's Kingdom on the earth from the forces of darkness. It has involved the restoration of our God-intended dominion that was lost through Adam's disobedience.

The Kingdom perspective is at the forefront of God's move into the marketplace, with God's people moving into positions of authority in seats of power in business and governmental circles. It reflects the operation of God's Kingdom rule on the earth.

The Kingdom Perspective Distinctive in the Marketplace

The Kingdom perspective in the marketplace operates on the premise that there is a unique difference between a Kingdom executive, official, entrepreneur, or business-owner — with a calling of accomplishing God's purposes and agendas in the fabric of society; and an upstanding, moral Christian business executive or business owner. The Kingdom of God is pervasive and embraces every area of our personal and business lives.

The Kingdom perspective incorporates our passion and focus in life, which is drawn from God's desires for us to operate in wholeness, and oneness with Him in all that we do. It extends to the whole of life. It deals with the priorities we have in our everyday activities — business, family and community — based on initiatives and agendas that come from God's Throne Room. It entails the purposes and motivations from which we operate and make both short- and long-term decisions.

In the marketplace, God's perspective results in a *modus operandi* that incorporates His purposes and agendas in how we act and make decisions in our business activities. The Kingdom perspective is based on the operation of Biblical principles in:

- how business is conducted,
- the way decisions are made and
- how relationships are established and developed.

The Kingdom perspective places keen significance on the role and operation of the Person of the Holy Spirit, as well as the gifts of the Holy Spirit in giving purpose, leading and daily guidance to the Kingdom executive, official and business owner.

The Kingdom perspective lends a distinct difference to the business person's attitudes and utilization of money, people and power. This attitude reflects a different paradigm from the world's approach to business, because it is derived from spending consistent time in the presence of the Lord. This attitude reflected in the Kingdom perspective is strategic. This eternal perspective, in essence, God's perspective, becomes the guiding force for daily decisions.

For example, it reflects the fact that the true value of money is not in its possession, but in the way that it is used. The Kingdom perspective impacts how the business executive or business owner makes money, how he or she spends money, and the basic purposes and approach they have to money. The Kingdom perspective toward money might be best summed up by the scripture in 1 Timothy 6:17-19.

"Command those who are rich in this present world not to be arrogant or to put their hope in wealth, which is so uncertain, but to put their hope in God, who richly provides us with everything for our enjoyment. Command them to do good, to be rich in good deeds, and to be generous and willing to share. In this way they will lay up treasure for themselves as a firm foundation for the coming age, so that they may take hold of the life that is truly life."

New Mind-Sets

To embrace this Kingdom perspective will require new ways of thinking. New mind-sets. What Jesus referred to as new wineskins. In three of the Gospel accounts, Jesus addressed the need for relevant methods. In Matthew 9:16, 17, He said:

"No one puts a piece of unshrunk cloth on an old garment; for the patch pulls away from the garment, and the tear is made worse. Nor do they put new wine into old wineskins, or else the wineskins break, the wine is spilled, and the wineskins are ruined. But they put new wine into new wineskins, and both are preserved."

Although the Kingdom perspective and God's move into the marketplace are very biblical, they do not fit a modern-day mind-set of how the church typically views the role of Christians in business. Christians in business are typically not viewed as serving in a front-line role in the building of God's Kingdom. The prevailing mind-set is that operating in the business world has little spiritual significance, and is simply "worldly."

Yet, this current-day move into the marketplace has its foundations in the business communities developed by Abraham, Isaac and Jacob. In the emerging move into the marketplaces of the world, God is birthing business communities that bypass the economic downturns of a region. It is a move in which the Lord is positioning uniquely prepared individuals, as instruments of His purpose, to work within and alongside seats of power in industry and government. They will operate in the secular realm as His emissaries in accomplishing His agendas. Just like in the days of Joseph and Daniel.

As we address old mind-sets, we see, for instance, that engrained in the thinking of many in Christian leadership circles is a concept of "the sacred versus the secular." Alongside that mind-set is the issue of separatism from the world. The modern-day premise which is commonly referred to as the separation between church and state. This premise underlies how spiritual matters both within and outside the church are approached and handled.

But this non-Biblical notion of keeping God's people in the "secular" arena operating according to the world's standards is one of the *most effective strategies* the enemy has ever conceived to keep the church feeble, frail and ineffective. It has no parallel to the original models set forth in Scripture. Old mind-sets. In the Words of Jesus, old wineskins.

The old mind-set is that business is worldly. The old mind-set positions entrepreneurs, business-owners and business and governmental leaders as serving in secondary functions in relation to building God's Kingdom.

Similarly, the concept of the "laity" is one that is not found anywhere in Scripture. Yet, it supports this separation between the lives we live at home and at work — the secular — and the events that take place when we enter a church building — the sacred. Once again this is a strategy of the enemy designed to keep God's people feeble, frail and ineffective. God wants to mobilize His Body. Indeed, Ephesians 4 states that the role of the church is to perfect the saints for the work of the ministry. And that means going into what one Christian leader has referred to as "every man's world." When Jesus said we are to go into all the world, that included the infrastructures and fabric of our society. Business, government, education, entertainment, the media.

God's Purposes in the Marketplace

So then, why? Why is the marketplace calling so important to God's purposes? I've already noted that it follows the Biblical prototypes represented by Abraham, Isaac and Jacob. They established small kingdoms, that, in essence, were enterprises. Their business communities were a light in a very dark world. Their *modus operandi* exemplified their relationship with the Lord, how His principles operated. Isaac sowed in famine and he prospered! God has always intended for His people to be witnesses and ambassadors for Him and His truths.

In the era WE have entered, the entrepreneurial spirit exemplified by the patriarchs of old is again emerging. It is emerging as a move of God in which men and women of God are being moved by the Spirit of God to launch out – as instruments of God's purpose; as lights shining in a world where the darkness is increasing.

This CALL into the marketplace has a keen parallel to the patriarch Joseph and the prophet Daniel. Joseph and Daniel were thrust into seats of power as gifted administrators. They were administrators operating according to God's wisdom and principles and prophetic insights; to be ambassadors for the Lord with His answers and insights and solutions.

Today, there is a move of God releasing modern-day Josephs and Daniels to serve as ambassadors and emissaries to appropriate and redirect strategic resources for God's redemptive purposes.

Understanding the Times

To understand why the Kingdom perspective and God's move

into the marketplace are so important, we also need to understand what I refer to as the Issachar context — "understanding the times and knowing what to do" (I Chronicles 12:32). In understanding the times, these are and will continue to be times of change and times of shaking.

Sometimes I think we in the Western world are somewhat inoculated from the realities of the times and the seasons we are entering. We are blinded by materialism and the mainstream dominion of the secular humanists. But the impact of the change and shaking underway is something those outside the Western world have no trouble in grasping. And if I'm hearing the Lord correctly, we've just been feeling the tremors of the shaking.

Nations indeed will undergo major upsets. Regions will experience discontinuities — economically, socially, and politically. Major power shifts have been taking place for some time now. Third world powers will challenge the status quo in global politics and economics. New alliances are being formed — for good and for evil. Terrorism will continue to increase. Muslim and communist hierarchies will find common bonds.

There will be an increase in the tempo of the persecution already underway against believers and against the Jewish people. Israel's role as a prophetic pivot point in the nature and order of world events will mount even higher. With all the discontinuities will come widespread disillusionment and social unrest, as well as new meaning given to ethnic hatred.

So, in the midst of the change and shaking taking place, people will be looking for answers. Answers that break the bonds of the superficial way of the world and offer genuine hope. AND THAT is one of the most significant reasons WE have been called into this arena of the marketplace. We are those who are going to have answers and solutions — both practical and spiritual answers and solutions.

In the Words of Jesus: (Mark 13: 7-10) *"When you hear of wars and rumors of wars, do not be troubled; for such things must happen, but the end is not yet. For nation will rise against nation, and kingdom against kingdom. And there will be earthquakes in various places, and there will be famines and troubles. These are the beginnings of sorrows. But watch out for yourselves ...."*

So, with the discontinuities and disillusionment will come increases in the risks and dangers for God's people. But with the increased dangers will also come increases in the opportunities. Kingdom opportunities tied to God's move into the marketplace. Opportunities that will not be obvious to those of the world.

Kingdom Opportunities

Globally, in the midst of the discontinuities, there will be bright spots. Unusual opportunities in the midst of the adversities. For example, economic systems based on biblical systems of business and new approaches to funding will be provided for those called as instruments of His purpose.

New approaches to funding? That reflects another dimension in need of new mind-sets: funding the work of the ministry. I believe we are fast approaching the time when those called and anointed for Kingdom service are going to have to develop a new mentality about financial resources.

The primary approach today among believers around the world seems to be centered on gifts — mostly from other believers. These are good and give believers the opportunity to share in the joys and rewards of the Lord's work everywhere. But needs associated with the times we are entering are so vast, that "gifts only" will not be enough — and certainly not solely from the existing resources of believers.

It will be a time when the wealth of the wicked is opened for the righteous! A time when new avenues of resources will be revealed.

But a change in the premises behind the traditional mind-sets for funding needs to be set in motion. We need to think in terms of resources. We need to look beyond the mind-set of one-time gifts. We need to recognize that our Father owns the cattle on a thousand hills. And in these unusual times, we need to embrace a mind-set of **revenue streams**!

The move away from being primarily focused on fund-raising models will result in new means to create revenues for Kingdom purposes. Investment funds are being established. Investment funds that involve alliances between Christian marketplace leaders and modern-day Pharaohs and King Cyrus types — individuals functioning as gatekeepers into the financial coffers of the world.

New business startup programs — business incubator programs are being put together by those called by God into the business world. Business start-up programs operated by believers that give positive impact to their communities and nations.

Kingdom opportunities are on the increase. These are opportunities that result in **God's people being those with both practical and spiritual answers.** Genesis 39 described Joseph as one being successful and prospering because people saw that the Lord was with him. Regardless of his circumstance — prison or slavery — the world recognized the God-difference in Joseph long before he was elevated to sit alongside of Pharaoh.

Kingdom opportunities are opportunities that dovetail with agendas high on God's priority list. This move of God into the marketplace is resulting in business-ministry alliances between key groups within the Body fulfilling the command in Isaiah 58:10 of reaching out to help the oppressed — the poor, hungry, and afflicted.

Isaiah 58:10-11 tells us, *"If you extend your soul to the hungry and satisfy the afflicted soul, then your light shall dawn in the darkness, and your darkness shall be as the noonday. The LORD will guide you continually, and satisfy your soul in drought, and strengthen your bones; you shall be like a watered garden, and like a spring of water, whose waters do not fail."*

With the discontinuities and upsets taking place around the world will be unusual opportunities to increase the focus of genuinely touching the oppressed — the hungry and afflicted — of reaching and rescuing those who are lost and without hope. These opportunities will reflect a shift from the ministry model of recent decades. The high profile, personality-based, fund-raising-focused models — a paradigm necessary for its time in building and connecting the Body will give way to models driven by cooperative inter-organizational efforts. Efforts like those previously described of the Joseph Project.

The old paradigm will undergo a shift to a model in which people called to the marketplace will play key roles. Key roles that will pave the way for groups implementing strategies fulfilling the charge in Isaiah 58.

For example, the Los Angeles Dream Center very well may be one of many new models of how the church will operate in the days ahead. Birthed from the ministry of Pastor Tommy Barnett, this comprehensive community center is a consortium of Christian ministries, humanitarian groups and marketplace organizations. This is a 24-hour, 7-day a week operation with 37 active ministries ranging from community outreach, rehab, feeding the poor, youth ministries, and more. It has been described as "God's mercy on display." The Dream Center operates from a 15-story former Los Angeles hospital in the inner city.

The Dream Center is not an isolated entity. Rather, its impact touches the entire surrounding inner-city community for the Kingdom. There are 500 people, including former addicts, drug dealers and prostitutes currently living there, undergoing an intense lifestyle rehabilitation program. The International Christian Chamber of Commerce and Businessmen's Fellowship International (BMI) have been given the entire 15th floor of the facility. Their role is to provide the skills training essential to enabling these on-fire graduates of the Dream Center program to break free from the way of life they knew in the inner-city. Tommy Barnett endorsed ICCC's role by saying that, to his knowledge, prior to this, no one from the business community has really caught the vision and filled this essential gap – of training transformed, on-fire inner-city converts to productively enter the marketplace.

As the Lord opens the gateways into the resources and systems of this world, there will be alliances between secular gatekeepers — key individuals of influence and power, and key leaders from among those called by God into the marketplace.

There will also be alliances between uniquely positioned Kingdom businesses and governments and governmental agencies. Alliances between businesses with overriding ministry objectives that will open gateways. Businesses with overriding ministry objectives and this new, emerging breed of church and ministry organization — groups that will be a conduit to give hope, both practical and spiritual, to the lost, displaced and oppressed.

Whenever we talk about Kingdom opportunities, I'm reminded of my good friend Don Shooster. Don is gifted in his ability to spot business opportunity in some of the most unlikely places. He exemplifies a unique group of Christian business persons who are simply awaiting God's timing coupled with the right Kingdom opportunities — in the strategic role they will be playing in this interlinking between business and ministry.

One of the most, if not the most pivotal, agendas emanating from God's Throne Room is Israel and Jewish revival. God's agendas, especially those involving His chosen people, always challenge the false, perverted ways and agendas offered by the god of this world. That is why anti-Semitism and anti-Israel rhetoric has been increasing at an alarming rate around the globe.

There is a spiritual polarization underway between those who are controlled by the prince of this world and the Jews, those referred to in Scripture as God's chosen. We have entered a time of great lawlessness. As discontinuities, disillusionment, social unrest, and ethnic strife increase, misguided leaders and spokespersons across the globe will be increasingly pointing to scapegoats, especially to the Jews and to Israel, as a means to mask their inabilities and inadequacies to provide solutions.

Zechariah 12:13 tells us that one day all nations will come against Israel. Indeed, the General Assembly of the United Nations has a history of votes and proclamations that have treated Israel as nothing more than an illegitimate nation. Ezekiel 38 and 39 describe a great war that will be coming against Israel. That war is imminent.

Yet we also know from Genesis 12:3 that *"the Lord is going to bless those that bless Israel and curse those that curse Israel."* Jeremiah 16 speaks of a time when the Lord will draw the Jewish people back to the land of Israel, the land of their heritage and inheritance. The anti-Semitism underway already has precipitated the exodus of Jews from many nations around the world.

The Church and Israel share a common heritage and a common destiny. In the midst of this time of anti-Semitism and pressures against Israel and the Jewish people, a select group from the Church and the Christian business community will emerge. A group that will play pivotal roles in standing alongside of Israel and along side the growing number of Messianic Jewish believers who are at the forefront of the agendas associated with Jewish revival.

These strategically-called marketplace leaders will become facilitators in developing unusual alliances to counter the amassing of forces coming together against Israel. The alliance between Joseph and Pharaoh is an apt parallel to alliances that select marketplace leaders will have with high level gatekeepers of our era. These alliances will open doors to unique opportunities in the accomplishment of God's agendas for Israel and the Jewish people. The fact is that the unorthodox Joseph-Pharaoh model was indeed an unusual, unconventional alliance for its time. And the alliances the Lord will be initiating to support Israel and the Jewish people will likewise be unusual from a natural or even traditional religious viewpoint.

We have entered a time when the Lord anoints gifted believers in the marketplace, in similar fashion to Daniel and Joseph of old, with favor and wisdom to penetrate and operate in the midst of the seats of power within business and governmental circles. The seats of power in communities; in the marketplace; and even in government — to bring about His purposes for His people and to offer hope to the hopeless.

We have entered a time of unusual strategic alliances between those called as modern-day Josephs and uniquely chosen persons of the world. Alliances with those representing modern-day Pharaohs like in the time of Joseph, or like King Cyrus who was responsible for returning the Jewish exiles to Jerusalem. Strategic alliances with persons in pivotal positions who are inclined toward the Lord, His people and God's purposes.

So, in the midst of the growing discontinuities — and opportunities, the Lord is releasing His marketplace ambassadors to penetrate seats of power and appropriate resources for the restoration of His Kingdom. The Lord God Almighty will not be bound by the traditions of men as He accomplishes His purposes. Just like Joseph and Daniel of old, the Lord will have His chosen in the direct center of the discontinuities — with solutions. They will have practical solutions that minister to the lost and the hopeless in the Name of the Lord. Zechariah 8:13 says: *"So I will save you, and you shall be a blessing. Do not fear, Let your hands be strong."*

Understanding the times and knowing what to do is not an option in times of upset. Indeed Daniel reflects that when he says that "...*wisdom and might are His. And He changes the times and the seasons. He removes kings and He raises up kings. He gives wisdom to the wise and knowledge to those who have understanding. He reveals deep and secret things. He knows what is in the darkness and light dwells with Him."* Daniel 2:20-22

CHAPTER 10

KINGDOM RICHES

For there is no distinction between Jew and Greek. The same Lord is Lord over all of us and He generously bestows His riches upon all who call upon Him in faith. (Romans 10:12 Amplified)

The principles of the Kingdom of God defy the odds of the most adverse of situations.

During one of our trips to Israel long after the start of the intifada, the Lord brought home to me — the cost and realities of living in the land of promise. Aside from the constant threat of terrorism and the uncertainty of the future is the reality for the majority — of simply making ends meet. Poverty in Israel is increasing. Unemployment is rising. And peace has become even more fragile and elusive.

The pressures and threats and tragedies created by the insanity of the intifada have a broad segment of Israel's secular community struggling with hopelessness and asking questions. Many recent immigrants have left Israel disillusioned. Even some Israeli-born citizens have given up and emigrated to nations that have taken public stances against Israel's very existence.

Yet within Israel is a community with hope, a community of Jewish believers. For the purposes of our ministry activities, these are the ones at the forefront our Lord Jesus was speaking of with

His admonition in Luke 22:32 to *"strengthen the brethren."* They are an infrastructure of Israeli citizens; a community of what some estimate to be some 7000 Israeli Messianic Jewish believers.

They are the ones best equipped to offer hope to their neighbors, co-workers and leaders — with both spiritual and practical answers and solutions. They are paying the cost like their neighbors and co-workers. But it is a cost that is compounded by an organized persecution directed by a small, but politically powerful minority who view Jews who believe in Jesus as their Jewish Messiah as a curse to Israel — and who make every effort they can to drive them out.

We've been involved with initiatives in other nations where the Body is persecuted and only operates underground. But in Israel, operating underground is neither an option nor desire for those Jews who have found their Jewish Messiah. The spotlight is on Israel — and it is the spiritual focal point for believers around the world. This is the Holy Land — the Land of Promise. But with the persecution of the Body in Israel is emerging a Body that is engaging the incredible spiritual onslaught to destroy them — and is bearing fruit. One congregational leader, born in Israel, shared with me that ten years prior, it was considered a major accomplishment for an Israeli Messianic congregation to have a handful or two of new, born-again believers in a year's time. But because of the desperation created by all the uncertainty, individual congregations are seeing those same numbers coming to the Lord on a weekly basis. Significantly, these new believers are largely Israeli-born.

Practical Answers and Kingdom Principles

At least part of the reason for the change is the fact that in an environment of hopelessness and uncertainty, people will listen to spiritual answers from those offering help with practical ones. When Jesus came 2000 years ago, He announced His ministry with the Words, *"The Kingdom of God is at hand."* Using the standard of the Old Covenant, He taught the Jewish people about the Kingdom of God. Through the parables he unveiled principles that underlie the operation of the Kingdom of God. With those Kingdom principles, He taught about practical things that might be summed up as Kingdom riches.

While Jesus pulled aside a smaller group who traveled with him and received special focus, His typical audience, as He imparted these practical truths of how the Kingdom of God operates — were everyday people. People who were disillusioned by the heavy requirements laid upon them by the religious community. People who lived in an occupied land filled with uncertainty and hopelessness. People in need who were hungry spiritually and looking for something real. People who were looking for answers — practical answers. People not unlike the people of Israel today.

Kingdom principles are practical. They serve to strengthen, mobilize and equip those with hearing ears and seeing eyes. When these truths are embraced, along with the Author of Truth, they transform lives, build communities and impact nations. They serve to make the adherents of these truths to be the head and not the tail.

The practical and the spiritual dimensions of God's Kingdom are uniquely tied together throughout Scripture. The practical provides principles and wisdom needed for the social (community) and economic requirements of life. The spiritual deals with our souls, with standards of righteousness and our relationship with the Lord. The approach Carol and I have to our ministry incorporates the spiritual, the social and the economic dimensions of what we see in Scripture. They work in concert with one another.

Kingdom Riches: Spiritual, Social And Economic

A clearer grasp of the operation of the spiritual, social and economic dimensions outlined in Scripture can be gleaned by viewing what the Word refers to as "riches and wealth." Riches and wealth are referred to again and again in both the Old and New Covenants.

The operation of the "spiritual, social and economic" dimensions of Kingdom riches is uniquely tied to the dynamic operating when faith is released and the promises received.

The Western Church is very big on the release of faith to obtain the promises on an individual level. So am I. But within the Jewish culture; within the culture that brought us the Word of God and the Messiah; and within the realities of a pressure-cooker type of environment like Israel, the connection between "the release of faith and the promises received" has got to flow at the community (social) level — for there to be the "release" needed to overcome the incredible forces of darkness arrayed against this most spiritually significant people and land.

The operation of our faith is tied to a Kingdom principle referred to in Scripture as dominion. Spirit controls matter. That's the foundation on which prayer is based. It's tied to the authority the Lord has invested in us as His emissaries. An authority that reflects service and humility.

Around the world, there is a fierce battle underway over dominion. It is a battle that can be summed up as the clash of all ages — the battle between good and evil. Yet nowhere is that battle more evident than in Israel. Globally, Israel is the pivot point. Evil hates and would like nothing better than the destruction of those who are God's people. While that certainly involves those grafted in as God's people, the Church, it especially hates those who are the original covenant people of God. The people the Scripture refers to as God's chosen. The Jewish people. Within those who are God's chosen are a remnant who by the Spirit of the Lord have had the revelation of their Jewish Messiah — and are walking out a most strategic calling for our day.

The Spiritual Foundation to the Clash

This issue of dominion ultimately deals with the hearts and minds of people — which is the spiritual dimension. But dominion also involves "ruling over the work of His hands" — the economic, practical side of things — that is time and again referred to in Scripture as wealth and riches.

So while the foundation in this clash between good and evil is spiritual, and the clash between good and evil most clearly manifests in the struggle over control (dominion) of the economic and political; the impact is upon the social or community level. The leverage point over the quest for the spiritual and social (community) is the economic dimension.

The Bible gives keen reference to each of these dimensions of riches or wealth — the spiritual, the social and the economic. My good friend Dr. Bill Bolton very aptly describes them as biblical dimensions of spiritual, social and economic capital. He describes a wonderfully apt analogy of the fixed versus the working capital that is tied into our inheritance in the unsearchable riches of Christ. Dr. Bolton's observation is that far too many within Christendom try to stand on only one leg of the "three-legged" stool of this truth.

Yet all three dimensions of riches or wealth are developed very well throughout Scripture. The Old Covenant has one example of the "spiritual" riches from Isaiah 53, the "social/community" riches from Isaiah 58 and the "economic" from Isaiah 60. The book of Deuteronomy hits them all as it outlines the principles for a God-centered entrepreneurial community. Jesus' parables land strongly on all three.

The fact is that the dynamic operating between the spiritual, social and economic reflects a progression that has its foundation in the spiritual. It is the balance of this progression that reflects the principles that enable the Lord to operate in every dimension of our lives.

The world has tried to seize the economic, but without both the spiritual and social, it is destined toward cyclic ups and downs. Likewise, the social can't operate without both the spiritual and the economic. And far too often, the Church's approach to the spiritual is a focus that ignores God's place regarding the social and economic.

The Challenge in Israel

So how does all this tie back to Israel and to what I see emerging within Israel's Messianic Jewish community?

It's this. As a whole, the Church has floundered in its operation of the community (social) and economic dimensions of God's riches. Unity is required for God's riches to operate together.

We all talk about Paul's strong Ephesians 4 admonition for unity in the Body. But we've fallen short. This passage in Ephesians says that without this unity that we will all be tossed about by craftiness and every wind of doctrine. It says basically that if we fall short on the issue of equipping the saints for the work of service that builds up the Body, we will be like children being tossed about.

Likewise, if we expect there to ever be a time in which "all Israel is saved," we are going to have to take a look at another dimension of what we refer to as the "full Gospel." Because the teaching of Jesus — on how God's Kingdom operates — is based on Kingdom principles that connect the dots from the truths forming the basis of Judaism. These truths involve the melding and operation of the spiritual, community (social) and economic riches outlined in Scripture.

Scripture indeed refers to a time in which "all Israel will be saved." But to have a realistic expectation of the fulfillment of this eventuality, the Church is going to have to rethink how it views its essential role of standing behind and strengthening that remnant of believers in Israel, who represent the front-line of those called to reach the Jewish people.

Yet, the Church is fractionalized. That "divided house" is just not a reflection of the Gentile segment of the Body. The Messianic Jewish community in Israel is just as fractionalized. So, with the spiritual forces of darkness arrayed against Israel, the Body in general is approaching this most significant spiritual task of "all Israel being saved" — divided and on a one-legged stool.

Likewise, these issues of division and the short-sided approaches to the community and economic dimensions of how the Body generally operates — the practical outworkings of our faith — become the basis of our witness.

Another friend of mine, a ministry leader in Israel, recently shared this story with me: *"The Orthodox Jewish community in Israel has created such a network of Tz'dakah (charity) that virtually no one who is part of the community is ever on the street. No one goes hungry. No bride goes to her wedding impoverished, no one is forced to remain alone and lonely. Among the Orthodox, an entire social system exists to care for the needs of their own people. One believer we know lived among the Haredim (Ultra-Orthodox), and experienced the warmth and security of this community. But when she became a believer in Jesus, she was forced out of her home. Then, as a Messianic believer, things got worse. She wound up on the streets of Jerusalem. She has been hungry. She has been lonely. She laments the fact that 'Believers in Jesus should be putting those who do not believe in Him to shame in their acts of Tz'dakah (charity), but instead they put us to shame.'"*

So, in light of the economic struggles and poverty that have impacted Israel's Messianic community; and in light of the persecution directed against believers in Israel, the question is "how."

How can the Israeli believing community stand up to become the head and not the tail? How can Israel's Messianic Jews assume the mantle of their calling — perhaps for such a time as this — while figuratively being shot at from both sides? That's the issue. That is what is at the crux of our ministry to Israel's Messianic Jewish community, *"to strengthen the brethren."*

The Keys of Unity and Intercession

Kingdom "riches," in essence, connect the dots to the operation of the Kingdom of God when the spiritual, social and economic capital the Lord has made available to us begin operating together.

My observation is that most congregational leaders in Israel are doing all they can to nurture and build up their flocks — from the spiritual riches dimension of these Kingdom principles. Some are instituting programs to help those impacted by the mix of poverty and persecution. But for the most part, they are operating on a one-legged stool with one hand tied behind their back, due to the issue of the Body being fractionalized.

Essentially, the Body in Israel is doing what the Body elsewhere is doing in a quest to grow and to bear fruit. Yet the spiritual warfare surrounding Israel is in some instances far more intense and in others, far more subtle.

Ephesians 4 calls for an equipping that results in a mature Body — and a mature Body is one that operates together. A mature Body is one that builds bridges, rather than burning them or tearing them down. A mature Body is one that is equipped for *"the work of service"* as it is phrased in verse 12 of Ephesians 4 of the NAS version.

While we all generally agree on these points in Ephesians, the key is tied to unlocking these principles of God's Kingdom and putting them into practice.

The answer to "how" Israel's Messianic Jewish community can be released to be the head and not the tail, against an incredible array of odds, is tied to the release and balance in the operation of these three dimensions of Kingdom riches.

Each of these dimensions of Kingdom riches is incorporated in the principles of the Kingdom of God taught by Jesus during His earthly ministry. But the answer to "how" our Israeli Jewish brethren can begin to most effectively implement them with the result of operating with the vibrancy of the early Church is not one that can be approached simply in the natural.

I personally believe that unity will unfold as the prayer initiatives toward this end mount and begin amassing — prayer initiatives that are initiated from within and among Israel's Messianic community. Likewise, it wouldn't hurt to have an army of intercessors from around the world mobilized and praying with them toward these ends.

On this issue of unity, we all need to be wise to the schemes of the evil one.

Unity doesn't mean everyone has to agree on everything. It does mean you start working together. Unity is tied to the operation of that working capital of the truths of His riches. Truth among the brethren is not brittle. At least not when it operates in love. The precepts of men are brittle and create dissension. Our salvos of ammunition need to be directed toward the enemy's camp, rather than our own.

Unity based on community is an operational reality that is the outworking of truth on more than an intellectual level. It is Spirit and Truth operating together. It operates on a foundation of service and charity — both the 1Corinthians 13 charity and the *Tz'dakah* type charity. This Hebrew word "charity," *Tz'dakah* interestingly is the same one used in Proverbs 14 where it says that "righteousness" exalts a nation: *Tz'dakah (charity) exalts a nation*. The implication of the Hebrew word flows both ways — there is a righteousness in *Tz'dakah* charity and charity in *Tz'dakah* righteousness.

Yet, even the best of us can be blindsided by the subtle ways the enemy works overtime to undermine this factor of unity within the Body. Many years ago, a major Christian leader was invited by the heads of a Native American tribe to speak to their people. He was met by a delegation of leaders from this Indian nation. They dressed him in the traditional headdress of one of their tribal chieftains and with accompanying pomp and ceremonies had him lead a parade through the reservation. Afterwards he preached. A number in the audience came to the Lord. But despite the appearances of a marvelous event, something very significant was missing. There wasn't one Christian leader from this tribe in the delegation invited to meet with him. And after this man of God left, the non-Christian tribal leaders faced their tribe's Christian leaders and told them: "Your big Christian leader came here and honored our traditions and religion. He didn't even need you, and neither do we." According to Christian leaders of this tribe, that event set the efforts of the believers in that tribe back a decade.

The Issues for Change

This is not unlike what has been happening in Israel. The Church genuinely loves Israel — and tends to be enthralled at the prospect of invitations from secular and pseudo-religious sources to play a role in events and initiatives in Israel. But in most cases, these "opportunities" tend to ignore the believing community. It's time for change.

It's time for the Church to understand what it truly means, *to stand alongside of Israel.*

It is also time to begin employing the full range of Kingdom principles and the "working capital" of the riches with which the Lord has entrusted us — so that the spiritual, the social and the economic begin operating together.

There are initiatives underway and others in the birthing stage that hold much potential of enabling our Israeli brethren to face the issues before them with the strength needed to be that vibrant Body the Lord has called them to be. To be the head and not the tail. The efforts of Carol's and my treks to Israel have been and will continue to be focused on initiatives that bear on these goals.

It is time for the Church to recognize and come behind what the Lord is doing through the fervent pioneers comprising Israel's Messianic Jewish community. It is time for the Messianic community's infrastructure to be strengthened through the development of business enterprises. It is time for wholeness and healing to begin manifesting so that our brethren are equipped individually — but also as a community to be that light shining in the darkness that they are called to be.

It is time for intercessors to embrace this incredibly strategic issue of seeing the release of God's Kingdom riches. It's time to face the realities of the one-legged stool and to begin coming together with the wisdom, strategies and initiatives that will begin changing the posture of the Body from being on the defensive to advancing His Kingdom on the offensive.

It is time for both the Church and the Body in Israel to begin addressing the practical side of this issue of unity and begin working together in their efforts of service that provide the tangible outworkings of the social and economic riches of His Kingdom.

I've seen Kingdom initiatives in operation in which the fullness of His riches ARE operating together and it is an awesome thing. I know that as the release of the three sides to His Kingdom riches gains momentum, we can expect to see unusual signs and wonders and miracles. Signs and wonders and miracles that will change lives, build communities and change nations

Against All Odds

Against all odds, it is time for the operation of the faith that receives the promises. The missing link for the really strategic issues unfolding is the Body working together.

There is no question that for many, the issues our brethren in the Land of Promise are standing for are ones they have been praying for, for years. I have repeatedly heard the statement from believers in Israel that it is hard for those who live in the economy in Israel. However, God's Word says that He has made them to be the head and not the tail.

One member of the Messianic community tells the story of how the Holy Spirit led him to expand his business into catalog sales — eighteen months prior to the beginning of the intifada. Eric Morey's business, prior to that time, was totally dependent upon tourism. When the intifada hit, tourism in Israel hit the skids and at one point was down over 90 percent. Eric's tourism-related business was no different. But because of the catalog sales of products that he had previously sold only to tourists, his operation grew while others floundered.

That's God's economy. When God's economy is in balance with the spiritual and community dimensions of God's Word, it is the edge that operates against all odds. It's the edge that enabled Isaac to sow in famine and to prosper.

There is no question that the spiritual battle over Israel is intense and deadly. But like the example with Eric's business, the reality of the times demands this community of our brethren to start entering a new dimension of realizing the promises. Against all the odds arrayed against them, it is time for them to begin embracing the full availability of the working capital of God's unsearchable Kingdom riches in Messiah: the spiritual, the social and the economic.

The simplicity of our efforts of obedience through my wife's trauma counseling and my activities with entrepreneurial Kingdom business startup workshops often seem meager to us in light of the significance of the issues unfolding in Israel. But the fact is that it is through this Spirit-led simplicity of our service that we have time and again seen the Lord intervene and begin doing *"far exceedingly above all that we might ask, think or even imagine."* We likewise have come to recognize that the Lord often sends us into situations at timely, pivot points — to serve as catalysts for what He is releasing from His Throne Room.

The world is looking for answers. Answers we've already been given — answers tied to the principles of the riches of His Kingdom. We each need to assume our roles as those "living stones" giving evidence to His love and power — and the reality of the Lord operating in our midst.

CHAPTER 11

ENTREPRENEURIALISM AND MODELS OF GOD'S ECONOMY

Penetrating the marketplace with God's principles, God's love and God's Kingdom perspective and agendas will require an understanding of the dynamics involved in entrepreneurialism. The basic principles of entrepreneurialism are biblically based, and they work — regardless of whether the business is a family business, a community business or a larger corporate enterprise.

Change, Disruptions and Opportunity

Business start-up specialist Dr. Bill Bolton states that *"entrepreneurship is the single most important factor in deciding whether or not a region or community achieves its full potential, both economically and socially."* He indicates that this observation is true whether you are dealing with prosperous areas or deprived ones, whether it involves the developed world or the developing world.

He also notes that "entrepreneurship also determines whether successful regions stay that way. Businesses and societies are able to continue fairly well until they are threatened by change." (Bolton, Bill; *Building an Entrepreneur Community*, unpublished paper, January 2001)

Responding to Change with Strategic Entrepreneurship

An important key in God's move into the marketplace is to rekindle the entrepreneurial spirit and to provide the opportunities for entrepreneurs that can make a difference. Abraham, Isaac and Jacob operated family businesses that provided for not only their families, but for the people they hired as well. The marketplace calling will impact those around us.

Dr. Bolton indicates that maintaining the entrepreneurial spirit is essential to maximizing opportunity and maintaining growth — especially in distressed environments and environments of change.

He explains that the temperament of the entrepreneur is one that creates. This is a God-given quality. The entrepreneur innovates. He is a person of vision. Entrepreneurs see opportunity where others do not. They know how to turn opportunity into reality. They are team-builders.

People with organizational or managerial profiles or temperaments tend to stifle the entrepreneurial spirit. Where the entrepreneur creates, the manager temperament tends to work to maintain. Where the entrepreneur sees opportunities, the manager just sees problems. In situations where the entrepreneur is inclined to make things happen, the manager is focused on just doing things right — on operating "within the box," instead of outside the box. Where the entrepreneur operates on principles of building a team, the manager tends to concentrate on simply controlling things. (Bolton, Bill; *Building an Entrepreneur Community*, unpublished paper, January 2001)

So who is the entrepreneur? Here's the Bolton definition: *An entrepreneur is a person who habitually creates and innovates to build something of recognized value around perceived opportunities.* (Bill Bolton and John Thompson, *The Entrepreneur in Focus*, Thomson Learning Publications, London, 2003)

Dr. Bolton and co-author Professor Thompson also assume that we all have talents of one kind or another. Jill Garrett, the Managing Director of the UK Gallup Organization has said that *"Every person can do something better than 10,000 other people."*

This premise applies to the poor and disadvantaged as much as it does to the prosperous and well educated. Identify that one talent

— and line it up with a market need — and you have the foundation for opportunity. (Bolton, Bill & Thompson, John; *Entrepreneurs, Talent, Temperament, Technique*; Butterman, Heineman Publishing, Oxford, 2000)

Jacob is an example of a man with unique entrepreneurial talents. But he had two pivotal experiences with God that illustrate the distinction between simply operating according to the principles — and the change-in-venue that takes place when nothing will do other than God at the forefront.

It was after Jacob met the Lord at Peniel that he genuinely became God's entrepreneur and representative. His first experience at Bethel seems to parallel that of many Christians in business who may have had a very real experience with the Lord. However, they see their business and the Lord on the same footing, which is based on the premise of "You bless my business and I will serve You." But Jacob's Peniel experience changed him and resulted in him becoming Israel — a man who from that point operated according to God's agendas rather than his own.

The Significance of God's Economy

So why is the Biblical premise of entrepreneurialism so pertinent? The short answer is that it comprises a key part of the solution that God's people will offer to the world in these troubling times. During times of upset, God's people are going to be those with both practical and spiritual answers and solutions.

As growing disruptions bombard markets and economies, God's people will be at the forefront by offering an **alternative** to impoverished and distress-impacted regions, as well as to the increases in the cyclic aberrations impacting what we refer to as the "world's economy." That alternative is a biblically-based economic system I refer to as *God's* economy.

The Torah, as well as the Bible as a whole, is replete with wisdom for the ages on economics and business. The book of Deuteronomy alone addresses business issues such as: fairness and customer service, unrighteous gain, God's intention in the ability to create wealth, principles for business loans, the use of collateral, parameters for eliminating poverty, accountability and stewardship, worker's rights, community support of one another, and the conditions for God's blessings.

These are principles that believers in business need to understand and be acquainted with. They reflect the wisdom needed to be the head and not the tail. They are foundational to operating in challenging times. God's principles of business and enterprise form the basis of entrepreneurialism.

God's principles combined with God's values work — whether the enterprise is a family business, a community business, or a multinational organization.

Operating in God's economy also has its foundation in Proverbs 3:5, 6 that we *"trust in the Lord with all our heart, we lean not unto our own understanding; in all our ways we acknowledge Him, and He WILL direct our paths."* I've previously mentioned Stanley Tam. The title of his book tells it all: GOD OWNS MY BUSINESS. Make the Lord your senior partner. Then insure that you give Him at least the same priority that you would any other **covenant senior partner**.

Operating in God's economy requires a giving and generous spirit. Giving off the top is an act of faith and an act of obedience. Participating in and supporting the Lord's work involves looking to Him as the source of our provision rather than to our talents and capabilities. It means looking to Him to meet our needs, rather than being restricted to the confines of what we can do for ourselves.

God's principles in Deuteronomy are based on generosity toward employees and towards those in the community who may be poor and needy. God's economy operates on integrating reverence and worship of the Lord into every facet of our lives. That means that those called into the marketplace will serve a function of both **working alongside** of and **in support** of those called into traditional priestly roles in the church and parachurch operations.

Kings and Priests

Revelations 1:6 says God has made us to be "kings and priests." Over the centuries, the Church has fostered a ministry-laity paradigm to emerge that the Lord never intended.

God's economy is based on the operation of the Old Covenant

model of "kings," which reflects the central role of anointed, kingly leaders in the accomplishment of God's purposes. It was these "kings" who time and again changed the course of nations and brought redemption to God's people. Kings like Abraham, Isaac, Jacob, King David, Joseph, Mordecai and Daniel.

Kingly, servant-leaders: who understand the times and know what to do. Kingly leaders with a priestly anointing that is clearly described in Deuteronomy 17. Kingly leaders: who head up enterprises, communities and empires. Servant-leaders: who are the warriors and administrators.

Kings who go out and take dominion. Who pave the way, provide protection, and facilitate and undergird the strategic purposes of God with a focus on the redemption of His people. Kings who work closely with the priests and the prophets within their sphere, but who lead and pave the way for God's agendas. The Biblical kingly model — as it was intended — is something a great deal more than the mind-set which says, "Give me your shekels, and go about your way."

The Joseph-Pharaoh alliance took the kingly paradigm even a step further. It is an apt parallel to the unique opportunities God is initiating for the times we are entering. The fact is, the Joseph-Pharaoh model was one that was completely unorthodox in terms of the expectations of God's people in that era. It didn't fit with their religious mind-set. It was indeed an unusual, unconventional alliance. They definitely will not fit with the religious mind-sets of what is considered sacred and what is secular; nor will they fit into the constraints of the concept of the laity.

Dual Economic Systems

Isaiah 45 speaks of "double gates." The context of these passages lead me to conclude that this refers to dual economic systems. We indeed operate in the economic system that the world controls. But the Lord is sending forth modern-day biblical entrepreneurs to use both the world's system and God's economy in the accomplishment of His purposes.

In the days before us, those called as God's marketplace ambassadors will move in and out of the world's system — but will bring to bear the principles governing God's economy into both spheres. In this process, there are models being established that bypass the upsets and the impossibilities being experienced by the world's system.

In God's economy, there will be some high-level economic initiatives that surpass the controls and normal order of doing business for major resources and commodities. Beyond the cartels.

Likewise, there are resources yet to be discovered. Again in Isaiah 45 reference is given to hidden riches and treasures of darkness that will be released by the Hand of the Lord. Incredible realignments of global alliances and distribution systems can be expected in the days before us that will bypass the old and supercede existing economic power structures.

There should be no question in anyone's minds that we have entered an era of incredible change. Changes in the infrastructures and assumptions that govern the nature and order of business and the affairs of men. There are now economies without borders. Seats of power in this emerging global economy are no longer limited to the economic and political bins of superpower nations. This is a radical departure from the basis of conducting business in days past.

After Sam Walton of Wal-Mart stores had seventy-eight of his huge chain of stores in place, it took him ten years to build to the point of reaching $150 million annually in revenues. BUT, with one warehouse and one web site, Amazon.com did the same thing in just three years. For the first time in history, with very little capital down, a global business can be established from any point in the globe that is connected to the Internet. Customer mailing lists are available. Web sites can attract customers from all over the world. This is a new day with new paradigms for pursuing opportunity.

Micro-Enterprises. In talking about God's economy, micro-enterprises represent an important alternate economic system. Micro-enterprises can take a variety of forms. They can be individual or home-based enterprises, like a seamstress shop in a remote village. Or a vendor on a local or city street-corner. The concept of micro-enterprises may involve neighborhood or community-run businesses established in economically distressed areas, with distribution outlets operating outside the distressed area.

A Micro-Enterprise Development Model.

I've already briefly mentioned Enterprise Development International of Fairfax, Virginia. This is a unique operation that provides micro-loans for the establishment of micro-businesses. In most instances they approach their work from a community standpoint. When they move into an area, it begins with them raising the funds to do a business startup program in a particular community. They begin with a feasibility study to determine the market needs — realistic opportunity — that might exist locally that could be supported by individual or group-run businesses. That study includes looking at the unique talents of those in the community. It includes the potential for distribution outside the community.

Once a good assessment of market needs, opportunity, local talent and distribution points to a realistic direction and business focus for those in the community, then a business coordinator is hired. This will be someone with business expertise who will live within that community. It is also someone who can provide leadership for the new business owners on a spiritual basis. A wide diversity of individual businesses typically results. The micro-loans will vary depending on the part of the world they are in, but typically they are between $250 and $1500. The micro-loan serves to provide something essential — like the purchase of a good sewing machine for a new seamstress business.

Potential recipients of these loans apply and are interviewed. Those selected go through some basic training in the principles of operating a business. How to budget. How to keep the books. How to set pricing so that you make a profit and provide an affordable service at the same time. Basic "how to run your own business" stuff. After the training the coordinator makes frequent visits to the new businesses and answers questions, encourages and provides ideas.

Then, once a week, there is a gathering of the new business owners — as a support group and a prayer group. This weekly gathering is moderated by the coordinator. But in most instances, the value of the group business-wise, comes from within the new members. The members of these groups, believers and non-believers alike, are again and again touched by the reality of the Lord operating in their midst.

Their success rates might be measured by the fact that over the years 96% of these micro-loans are paid back — to be recycled into other community-based startup ventures.

A Dual-Level Business Model

A dual-level mode of operating a business is another God's economy model which I've seen operating very successfully. This model of business is set up in a way that involves a two-step process involving a successful medium-sized business operation that supports micro-business startups in impoverished areas.

This model is best illustrated by the previously shared story about the unique Singaporean-based business that was birthed between a British geo-physicist turned missionary and a Singaporean Christian businessman. Their objective was to establish a business that would make a powerful spiritual impact. A genuine Kingdom business resulted.

The first level of this operation — the level that creates the majority of the revenues — has offices in several major Pacific Rim cities with their headquarters in Singapore. However, part of the main business includes offices in closed-access nations. Nations hostile to the Lord and closed to any form of Christian proselytizing. But, then there is the second-tier to their operation. This second-tier involves micro-businesses being established in economically distressed rural areas — in these closed-access nations.

One of the examples resulting from this Singaporean Kingdom venture is of a community business that creates attractive, hand-crafted, decorative products that have become extremely popular in Western gift shops. Each product carries a card that says:

> *"The beautiful Southeast Asian country where this product was produced is rich in heritage and culture and its people are warm and hospitable. However, their homeland has been ravaged by years of civil war and strife. Today, these people are rebuilding their shattered lives. Community Hope* (name changed) *is a company dedicated to investing in the lives of the poor in developing nations. This product*

was hand-crafted by one of the people from this
community working with Community Hope. Profits
from the sale of this article help change the lives of
those in need."

A Community-Based Business Startup Model.

Another example is that of a business start-up program
currently taking place among believers in a former CIS country.
This is an economically distressed area. At the time of this writing,
a unique group of UK business owners and executives, led by my
friend Mike Bundock, has birthed 50 new businesses in four years
with only one failure. The new businesses include: bakeries, the
sale of cooking oil, farming, handicrafts, dairy products, computer
training, meat, salt, and other practical needs. Six of these businesses are run by local pastors.

This program includes three phases of training sessions that
provides the basics on putting together a business plan; then a
second session of refining and coaching those who have completed
their plans. The plans that result are then submitted to potential
investors and sponsors who work together with a charitable foundation that serves in the support and adoption of the start-ups. The
third phase of these training sessions then goes on-site with the new
startups to coach and give advice and encouragement.

Personnel in the program reflect one local person plus one
expatriate on the ground to provide ongoing support, advice, and
accountability. **Training** involves visiting teams of business people
sharing expertise and teaching. Many have long-term relationships
with local businesses and also coach them from a distance. **Finance**
in most instances is handled by loan financing. Full repayment
takes place by the end of year-three. Funds are then recycled into
new loans. Supportive ties to local fellowships are a standard part of
the program. Ten percent of profits are given to cooperating congregations. **Long-term** control of the program is handed over to locals.
Year-one entrepreneurs help with year-two businesses. By year-
three they also do some teaching.

In addition to providing for the welfare of their own families,
these Christian business-owners are also making an impact on their

otherwise economically distressed communities. They let their Light shine and are becoming community builders.

In a later chapter, I will be describing a parallel entrepreneurial program, instituted through our ministry of Global Initiatives Foundation, that specializes in assisting the Messianic Jewish community with business startups in Israel and the Former Soviet Union.

Business-Ministry-Foundation Model

One of the more effective models I have encountered is simply an outgrowth of a successful business run by a group of Christian business owners. It is not unlike the models reflected by Robert LeTourneau and Stanley Tam, where business profits are fed into a foundation or ministry or both.

In this case, the model includes a business, a ministry, and a foundation. The lucrative business operated by these six Christian business partners is well respected and in demand in the communities they serve. The proceeds from the business serve to support its own ministry, which among other activities includes Christian orphanages around the world. But then, business-levels grew to a stage in which the owners formed a foundation that invests several million dollars (US) into the efforts of other strategic ministries.

Venture Fund Model

I have seen a variety of funds that serve the purpose of launching Kingdom enterprises. They range from community-based support of small businesses run by believers to funds that parallel venture capital funds, but with a specialty for ventures that are Kingdom-related in nature.

One particular Kingdom venture fund describes itself as a faith-based products group dedicated to the Christian marketplace and the business community. The mission of this publicly-traded fund is to become the foremost Christian products company by providing services and products that distinguish and mobilize the largest affinity group in the world: the Christian Community. The bottom line: to impact the market-driven world culture with a united Christian voice and perspective.

The Nehemiah Trustees Covenant Fund (NTCF) serves the primary purpose of providing grants to Israeli Messianic Jewish believers in distress. But they have also served a very significant function in assisting small business development across the congregational boundaries of Israel's 7000 member Messianic Jewish community. Their pre-intifada efforts resulted in 105 successful businesses being launched.

Business and Technology Ventures

The days before us will see an increase in Kingdom ventures representing unusual investment and resource generation opportunities, creative inventions and ideas, and technology transfers.

Richard and Nancy Speck's operation of MicroSpace, Inc. represents a unique entrepreneurial innovation effort. Another firm they started and sold, Spectron Engineering, is still known for the state-of-the-art, precision jet aircraft test equipment that Richard designed. Their success with Spectron has enabled Richard to pursue the research and development of a low-budget alternative to today's expensive satellite launches. His technological designs in the area of rocketry hold the potential of changing the face of the aerospace industry and blessing the Kingdom in the process.

Business and technology incubator programs will foster a generation of new business opportunities. These will be opportunities the Lord will reveal and entrust to Kingdom business persons He has prepared, who hear his voice and have a heart for furthering His agendas and initiatives for this day.

What is emerging should not be confused with the high-powered, get-rich-quick investments and sales schemes. These will be sovereignly designed opportunities with strategic market implications reflecting new inventions and technologies along with the development of untapped resources tied to timely, critical market needs. Among these Kingdom ventures will be corporate alliances that result in the release of new avenues of resources. New models for funding these ventures will evolve and be directed by Kingdom professionals.

As the Body grapples with the changes and challenges that have been unfolding since 9/11, there is a growing awareness of the potential of these biblically-based economic models and an expectation of the potential involved by embracing God's economy.

Counterfeits

Those emerging as anointed Kingdom business leaders will be untouched by the greed of mammon or the lust for power. Their impact will exemplify the difference outlined in Malachi 3:18: *"Then you shall again discern between the righteous and the wicked, between the one who serves God and the one who does not serve Him."*

There will be a clear difference in their mode of operation and purpose. Daniel 1:20 describes that difference: *"In all matters that the king inquired of them, he found them ten times better than all the magicians and astrologers that were in his realm."*

Simultaneously, the enemy would like to infiltrate the camp of the righteous to pervert, discredit, divert and bring disarray to the thrust of God's move into the marketplace. There will be those who are sent to masquerade as God's emissaries in the marketplace. There will be counterfeit programs and opportunities, as well as business people posing as Christian entrepreneurs and business-owners.

The counterfeit programs will be designed to be part lie and part truth. Counterfeit opportunities, designed to deceive the very elect, which will resemble important God-directed agendas. The counterfeit initiatives may appear at first glance as right and good, but they are designed to create a flurry of activity and consume the energies of those they attract. They likewise are designed to undermine and divert the focus away from genuine initiatives the Lord is releasing. Not every testimony will reflect truth. But God's people and God's ventures will stand the test and bear witness. There will always be clues that give discernment and alert us to the deceivers and the phonies.

Strength in Community for Kingdom Entrepreneurs

While there are always exceptions, as a rule, very, very few will be called to go it alone. As Kingdom business owners and entrepreneurs, and as facilitators and operators within God's economy, the business community can profit and grow by meeting and praying together. Aside from the basic support and accountability of gathering together, there is much to be gained through sharing and pooling of business expertise, wisdom and spiritual insight.

Business ownership involves responsibilities and challenges that quite often are genuinely understood only among those who walk that pathway. The wisdom reflected in the start-up programs in which new entrepreneurs meet to share and pray is a venue that should be extended to Christian business-owners in general.

As the scripture says, "*one will put a thousand to flight and two, ten-thousand.*" There is strength in community and by fostering that strength, the potential impact for the Lord is greatly multiplied.

CHAPTER 12

KINGS, RULERS AND LEADERS

The Word the Lord spoke to me in the mid-seventies that would shape and define my calling alluded to my role in working along side kings, rulers and leaders.

That Word was: *"Just as in the days of Joseph and Daniel, God will bring out mighty works at your hand; as you are led into the midst of the world, kings, rulers and leaders will be converted and humbled; you shall work beside them and be given authority and your counsel will be heeded for their good."*

Understanding who the "kings, rulers and leaders" this Word refers to is significant. We are in a day in which God is anointing Kingdom ambassadors with the authority of Joseph — who will be used as catalysts as they work alongside modern-day Pharaohs to build the Kingdom of God.

So, just who do these kings, rulers and leaders represent? Our modern-day concept of a king is that of a reigning monarch, a political ruler over a nation or territory defined by borders. While the Merriam-Webster dictionary offers a definition that coincides with this concept of king, it also expands it by describing a **"king"** as: "one that holds a supreme or preeminent position in a particular sphere." This definition parallels that of **ruler** as being "one who exercises authority, command, or dominating influence in some specific sphere;" and a **leader** as "a person who by force of example, talents, or qualities of leadership plays a directing role, wields commanding influence, or has a following in any sphere of activity or thought."

The English word "king" is derived from an ancient Germanic compound whose first constituent is represented by the English word "kin," and whose second constituent is represented by English –"ing." In other words, a "king" originally was one exercising rule over an extended "kin" or family community. This insight finds a strong corollary to those considered kings in days of Abraham, Isaac and Jacob.

In the days of these early biblical patriarchs, kings were those who were the overseers of the economic communities which had at their core an extended ruling-family.

Historically, the world has had major seasons in terms of the type of dominant governing rule it has gone through. Over time, the extended family communities have grown into city-states and then become nation-states as the primary means of societal order, community, law and rule. In that context, there have been seasons in which the dominant means of rule has been by military leaders. There have been other seasons in which the prevailing rule has been through religious leaders. There have been still other times throughout history with governments ruled primarily by autocratic monarchs. For the most part for each, the dominant rule was established by power or economic wealth, and in most cases both.

In our most recent history, the dominant ruling structure has been through independent nation-states: territories with borders. But there is strong evidence to support that this approach to how our world is governed is undergoing some very subtle and unusual change.

That change bears not only on the structure and role of traditional and non-traditional nation-states, but on those who wield the influence and occupy the seats of power that impact the course of world events. But before addressing the change underway, the emerging seats of power and a distinct shift in our traditional understanding of "kings, rulers and leaders," I want to review the concept of God's Kingdom rule.

God's Kingdom Rule
God's original intention was for man to be in fellowship with

Him and for man to rule over the works of His hands. But through disobedience in the garden, man fell. With the fall, evil entered the world. God's plan of redemption and restoration came through God's chosen people, Israel. Through Israel came the Word of God and the Messiah.

Jesus came to restore and to redeem. In a world driven by passion and power, Jesus came to reestablish God's Kingdom rule with the authority and purpose that comes from above. In a topsy-turvy world that calls black white and white black, Jesus came to reintroduce truth and righteousness, reclaim God's sovereignty and extend His principles and blessing into every facet of the operation of this world.

Again and again, Jesus announced His earthly ministry with the Words, *"the Kingdom of God is at hand."* God's Kingdom rule, which was God's intention from the beginning and the prototype established through the patriarchs, was being brought to light and entrusted to His followers — through Jesus' earthly ministry.

What Jesus unveiled, with principles comprising God's Kingdom rule, had its foundations outlined in the Torah. The principles governing the operation of the economic-communities operated by Abraham, Isaac and Jacob are found in the book of Deuteronomy.

While there was a parallel between the communities operated by the patriarchs and the kingdoms of the world around them in their day, there were two distinguishing differences. First was the central role placed in their covenant relationship to the Lord, which shaped the principles of community government to be outlined in Deuteronomy. Second was the type of authority wielded by their leaders: they were subject to the law and principles of God's covenant rule like everyone else.

God's Kingdom rule was and is people-centered, rather than power centered. It incorporates a different type of authority to govern. Likewise, God's Kingdom rule reflects a Gospel that incorporates every facet of our lives: spiritual, community (social) and economic.

These unique characteristics were a major divergence from the general operation of other kings and rulers during the days of the patriarchs. God's Kingdom rule in the days of the patriarchs reflected economic communities designed to support and bless its members.

The distinctiveness of these God-centered economic communities operated by Abraham, Isaac and Jacob was tied to their covenant relationship with the Lord. Their covenant relationship with the Lord was based on His ongoing guidance, protection and blessing through these kingly leaders that was extended to their community as a whole.

These truths were foundational to the central teachings of Jesus' earthly ministry — which were centered around God's Kingdom principles and how they operated in practical ways to meet the needs of everyday people. While Jesus taught the people practical dimensions of how God's Kingdom rule would work in their lives; he extended those truths to His leaders-in-training, by imparting to them how to operate with the authority that accompanies one in leadership in the Kingdom of God.

As such, the teachings of Jesus outlined these spiritual, community (social) and economic dimensions that undergird the principles of God's Kingdom rule.

The parable of the talents carries a strong message that God expects us to make our assets work for us. The parable of the good Samaritan provides a clear illustration of how our assets should be used to help those in need, who should be considered our neighbors. The parable of the ten virgins gives an apt message on the need for planning and being prepared for the unexpected. Jesus taught us about reciprocity and generosity with the Words, *"give and it will be given unto you."* He taught about responsibility with *"unto him that much is given, much is required."* And He taught us about the spiritual and practical power of unity with the Words, *"If any two of you AGREE on earth about anything that they may ask, it shall be done for them by My Father who is in heaven. For where two or three have gathered together in My name, there I am in their midst."*

So, how does all this relate to my questions about the nature of the "kings, rulers and leaders" the Lord spoke to me about in the mid-seventies?

Economic, Community and Spiritual Dimensions of Kingdom Leaders

In the context of God's Kingdom rule, authority for governing is a God-centered, economic-community-based model. The balanced operation of the economic, community and spiritual in a given sphere will define those who are today's Kingdom leaders. This will be the case whether the sphere of operation is economically-driven or community-driven. With God at the center, economically-driven enterprises will operate as communities and genuine Kingdom communities will incorporate the economic.

So what is it that defines "kings, rulers and leaders" who will be making an impact for the Kingdom of God? The kings, rulers and leaders among the patriarchs were God's chosen. They were models in establishing God's principles and God's rule in the world in which they lived. They were lights shining in the darkness of their world. They were an example to the peoples around them of how the God of Israel protected and blessed those who were His own. They operated economic communities that had a spiritual foundation because of their covenant with the Lord. They were blessed when they were faithful and obedient to their covenant; and when they were not, the blessings and protection of God were gradually choked out.

So, how does that apply today? As believers, we are ambassadors of God's Kingdom. Our function is in reestablishing God's Kingdom rule: not only on a spiritual level, but at the community and economic levels as well.

Those the Lord spoke to me about as kings, rulers and leaders are those paving the way for God's Kingdom rule at the economic-community level, with its foundations based on the principles of God's Kingdom outlined by Jesus.

While individual entrepreneurial entities form the basis to support the communities of which we are a part; there are also entrepreneurial endeavors that have grown and become communities in their own right. And when entrepreneurial endeavors grow to become communities AND are led by God's people — those leaders take on a role that is not unlike those of the kings and patriarchs of old.

Righteous Authority and Power

Righteousness and right-standing with God defines the power and authority that comes from above. Likewise, righteous authority and power determine those leaders who are ordained by God and those who are entrusted with God's Kingdom rule.

There are two levels of kingly authority through which God works His divine purposes. The first are the non-believers God uses because they are God-seekers who are both sensitive to and willing to embrace God's will when they recognize it. Pharaoh during the time of Joseph was ordained and chosen by God, as was King Cyrus, who was described in Isaiah 45 as God's anointed.

The other category of kingly authority through which God achieves His purposes are those who believe in Him, are called according to His purposes and whose sensitivity to His principles and His voice are a pivotal priority in the outworking of their gifts in leadership and administration. Joseph the patriarch was a man who understood the heart of God, God's Kingdom rule and the authority God had entrusted to him to bring about God's redemptive purposes during the time of crisis and famine that was to strike the world in Joseph's day.

Daniel operated under a similar calling, authority and anointing to that of Joseph. The foundation to how they impacted both the course of the nations in which they found themselves and the destiny of God's people is a reflection of the heritage and principles reflected in the governing leadership of Abraham, Isaac and Jacob, which was outlined by Moses in Deuteronomy.

In other words, whether it was a community of some 300 persons during the early days of Abraham; the 600,000 men, not counting women or children, led by Moses at the time of the Exodus; or the remnant of God's people in the nation of Babylon during the days of Daniel; for each, there were people of God either at the helm or in seats of power who were kings, leaders and ambassadors of God's Kingdom rule. They wielded authority and influence. They made a difference from the perspective of God's purposes. They were community builders and nation-shakers who understood and operated in a way that reflected the spiritual, community and economic balance needed to govern according to God's Kingdom rule. That was what was operating whether it was within the community-nations governed by God's covenant or the secular nations God was using to bring about His purposes for His people.

But there is a change underway that will govern the way we define the "kings, rulers and leaders" of our day.

The Change

A recent book entitled, *Global, Inc.*, (Gabel and Bruner, 2003, The New Press, New York) makes the following observation: "*Of the 100 largest economies in the world, 53 are corporations. A handful of corporate giants control most of the world's energy, technology, food, banks, industry, and media. Yet despite the ubiquity of enormous multinationals and their tremendous economic, social, political, and environmental presence in the world, the history and character of corporate entities remains largely unknown, daunting, and inaccessible to the general public.*"

The change underway reflects a shift in power toward the economic. The economic dimension — with the pivotal focus on "*energy, technology, food, banks, industry and the media* — has become as central to the order and course of world events as the political. The underlying clash is between the forces of evil and the Kingdom of God. The forces of evil are targeting the power tied to the financial, energy, technology, food, business and media resources and structures of this world, while the Church too often has proved content with not dirtying its hands with the economic dimensions tied to the community. But the separation of the sacred and the secular-profane was never God's intention: as from the beginning He gave His people authority to rule over the works of His hands.

This thought brings us back to the issue of better understanding who these modern-day kings, rulers and leaders are that the Lord will be using for His purposes in the days before us. I noted that the Merriam-Webster dictionary provides a definition of "king" that goes beyond either the political or territorial. A "king" is one who holds a supreme or preeminent position in a particular sphere. A ruler exercises authority, command, or dominating influence in some specific sphere. A leader is one who by force of example, talents, or qualities of leadership plays a directing role, wields commanding influence, or has a following in any sphere of activity or thought.

Leaders of corporations and communities — whether redeemed or simply prepared-by-God for His purposes like Joseph's Pharoah or King Cyrus — clearly fit into a modern-day category of kings, rulers and leaders that the Lord spoke to me about in the mid-seventies. These corporate entities are in reality nation-states without borders. While in most cases these larger corporate enterprises that control 53 of the world's 100 largest economies may be without the spiritual and essential covenant dimensions of Kingdom enterprises; they do incorporate the community and economic dimensions that may simply be awaiting a modern-day Joseph or Daniel to enter the picture to fulfill their God-ordained destiny.

Ben Ronn is an Israeli-American who is a leader in the Jewish community of a major U.S. city. He flew for the IDF in Israel's '67 war. For years, he was CEO of a $60 million multinational firm. Currently, he operates a low-key, but potent- consulting firm that facilitates strategic alliances between Israeli and U.S. businesses. Ben is a man who recognizes the value of the role being played by modern-day Josephs. He is a man who undoubtedly will open doors for Kingdom ventures.

George Allison was the head of a $1.4 billion corporation. He had been hired as president of this firm to bring about a reversal to the huge losses they had been experiencing. He in turned hired me as a senior vice president whose role was to put the institution back in touch with the marketplace. I proceeded by making major changes internally and externally. We conducted values-oriented advertising and made a point of acknowledging and working hard to uphold our responsibility to the community. Internally, I awakened believers to their role in the needed change by initiating Bible studies and also attending prayer gatherings that prayed for the organization.

While I got flak for my high profile Christian posture from those at my peer level, George Allison, a nominal church-goer at the time, supported my efforts. Our results not only achieved a successful corporate turnaround, but they had a ripple effect throughout this firm and across the communities it served. First believers in both this organization and its communities began taking a stand for righteousness and became community builders. But then, complemented by the values-based ads and programs we sponsored, there emerged a bridge of cooperative initiatives between believers and their communities that extended far beyond what our corporation was doing. George Allison, as the head of the corporation, served as a modern-day king.

The Change, Kingdom Entrepreneurs and Alliances

I see still another dimension to this emerging change that bears on the potential role that can be played by modern-day "kings, rulers and leaders." It involves entrepreneurial Kingdom businesses that are beginning to recognize the power of alliances.

An August 11, 2002 Wall Street Journal article, *"Independent's Day,"* describes the power of an entrepreneurial coalition of smaller advertising agencies bidding on the enviable Chrysler advertising account. The article made the following observations: *"The Chrysler competition illustrates why independent-business alliances are hot. What's striking is how adamantly Bell [Chrysler's VP of Marketing] opposed hiring a large ad agency. He valued the creativity of the independent entrepreneurs. But he also wanted scale. Hey, customers want what they want. Clearly, the changing face of customer needs (or make that demands) is driving more entrepreneurs to team up in groups of 5, 50, or 100 companies. It's a great hook when you can present your alliance as a single-source solution, especially in a tough economy."*

The article made the following conclusions: *"An alliance's mission is often simple: increase sales and profits. But many alliances also appeal to an entrepreneur's deep-rooted sense of identity. The people who start and join alliances believe unceasingly in the advantages of remaining independent and are willing to defend that unalienable 'right.' But the best of the alliances are pushing the boundaries of what independent means in some very inventive ways. And by joining forces they're finding even more freedom — truly the best of both worlds."*

In still another arena, Ariel Sharon, in his autobiography *"Warrior,"* described the steps that resulted in the formation of

Israel's Likud party: "*Angry opposition was growing .... among those resenting the stranglehold Labor and its daughter institutions often held over their jobs, their housing, their bank loans, their children's education, and other basic facts of their existence. A proliferation of bureaucratic organizations that paralleled government agencies fed thousands of Labor Alignment functionaries and imposed a heavy burden on almost all the country's economic and social endeavors.*"

Mr. Sharon's initiative brought together a coalition of some of the most unlikely participants in the formation of the Likud party some years ago. It was not unlike the independent entrepreneurs bidding on the Chrysler account or the array of fractionalized entities operating within the Body today.

The story of this phenomenon in Israel speaks volumes of what the power of unity can overcome and achieve, even when comprised of players with wide divergences in their views and positions. But it will take a new breed of modern-day kings, rulers and leaders with a genuine Kingdom -perspective to cross this bridge. It is a bridge that is being crossed and led by pioneers embracing the Kingdom economic-community-spiritual paradigm.

I've already mentioned being a part of launching an initiative that has been just such an alliance. The Joseph Project is a coalition of Christian and Messianic Jewish ministries, working together with businesses in an effort to address a serious problem being faced in Israel. The results of this Israeli "faith initiative" in-action have to date, far exceeded anyone's expectations. The results speak of the synergy and exceptional level of change that come from cooperative efforts and alliances.

What is reflected in the examples of the Chrysler account alliances, the coalition that birthed the Likud party and this business-ministry coalition for Israel — and what is sorely needed at the forefront in today's power struggle between righteousness and darkness — is the unity that comes from community.

Community that is not necessarily defined by borders, but by the seats of power that are the subtle drivers of the economic foundations manifesting across the globe. Seats of power, with kings, rulers and leaders who are responsive to God's Kingdom rule and as a result will anticipate, bypass and simply override the famines, reversals, threats and terror of our day in order to accomplish God's purposes.

A New Breed of Kings, Rulers and Leaders

Proverbs tells us that *"righteousness exalts a nation."* That principle applies as we realize the definition of a "nation" can extend to include a community without borders or a business enterprise. Righteous communities according to God's principles will grow as a result of God's blessings, which will be the result of operating under His Kingdom rule and according to His Kingdom principles.

Yet the world is in turmoil because of the perversions of power operating in the seats of authority in business and government. These perversions of power are not the result of the businesses or governments, but rather the kings, rulers and leaders at their helms.

Perversions of power are aligned with perversions of truth. Almost three decades ago, I came across a book about the media, entitled *"The Fourth Branch of Government."* There are alliances in the highest seats of power serving the god of this world and his agendas. Hitler's number one strategy in his quest for world domination was the concept of the "big lie." His demonic premise was that if you make a lie big enough, people will be overwhelmed by it and tend to believe it, especially if it plays into their fears. Hitler represented one of the most insidious perversions of power in modern-day history.

These types of distortions of truth, generated from the pits of hell, are still running rampant and being promulgated from the ranks of modern-day religious and political despots. Those who call black white and white black. It is this same demonic strategy that is being played out today in even more subtle ways, as the devil has infiltrated the ranks of the media with its big lies on values and goals and realities tied to current issues, such as peace and terror. Kings, rulers and leaders are wielding these perversions of power and truth.

It is time for those who are called by His Name, especially those called as modern-day Kingdom rulers and leaders to begin emerging and coming together in the accomplishment of God's big picture purposes for our day. The days we have entered are evil.

But just as in the days of Joseph and Daniel, God has been preparing a key group of "kings, rulers and leaders." Those who have been paying an incredible cost for the responsibility and calling they are or will be embracing. But these are ones who will be community builders and ones who will change the course of nations. They are Kingdom ambassadors, who will guide the Pharaohs and Cyruses of this hour. They are the ones who will serve to reestablish God's Kingdom rule within key seats of power in this world.

Examples of Modern-Day Kings, Rulers and Leaders

The focus of this book limits elaborating on the many just within my sphere, who have and are serving as modern-day Kingdom rulers and leaders. I have been blessed to serve and work alongside many of these Kingdom rulers and leaders whose faithfulness and obedience have changed the course of events so that they line up with God's purposes and initiatives.

I have been honored to have served numerous secular and ministry organizations over the years. In most cases, there has always been a "God-purpose" that has superceded the immediate assignment. Secular clients have told me that my recommendations have proven to be "prophetic."

In recalling executives, organizations, governmental and ministry leaders I have been honored to work with, there is a strong sense of many of them being modern-day parallels to the heroes of faith noted in the book of Hebrews — heroes of whom the world is not worthy.

In the governmental arena, I recall Jim Head. God spoke to Jim to run for the office of governor of Oklahoma. I helped him to define the issues. "Family-values" was his platform. For a year he traversed the state giving speeches and holding press conferences — with a focus on the issue of family-values. This was prior to the time CBN ever picked up and began their key role in taking this issue nationally. Jim Head lost the Republican primary and at the time thought he had missed God. Yet, from his "unsuccessful" mid-America run for office, this faithful servant of the Lord set in motion an issue that has changed the course of this nation.

Likewise, there are many, many within the corporate sphere, whose individual roles have impacted industries and the communities they serve. I've previously mentioned Bill Bartlett. Bill is a genuine Kingdom entrepreneur-leader. Since the launch of his organization, I've been honored to be a part of numerous consulting assignments for this first-class Christian CEO. Bill uniquely fits the role of the modern-day kings, rulers and leaders the Lord spoke to me about back in the mid-seventies.

In my most recent assignment with Bill, I accompanied him on a number of visits with a cross-section of his firm's clientele. I witnessed first-hand the response of his clients, leaders in their own right, to his industry leadership.

In less than a decade, not only has he taken this Fortune 500 startup to the place of being a respected, global industry leader, but he and his team have come to command the respect of their clientele as being innovative forerunners changing the course of their industry. They've done so as people you can trust and depend upon. As an organization, they strive for excellence and go the extra mile in their service to their clientele — contrary to the dog-eat-dog approach that has prevailed in their industry. Yet they are not bashful in letting people know that their success is the result of prayer and God's favor. Kings, rulers and leaders!

Mike McGowan and I first connected and became close friends back in early 1969 when I took over his position as Senior Battalion Advisor of a battalion of Vietnamese Marines. Mike had previously been a White House aide to Lyndon Johnson. Now as a retired USMC Colonel and business owner, he is a genuine community builder. He has served as the head of civic business groups and made a big impact in the area of Christian education, as well as strengthening the Christian business community through the regular weekly prayer meetings he hosts.

Another example is Mike Steen. Mike, a man who has become one my closest friends, served as the Marketing and Merger-Acquisition Director for a Fortune 500 company. Mike was responsible for re-positioning his operation to the marketplace and the public at the time this firm entered a major growth cycle. I was responsible for conducting a series of strategic assignments key to the planning and development of their new corporate image, along with evaluating the market potential of a number of their acquisition candidates. In a three-year period of time, Mike was responsible for acquisitions that totaled almost $900 million (US). During that tenure his firm's stock went from $7 per share to $70. I have frequently had the pleasure of praying and sharing with Mike as God progressively became first priority in his life.

Just within my own sphere, the array of modern-day kings, rulers and leader I have served, collaborated with and worked alongside are too numerous to mention. They are kings, rulers and leaders making a difference for the Kingdom of God. Taking bold stands for righteousness. Opening doors of opportunity. Building communities. Changing the course of industries and nations. Serving as catalysts to release Kingdom initiatives in the establishment of the Kingdom of God.

Traditional seats of power are indeed being redefined. Territorial and political boundaries do not necessarily reflect the dominant influence. While coalitions of evil and alliances designed to undermine righteousness are globally emerging under our nose; in the form of political, media and financial power brokers in today's systems; there is a groundswell of "Kingdom enterprises" coming to the forefront that reflect the covenants, economies, community-social and divine purposes established as models by the patriarchs. With them are a new breed of "kings, rulers and leaders," who range from entrepreneurs to corporate executives, to those who will stand alongside the Pharaohs and Cyruses of our day as God's ambassadors.

The emergence of this new breed of movers and shakers is a means to anticipate the destructive strategies of the evil one. This new breed of "kings, rulers and leaders" is a move of God designed to reestablish God's Kingdom rule within their spheres of influence, while impacting and building the communities and nations of which they are a part.

CHAPTER 13

THE BIG PICTURE

"When the enemy comes in like a flood, the Spirit of the Lord will raise up a standard against it." Isaiah 59:19 NKJV

What are the practical dimensions that connect the dots between the operation of the Kingdom of God and the big picture realities being faced in our day?

Since the turn of the millennium there has been a marked increase in activities Satan has been unleashing against God's anointed and God's chosen: the Body and Israel. These assaults have carried with them a level of viciousness previously unseen in this generation. In addition, these assaults have increased in targeting strategic-level initiatives and leaders.

The confusion and deception levels that sway and persuade those in the ranks of the spiritually vulnerable and blind have resulted in gross distortions of reality at the highest levels in global leadership. Alarmingly, the level of anti-Christian and anti-Semitic sentiment has increased to levels that are no longer subtle or hidden.

Among those genuinely called by His Name, there is *the need for a more effective response* — a response that grasps the issues of significance for this hour. The issues that underlie the Issachar context of *"understanding the times and knowing what to do."* The big picture.

The truth in Isaiah 59 provides an apt glimpse into the response needed — a response that extends beyond our human efforts. It points to the Spirit of the Lord raising up a standard when the enemy comes against God's people. *The context in Isaiah 59 is judgment against the enemies of the Lord.* But for that judgment and the power of God to be unleashed, there is an alignment needed among God's people. That alignment is tied to the power of God, the judgment of God and His holiness.

"Understanding the times and knowing what to do" involves the need for an accurate big picture perspective. A perspective that guides our approach so that it releases the Spirit of the Lord to move against the enemies of God's people. That's the pivotal issue. Doing what is needed in both perspective and approach to unlock the power of God to operate on our behalf. This means not only being prepared, but having our hand at the plow with the focus on the right agendas.

The Battles versus the War

I recently read the text of a talk given by a man I knew many years ago. Tony Zinni and I were USMC captains and advisors to the Vietnamese Marines in the late '60s. General Zinni is now retired from the military, but as the former Commander in Chief over the US forces in the Middle East, his talk reflects a strategic perspective concerning how we are handling post-war Iraq. It also uncovers a truth that those segments of the Body of Christ who hear God's voice and flow in His Spirit need to face.

His talk was entitled *"Winning the War,"* and the premise of his message was that since WWII, *the US has had a tendency to win the battles, but not the war.* He posed some very key questions in terms of the role the military now has in post-war Iraq. He addressed *the very strategic issue of changing a nation.*

General Zinni's insights deal with some very poignant and strategic policy level issues. A big picture perspective. Each of his points was based on what is good and what is right — in terms of setting things in order in this world in which we live. But *the big picture dimension General Zinni missed is the spiritual one.*

The Course of Nations and the Spiritual Dimension

At the end of WWII and the defeat of Japan, General Douglas MacArthur called for missionaries to come in to play a major role in the rebuilding of that land. Four showed up. Some reports indicate there were only two.

While there has been a great awakening and maturing in the Church's role in the affairs of nations since Douglas MacArthur's day, much of the church is still not prepared and doesn't have a clue. There has been however, an emergence of some who do. It is a substantial number. But the issue for those awakened and active segments of the Body of Christ being led by the Spirit today is one that dovetails with the premise which General Zinni postulated. We tend to win the battles, but not the war.

For those who understand the spiritual foundations of the drama being played out in the nature and order of world events — there is a need to also understand that to win the war, we need to understand the times and to know what to do.

To win the war, as General Zinni suggests, we need change. This change places a huge responsibility on those with eyes to see and ears to hear, to not allow the spiritual dimension to be masked as it was during WWII. The change required involves a responsibility of the awakened and active segments of the Body of Christ to be about His business with a big picture perspective.

To win the war, we need nation-changers, like Joseph the patriarch. Nation-changers: who grasp and accurately address the spiritual dimension. Nation-changing efforts: that understand the key spiritual dimensions of the standard, the strategy and the goals.

Ignoring the big picture, spiritual dimension can only conclude with a blindness that will eventually result in eroding our ability to win even the battles. To adequately address what lies before us, we as believers need to adjust our mind-sets.

While the "war against terrorism" is indeed an encouraging step, it falls short. The big picture war underway today involves the enemy's infiltration into the power structures that undergird the free-world's infrastructures. Much like in the days of the Nazi rise to power.

As in the Nazi rise to power, the spiritual dimension operating behind the battles of terrorism and radical Islam are the age-old strongholds — referred to in Jeremiah 51 as Babylon and Chaldea. Mammon and sorcery. Power and witchcraft. Strongholds that have infiltrated the fabric of society. Strongholds that have penetrated political, religious and intellectual circles both within the West and around the world.

However, as these "battles" in Iraq are pursued, the difference is the fact that the battle is taking place where the strongholds of Babylon and Chaldea originated. Which is good — but only so long as the spiritual dimension is recognized, which more accurately uncovers just what is being dealt with.

Recognizing the Enemy's Modus Operandi

While the enemy is being forced out of hiding and dealt with in the very heart of darkness today, there simultaneously is a parallel move to bring acceptability to evil while discrediting righteousness and the confrontation of evil. This is not unlike the controversy, flurry and confusion during Hitler's rise to power, which was clearly fueled and directed by the spiritual dimension. A realistic big picture perspective has got to recognize the operation and alliance of the strongholds of Babylon and Chaldea, as pointed out by Jeremiah 2600 years ago.

Babylon and Chaldea. Mammon and sorcery. Today's Western perspective tends to view the primary evidence of mammon as being greed and materialism. It does certainly involve greed. But **the real operation of mammon** is fueled by its alliance with sorcery. Witchcraft. An alliance evidenced by the destruction that results from the operation of its wicked, corrupt power. An alliance that carries with it a lust for power. An alliance that seduces and controls and eventually curtails the operation of dignity and freedom and opportunity.

Mammon that operates in this mode tears down the communities and ultimately entire regions around its operation. Across the globe, the major clue to this alliance between mammon and sorcery is a region distinguished by abject poverty. The poverty is tied to false religion. In regions marked by poverty, a frail or no middle class, a minimum of entrepreneurial activity, and perverse or atheistic governmental-related religious activities: these are likely to be areas dominated by this alliance between mammon and sorcery.

The Lord is indeed moving the Church out of the passive modes evidenced when General MacArthur got such a pitiful response at the conclusion of WWII. Those being called as modern-day Josephs and Daniels have a very strategic role in the course of world events. Those being used to finance the mobilization of Kingdom initiatives and God's end-time strategies are coming forth.

Yet it shouldn't take a rocket scientist to discern that when those segments of the Church that recognize the spiritual dimension of the war underway are being consistently attacked in the area of finances; there is a need to get to the root of the matter and discern not only what the Spirit of the Lord is doing, but what our response needs to be. We need a better grasp of the big picture to realistically intercede and respond.

There is indeed a grand-strategy emerging. "Grand-strategy" is a military term, which refers to the highest level strategy driving all the other strategies.

As the Lord mobilizes and sensitizes His people to move into key roles in the course of world events, the battleground is being defined. As the Lord is mustering His army for battle, the big picture issues are being defined. As God's mobilization strategies unfold, the evil one is attempting to push the Church back in his attempts to keep it "in its place." The devil's goal for keeping the Church "in its place" is to see it enmeshed in the arena of "playing church" and business as usual. It is his intention to keep the Church as far away from the realm of impacting communities and nations, as possible. It is the evil one's aim to keep the Body of Christ focused on the battles, and unaware of the big picture of the war underway.

The Need for a Big Picture Mind-Set
The paradigm the Body of Christ operated from prior to 2001 is falling short. It is becoming increasingly clear that while we indeed embrace the spiritual dimension so desperately needed in this hour, that *something more is needed to bring us to the place to where we will not only win the battles, but be positioned to win the war.*

That something more will involve a fresh look at not only the standard, but how the standard can be most effectively wielded — the strategy. And with that, the mind-set that embraces the big picture goal required to win the war. We need to take a fresh look at the issues of revival, unity and dominion and how they operate together as the standard, the strategy and the goal for not only the assaults currently coming against the Body, but the course of world events.

The Issue of Dominion and Seats of Power

Since the time that General MacArthur called for missionaries to come, the Church has undergone an incredible process of maturing, awakening and preparation. While we will always have those who will resist change and be blind to the initiatives being released from God's Throne Room, we have in this hour entered a time in which the Lord is moving His people into the fabric of society. Like Joseph the patriarch and Daniel in Babylon, these men and women of God are prepared and aligned and entering the seats of power of this world to bring about God's plans and purposes. To serve as nation-changers.

For nation-changing efforts to work, the key will be the spiritual dimension. Joseph and Daniel were very bold in their roles to speak God's Words of wisdom into the dilemmas facing the kings and rulers of their day. They did so in a way, that everyone knew that the wisdom they operated from came from the Lord.

For this to work today, an adjustment of mind-sets is in order. The Church is still largely operating on the premise that separates the sacred from the secular. A premise that has rendered the Church anemic in restoring dominion into the hands of God's people, as God intended before the fall. A premise founded not on Scripture, but on the traditions and doctrines of men.

This present move of God in the marketplace with God's prepared vessels penetrating key seats of power in business and government will uniquely impact the course of nations. But there are certain perspectives that need to be recognized, that will release God's role in this equation, which is implied in these passages from Isaiah 59.

Dominion is a very pivotal matter in all of this. Dominion and authority. Dominion that results from the restoration that comes from revival and the unity released in a genuine move of the Spirit.

From this dynamic will unfold the operation of the Biblical dimensions of community, covenant and Kingdom.

Revival and unity give birth to dominion. While the redemption from revival may be an "act of restoring," dominion takes restoration to still another level. Jesus came to reestablish man's relationship with God and to restore that God-intended dominion. Within that context, Jesus again and again announced His earthly ministry with the Words, "*the Kingdom of God is at hand.*"

As the free-world faces the unsettling change and disruptions coming upon the earth, the reality is that this truth is as applicable today as it was in the days when Jesus walked the face of the earth: "*the Kingdom of God is at hand.*"

In the face of the enemy's growing offensive, it is time to reevaluate. It is time for a *response that exceeds our best human efforts and activates the principles releasing a mighty move of the Spirit.* It is time for a response that will reverse the posture of the Body from being in a defensive mode to going onto the offensive.

To win the war, we need nation-changers. But along with the nation-changers is the need to recognize the evil one's primary schemes in his quest to hang onto the dominion that man relinquished at the fall. The enemy's age-old occult strategies in his quest for power operate in conjunction with religious spirits. These religious spirits provide entrance to undermining plants that the enemy has among the inner circles of believers. Judas is a prime example of the operation of inner-circle religious spirits.

God's move in the marketplace, as well as God raising up modern-day Josephs and Daniels is about dominion. It's about restoration. It's about nation changers and winning not just the battles, but the war. God's move in the marketplace is about penetrating the fabric of society — where revival, unity and dominion will serve as catalysts to the release and operation of the often overlooked Biblical dimensions of community, covenant and Kingdom.

During our visits to Belarus, we have witnessed an incredible level of covenant and community in operation. Belarus is one of the two remaining dictatorships in the Former Soviet Union, where I have led ministry teams putting on Global Initiatives' God's economy business startup program. I'll be sharing more about this in the chapter "Against All Odds." What we witnessed there was this ancient biblical paradigm operating in a most unlikely setting. Believers operating as community builders. Operating as modern-day Josephs and Daniels in the fabric of that society. Speaking God's prophetic Words of wisdom into the issues and dilemmas being faced by leaders and rulers. Extending God's love and healing through the operation of the principles of Isaiah 58, of reaching out to the poor and oppressed, to the widows and the orphans.

When God's marketplace ambassadors truly begin operating in dominion, there will be a release of the operation of God's Kingdom rule. Dominion and the operation of God's Kingdom work hand in hand. But the operation of God's Kingdom is predicated on community and covenant.

Community and Covenant

Nation-changing is built on the Biblical truths of community and the dynamic of community building.

Community building is one of the inherent principles outlined in the book of Deuteronomy. Abraham, Isaac and Jacob in essence, built entrepreneurial communities. Deuteronomy outlines the basic principles on how to operate a business-based, revenue-generating community. Principles of organization applicable to business and community. Customer and employee relations. Fairness. Generosity. Benevolence. Making your assets work.

Early pioneering communities of the old west in the United States reflected the dynamics of these biblical entrepreneurial foundations. At the core of these early pioneering communities were craftsmen and tradesmen whose talents and gifts were exchanged to the benefit of not only their own survival, but the other members of the community.

This biblical entrepreneurial dynamic of community building is built on a foundation of service. Service designed to meet the needs of the community. Helping others. Building the community. Taking care of your own. Community building ties back to dominion.

Community builders bring about change. Community builders are agents of change in the midst of obstacles and challenge. Community builders are visionaries who spot and seize the initiative when there is opportunity. They are those who face change and hurdles knowing that God has given them dominion — and their goal is to pursue the strategies that will bring about God's purposes in conquering the challenges before them. They are innovative and creative and determined and committed to build a future that will honor the Lord and bless the community.

Community builders understand the importance of shared values. Deuteronomy establishes principles of government and business and the associated relationships. At its core is putting God first and seeking Him for direction and guidance and working together toward common goals. Shared values not only establish higher standards, but provide the basis for a caring community. They communicate that there is meaning and purpose for not only our individual lives, but for our families and communities.

Marvin Kramer is an Israeli community builder-leader. He is a prince among men. This attorney businessman has sacrificially and successfully defended Jewish believers who have been targeted with unrighteous lawsuits leveled from the anti-missionary elements in Israel. He has served a significant role during the launch and operation of several strategic community initiatives including the Nehemiah Fund, the Messianic Action Committee and the Joseph Project. These initiatives are in addition to the right-to-life and outreach to women-in-crisis ministry (A Future and Hope/Acharit v'Tikvah), he and his wife Orit founded. Marvin Kramer's role as a community builder is making a difference across Israel.

Community is also based on covenant, or a shared understanding and agreement. Covenant is a central, unifying theme in Scripture. God's covenants with individuals and the nation of Israel and the Jewish people find their final fulfillment in the New Covenant in Jesus. God's grace in relating to His people by initiating covenants with them is a major theme throughout the Bible.

God's covenant is driven by His love for His people. God works for His covenant people. He protected them in the wilderness, gave them the land, and gave them the *"power to get wealth"* (Deut. 8:18; 29:9). But the blessings of the covenant are more than the promise of better lives for His people. The blessings of the covenant are foundational to God having a people who represent Him and through whom

He will accomplish His purposes for His creation (Deut. 8:18).

Communities are built around covenants or agreements and understandings that provide for order, but which also create the opportunity by which both the community and its individuals prosper. Community is based on covenant relationships that are based on unity. Community-covenant relationships create this corporate-level of dominion.

The Shaking and the Change

Over the last few decades, mobile, progressive Western society has begun losing touch with community. Many people don't know their neighbors. They work on one side of town and live on another. Friends may be in still another locale. Without community, we have lost our identity.

Yet it is community-based dominion that is needed to overcome lawlessness and the godless power structures that have infiltrated the political, information and economic circles of this world. An infiltration that perverts what God has created to serve the purposes of the evil one in this struggle over dominion. Community is significant because it represents the baseline from which nations are changed to bring the restoration of God's blessings.

There is a shaking going on. A shaking of this world's infrastructures. The shaking is tied to a clash of civilizations that is the age-old battle between good and evil. There is a struggle for the emergence of a new order.

It is a world driven increasingly by economic power. With this new order will come shifts in the political status quo. A recent report in Israel's Arutz-7 news service quotes European Union Parliament member Ilka Schroeder: *"The Europeans support the Palestinian Authority with the aim of becoming its main sponsor, and through this to challenge the U.S. and present themselves as the future global power."*

We are experiencing the birth pangs in the interim of this struggle for a new order. While the war on terrorism, Israel's intifada, along with the mounting anti-Christian and anti-Semitic movement is very real, the subtle and not quite so obvious battle is over economic sovereignties.

The issue is power. Behind these series of manifestations — such as terrorism against the free world and the assaults against ministry finances — are mammon and sorcery, Babylon and Chaldea. These demonic principalities are being rooted out of their lairs as God is releasing His initiatives for restoration.

The restoration and new order that begins with revival cannot overlook the need for community and community builders. Restoration and dominion that evolve from the biblical-principles of community are foundational to the release of the Kingdom of God. The issue of whether the Church is prepared as nation-builders will depend on its grasp of God's Kingdom rule.

The Kingdom of God

Jesus' earthly ministry was uniquely focused on opening the eyes of those who could see and grasp the revelation of the Kingdom of God — and showing them how it worked. Spirit controls matter and the blessings of God flow from the authority released when we exercise the principles of His Kingdom and dominion is operating. In Luke 6, Jesus made a simple, but very powerful statement. He said, *"give and it will be given unto you."* He told us, *"just as you want people to treat you, treat them in the same way."* He also told us to bless those who curse us! Love your neighbor as yourself.

For example, there is a Kingdom principle of reciprocity. It tells us that the standard of measure we operate with will determine the standard with which we will receive in return. If you are critical of everyone, you can expect to receive critical judgments from others. It is the principle behind biblical charity and offerings. It is the principle that undergirds operating with a generous and kind spirit.

The Kingdom of God is the integration of the principles and authority of God into the midst of the fabric of society — the world in which we live. It is the release, operation and manifestation of God's Kingdom rule into our everyday lives. It is the reality of the Lord consistently operating in our midst. Redemption involves restoration, of not only our souls, but of God's Kingdom rule. The Kingdom perspective incorporates wholeness and oneness with Him — in ALL facets of life. We are called to be a light in the darkness.

The Kingdom of God is at hand; and we're being called to advance.

The Kingdom of God and God's economy work hand in hand. God-directed dominion that results from the entrepreneurial and community dynamic modeled by Abraham, Isaac and Jacob will begin releasing God's Kingdom rule. Communities that have their foundations in the spiritual, but extend into the natural. Communities that have as their basis: revival, unity and dominion.

God's Kingdom rule is the basis of God's penetration of the marketplace, with His chosen ambassadors moving into positions of authority in seats of power in business and governmental circles. God's Kingdom rule is about the deliverance from the bondage of corruption that Romans 8 speaks of in referring to as the *"whole of creation groans and labors with birth pangs"* awaiting the deliverers from this age-old bondage.

The Holy Spirit revivals of the past few decades have been about redemption and restoration. Restoration of the role and operation of the Person of the Holy Spirit in giving purpose, leading and guidance to those advancing agendas that penetrate and interlink secular enterprises with God's purposes.

The role of birthing initiatives that merge business and ministry has been at the forefront of the activities of the International Christian Chamber of Commerce (ICCC). The Dream Center we've mentioned earlier is but one of numerous projects they have operating around the world designed to build communities and advance God's Kingdom. But foundational to all of them is the "You Can Start A Business Video Project" being spearheaded by Dale Neill. These videos, based on biblical principles of business, have been aired in a number of very unlikely places, such as the largest educational television channel in the People's Republic of China.

These revivals have challenged the traditions and doctrines of men that have undermined the power and authority — and Kingdom rule that God always intended for his people. These revivals have been the catalysts to bridging the gap between the sacred and the secular; with the current focus of reconnecting the gap between business and ministry. The shaking taking place in the area of ministry finances shouts to the fact that dominion for the Body extends beyond the boundaries of what have become the overworked traditions of fund-raising to support the work of the ministry. There is more to it than this single approach. Much more.

God's Kingdom rule will mark the difference from the Church's anemic response at the end of WWII to General MacArthur's prescient call for missionary nation-changers. It will be the point of demarcation that releases the power of God needed — to **extend beyond our human efforts**. It will provide the authority from which God's marketplace ambassadors will speak into the dilemmas being faced by the world with prophetic Words of wisdom that bring solutions to the problems of communities and nations.

As God's Kingdom rule penetrates, permeates and releases the goodness and blessings of God, there will emerge mature, unified and prepared believers. Kingdom ambassadors at all levels who are strategic in their outlook and response as they serve as mighty instruments of God's purpose in this clash of civilizations and age-old battle manifesting over dominion and Kingdom.

However, to fully enter into God's Kingdom rule in the midst of the changes underway, another very essential factor needs to be faced. A factor that will provide balance, stability and unity as God's Kingdom rule penetrates the seats of power of this world. A key factor to those called as nation-changers, but also requisite to seeing the Body evolve into the mature, functioning supportive type of unity spoken of in Ephesians 4:16.

This factor is identity. It is the identity that only comes when we genuinely know who we are in the Lord. When we know who we are in-the-Lord not only as individual believers, but corporately as the Body of Christ, the Body of Messiah.

This truth bears uniquely on our grasp of the Kingdom perspective and the response required to change nations. It becomes foundational to releasing the power of God in accordance with the big picture strategies needed for these times we have entered: times that are proving to be both times of peril and times of opportunity.

True Identity. In John 8 Jesus was teaching in the temple and was being challenged by a group of self-satisfied religious hypocrites, committed to the traditions of men. They were challenging Jesus' identity, but He turned it around to uncovering their lack of identity. These Pharisees told Jesus that they were "Abraham's descendents," but Jesus revealed to them that their identity was misplaced and until they recognized their identity "in-God," they in fact had no identity. Without God their traditions and precepts only left them bound in sin. Jesus uncovered to them the only gateway to identity — something that all but a handful had lost since the fall of man — when he said, *"IF you continue in My Word, then you shall know the truth and the truth shall set you free."* (John 8:32) He concluded his interchange with these religious leaders with the truth that *"whom the Son has set free shall be free indeed."* (John 8:36)

The world is searching for identity. Some are coming closer than others. George Melloan in a recent Wall Street Journal column (Dec 23, 2003) wrote about identity:

> *"The expression 'identity politics' has crept into the language to describe political messages designed to appeal to voters who find their identities primarily as members of a certain group, such as government employees or African-Americans. It is often used in a pejorative sense, and indeed is something to be feared when demagogues try to pit one group against another. The ardent nationalism that sparked two world wars or the 'ethnic cleansing' of more recent vintage are examples. But all humans have, and need, a sense of identity; and so, in a sense, all politics is 'identity' politics. That's why political freedom is such a positive force in the world."*

Mr. Melloan is right in his statement that *"all humans need a sense of identity."* But it's not our politics that defines who we are. Nor is it our heritage, as the Pharisees sought to convince Jesus. I'm not knocking the importance of either. Common purpose and heritage do play a role in our bigger picture corporate identities. But by no means are they the pivot points.

The bottom line is that it all begins and ends with the Lord and the truth of His Word. We will never know who we are or what we are genuinely here for — our destiny; until we go through the Penuel experience. This was Jacob's experience in wrestling with the angel of Lord — that resulted in his name-change to Israel. It was Jacob's pivotal encounter in truly facing God and himself — and embracing his true identity and destiny.

At the core of this issue of our identity being uniquely tied to God is overcoming the undermining effect of this unholy premise that separates the sacred from the secular. God never intended it that way. But until we bridge this gap between the sacred and the secular; between the ministry and laity; we will never be able to embrace God's Kingdom rule — and our callings as He intended — and we are constrained to operate as spiritual schizophrenics.

An Integrated Identity

Spiritual schizophrenics. It is the traditions of men that hold to this unbiblical concept of the sacred and secular. Among God's Throne Room initiatives, one of the most hated and resisted by Satan, is the Ephesians 4 premise of *"perfecting the saints for the work of the ministry."* The non-biblical concept of the laity, along with the concepts of the sacred versus the secular (which coincides with the separation of Church and state) are among the most diabolical strategies with which the devil has ever penetrated the Church. The Church will never be whole, nor will it see the full power of God released until we come into a time in which the saints are being perfected and mobilized.

To be perfected and mobilized to be in the world, but not of the world. Jesus' great high-priestly prayer in John 17 asked that we not be taken out of the world, but that we be protected from the clutches of the evil one — and that we be one. This will involve a major change in mind-set and *modus operandi* of church organization and goals. It's about identity. It's about dominion. It is about God's Kingdom — community building and changing nations.

There are segments of the Church with a keen understanding of its "identity" on an individual level — knowing who we are "in Jesus." The apostle Paul punctuates this truth in Colossians 2:10 in saying *"in Him you have been made complete."* But where the Church falls short is in understanding its identity on a corporate level for the Body. The result is a fractionalized, anemic and whiplashed Body.

We will never fulfill our destiny, either individually or corporately, until we get the identity thing right — on both levels. Our identity incorporates the sphere of our calling and the authority to complete it. When our individual identities are rightly and wisely connected to the big picture and the elements of our genuine corporate identities, then the results are integrated, multiplied and operating in support between the individual and corporate. When that happens, God's Kingdom begins manifesting and the awesome power of God spoken of in Isaiah 59 is released.

Proverbs 16 provides a passage that undergirds our individual identities that is also tied to our corporate identities. It says that *"he who rules his own spirit is mightier than he who takes a city."* As a former combat officer, that speaks to me. This scripture doesn't say that we won't take the city. It says that there is something far more powerful operating when a man rules his own spirit than that which is operating when a military commander takes a city. That's the commitment and discipline required to operate under God's Kingdom rule on an individual level. It is also the transition the Body of Christ needs to make to embrace God's Kingdom rule on a corporate level. Knowing who we are as individuals, in-Christ; but also knowing and being released into who we are as a Body — in-Christ. That's the integration of our identity in Him. It's John 17. It will incorporate service and sacrifice as the integration takes place, and the Lord anoints us to "take the city."

The traditions of men and the religious spirit driving these "traditions" resists the change involved in this revelation of our identity in God — on an individual level, as well as the corporate Body level. It resisted the impact of the miracle-working, tent revivals of the late '40s; the incredible Holy Spirit revival of the late '60s and '70s; as well as the rise of the Messianic Jewish movement in that same time frame. Before us is God's move in the marketplace — which will bring the issue of our identity in-God into the community, business, political and national arenas.

This present move of God is penetrating the fabric of society. It will also bring into fullness a dimension of our corporate Body identity needed to bridge the gap between Jew and Gentile.

The Messianic Jewish movement has sought to restore the foundational roots to what it means to be Jewish. The root of Jewish identity is found in a relationship with the God of Israel and His Word. Jewish identity is irretrievably entwined with Biblical Judaism. The Pharisees thought their identity was tied to their heritage. To a degree they were right. Judas was convinced his identity was tied to his politics of forcing the issue of restoring God's Kingdom. But both of these premises were and are incomplete — and can be stumbling blocks to operating according to God's Kingdom rule. Jewish identity is uniquely tied to God. And before there is a restoration of His Kingdom, the identity issue has to be settled.

There is a similar identity issue — between Jew and Gentile — for the Church. The Church has been grafted into the olive tree — and must address the identity issue of being a grafted-in branch in this tree. This big picture identity premise for believers — both Jewish and Gentile — is pivotal to "all Israel being saved."

The secular Jewish community has a far better grasp of the essential Kingdom rule elements of covenant and community than the Christian community. In essence, there is a large-scale issue of identity in need of being addressed in each camp. Very few segments of Christendom have a genuine grasp of the Hebraic roots to the faith. These truths will define not only issues of its corporate identity as the Church, but of its function, as it faces this clash of civilizations.

We will never understand who we are until we understand Whose we are and what we are here for. Likewise, we will never understand what we are here for until we understand our calling — individually and corporately.

Dominion and Kingdom and identity. It's the big picture. It is where we need to be giving primary focus. Paul wrote the Corinthians and said, *"After that comes the end, when He delivers over the Kingdom to God the Father after rendering inoperative and abolishing every [other] rule and every authority and power."* (1 Cor 15:24)

The biblical foundations of the big picture and the three-fold riches of God's Kingdom provide the practical principles that undergird the operation of God's economy.

CHAPTER 14

THE FOUNDATIONS AND PRINCI-
PLES FOR GOD'S ECONOMY —
ENTREPRENEURIAL
COMMUNITIES

The foundations of what we know today as free enterprise and capitalism were laid out long ago in the book of Deuteronomy and are elaborated on and illustrated in other major segments of the Bible. Free enterprise and capitalism are economic systems that are offshoots drawn from the biblical principles underlying God's economy.

Abraham operated an entrepreneurial community during times of social upheaval and challenge. The scriptures tell us that he was continually gaining in wealth and was very rich.

Genesis 26 gives an amazing illustration of how God's economy operates against all odds. It describes a time of famine being faced by Isaac. Yet God told Isaac to sow in that land of famine, with the caveat that He would bless him. Isaac was obedient and the scripture tells us that with God at the center of what he did, in the same year Isaac reaped a hundred-fold. Then it says *"so he began to prosper and continued prospering until he became very prosperous."* That is God's economy in operation.

We've already reviewed the covenantal foundations involved in a God-centered economic-based community. Now we will look at some of the specific principles of business contained in this amazing segment of Scripture.

Biblical Business and Entrepreneurialism

Entrepreneurialism has its foundations in the principles governing God's economy.

I've already noted that my friend Dr. Bill Bolton, author and expert on entrepreneurship has indicated that *"entrepreneurship is the single, most important factor in deciding whether or not a region or community achieves its full potential, both economically and socially."*

His observation applies in both prosperous and deprived areas. It is valid for the developed world and the developing world alike. Dr. Bolton and I agree that the principles of entrepreneurialism are universal — with their foundations outlined in Scripture. He notes that *"entrepreneurs are making the difference in regions as diverse as the Silicon Valley and the Central African Republic. In application, the principles are the same."* (W. K. Bolton, *"Building an Entrepreneur Community,"* January 2001)

He also explains that *"entrepreneurship also determines whether successful regions stay that way. Businesses and societies are able to continue fairly well until they are threatened by change."*

Entrepreneurship deals with *the management of change* and *risk and opportunity*. The advent of underground economies, black markets and hidden power structures carry a destabilizing effect on the economic systems that underlie capitalism and free enterprise. That reason alone should serve as a call back to the biblical basics for business: entrepreneurship and entrepreneurial communities.

Deuteronomy is the starting point in the biblical principles of how to create wealth. It incorporates the principles that believers in business need to understand and be acquainted with that reflect the wisdom needed to succeed in the business sphere. It outlines the principles needed to operate in challenging times. It provides the keys to avoiding unnecessary economic reversals. It depicts the principles of entrepreneurship and entrepreneurial communities — that undergird the foundation of God's economy.

To grasp the principles of God's economy and the operation of a God-centered entrepreneurial community, the book of Deuteronomy is the starting place.

Work Ethic. Deuteronomy outlines the importance and role of a work ethic. But it goes on to promise God's blessing when a strong work ethic is combined with excellence and the life of his people is centered around him.

Six days you shall labor and do all your work. Deut 5:13

> *The Lord shall open to you His good treasury, the heavens, to give the rain of your land in its season and to bless all the work of your hands; and you shall lend to many nations, but you shall not borrow.* Deut 28:12

Private Ownership. The Word of God continually speaks directly and indirectly about private ownership — of land, houses, vineyards and so forth, which is foundational to the operation of private enterprises.

> *When the Lord your God brings you into the land which He swore to your fathers to give you, with great and goodly cities which you did not build, and houses full of all good things which you did not fill, and cisterns hewn out which you did not hew, and vineyards and olive trees which you did not plant, and when you eat and are full, then beware lest you forget the Lord.* Deut 6:10-12

Risk and Opportunity. While the world addresses risk and opportunity with approaches such as "swimming with the sharks" and "doing unto others as they would — only doing it first;" there is something about knowing you are on the winning side that engenders confidence and fairness. It is the *God-advantage* that accompanies those who are known by His Name. It also is the reason those operating in God's economy can operate with generosity. Through faith they know that "if God is for us, who can be against us?"

Just like God's people are not meant to be like "everyone else," Kingdom businesses and the principles of God's economy are not supposed to be replicates of those of the world. Because of the importance of being God-centered, they are built on principles and foundations that honor the Lord.

> *Break down their altars and smash their sacred pillars. Erase the names of their gods from those places! Do not worship the LORD your God in the way these pagan peoples worship their gods."* Deut 12:2-4

Because of the orientation and uniqueness of God's economy being God-centered, the approach to risk and opportunity for Kingdom businesses will often involve the Lord providing wisdom and power to bypass the cycles and downturns experienced by the world's businesses.

In other instances, such as the example of the Lord telling Isaac to sow in famine, the Lord will do miraculous things that fly in the face of the *modus operandi* of the world's system.

Employee and Community Responsibility. Deuteronomy 15 addresses the issue of employee and community responsibility and the application of the principles governing debt and credit.

This chapter opens with the premise that credit is to be handled within the believing community. It will operate on a seven-year cycle. It is established and operated as a service among brethren. Credit outside the believing community does not carry the constraints exercised for the brethren.

The community and the enterprises comprising the community are responsible first to others in the community; for employment or for assistance in the establishment of their enterprises. By following God's principles — of a strong work ethic for individuals and a strong operation of community among the leaders and those who are successful — there should be no poor within the community.

Following these principles will indeed bring God's blessings on both the individuals and the community.

The believing community is designed to be self-sustaining; and by observing these principles, other communities and nations will turn to God's people and will never rule over them.

> *The LORD your God will bless you as he has promised. You will lend money to many nations but will never need to borrow! You will rule many nations, but they will not rule over you!* Deut 15:6

Generosity within your community will always be blessed by the Lord. Compassion toward the poor within your community will result in giving them a helping hand, helping them to get established and strengthening the community and blessing those participating in aiding the process.

> *If there are any poor people in your towns when you arrive in the land the LORD your God is giving you, do not be hard-hearted or tightfisted toward them. Instead, be generous and lend them whatever they need.*
>
> *When you release your servant, do not send him away empty handed. Give him a generous farewell gift from your flock, your threshing floor, and your winepress. Share with him some of the bounty with which the Lord your God has blessed you.* Deut 15:7,8,13-14

Verses 12-18 outline the principles for providing assistance to employees who want to establish their own enterprises. Do not hold them back after they have served as apprentices, interns and faithful employees. Help them on their way. There will be those who may choose to remain with your enterprise — recognize those who do and provide good opportunity for them and treat them well — and God's blessings will flow within your enterprise.

The firstfruit of the labors of your enterprise should be periodically set aside to simultaneously honor the Lord and bless your family and employees.

Excellence, Fairness and Honesty. Deuteronomy 17 begins with the principle that whatever you do, do it in a manner that honors the Lord. Never compromise in what you do, always give it your very best! Strive for excellence, fairness and honesty.

> *Never sacrifice a sick or defective ox or sheep to the*
> *LORD your God, for he detests such gifts.* Deut 17:1

Verses 2 through 5 demonstrate that whenever an enterprise is established for God's purposes, it becomes a witness, a representation of Him. Spiritual duplicity and compromise will not be tolerated among those who have become participants in His enterprises. Those who have been found to consciously choose to dishonor the Lord will be banished.

This chapter also emphasizes that care must be taken to ensure fairness in all decisions, especially those regarding upholding standards and discipline.

A strict standard of honoring the Lord will result in the fear of the Lord being released — which in turn will foster the type of wisdom that comes from humility and the fear of the Lord.

> *Then everyone will hear about it and be afraid to act*
> *so arrogantly.* Deut 17:13

Standards for Leadership. As your enterprises and community grow and prosper, remember the Lord and the principles of operation that have resulted in the blessing of this growth. The greater the growth and blessing, the higher the standards and requirements for leadership.

Be sure to select leaders who know the Lord and are intimately acquainted with the principles of His Word. Ensure that these are leaders who will honor the Lord and will genuinely serve the interests of the enterprise/community in the way they conduct the business of the enterprise and relate as God's ambassadors to those in the world that they do business with. In God's economy, leaders must abide by even more exacting standards than those they lead.

> *You will soon arrive in the land the LORD your God is giving you, and you will conquer it and settle there. Then you may begin to think, 'We ought to have a king like the other nations around us. If this happens, be sure that you select as king the man the LORD your God chooses. You must appoint a fellow Israelite, not a foreigner. The king must not build up a large stable of horses for himself, and he must never send his people to Egypt to buy horses there, for the LORD has told you, You must never return to Egypt. The king must not take many wives for himself, because they will lead him away from the LORD. And he must not accumulate vast amounts of wealth in silver and gold for himself.* Deut 17:14-17

The Priestly Role of Kingdom Leaders. Tradition tells us that Old Covenant kings were required to memorize the Torah and then to review its basic principles publicly on an annual basis. Historically, the times Scripture records trouble and distress for Israel were the times when their leaders fell away from the observance of these practices. God-centered Kingdom enterprises will operate on that standard when those called as Kingdom entrepreneurs, executives and officials assume their combined roles as kings and priests — and assure that the Lord is central not only to the way they operate, but to their very purpose for existence.

> *When he sits on the throne as king, he must copy these laws on a scroll for himself in the presence of the Levitical priests. He must always keep this copy of the law with him and read it daily as long as he lives. That way he will learn to fear the LORD his God by obeying all the terms of this law. This regular reading will prevent him from becoming proud and acting as if he is above his fellow citizens. It will*

*also prevent him from turning away from these
commands in the smallest way. This will ensure that
he and his descendants will reign for many generations in Israel.* Deut 17:18-20

Competition, Honesty and Accountability. The enterprises of
God's people will grow. That growth will be due to God's hand
being upon His people and the work of their hands. This growth
will be competitive in its result, displacing the roles and functions
of many within the world's system.

*The LORD your God will soon destroy the nations
whose land he is giving you, and you will displace
them and settle in their towns and homes.* Deut 19:1

But there is no room for dishonesty or compromise to be operating among those who are known by His Name.

*When you arrive in the land the LORD your God is
giving you as a special possession, never steal someone's land by moving the boundary markers your
ancestors set up to mark their property.* Deut 19:14

Verses 15-19 ensure that each person is accountable for his own
actions; and that any complaints need to be thoroughly investigated.
Legal actions will not be based on isolated cases, but only on
substantiated patterns of wrongful behavior.

Malicious witnesses and liars will be subject to severe punishment and penalties when identified. Operating as God's people
bears with it the responsibility of dealing rightly, fairly and honestly
with one another; and compromise, malice and lies will not be
tolerated.

*If an accuser is found to be lying, the accuser will
receive the punishment intended for the accused. In
this way, you will cleanse such evil from among you.
Those who hear about it will be afraid to do such an*

evil thing again. You must never show pity! Your rule should be life for life, eye for eye, tooth for tooth, hand for hand, foot for foot. Deut 19:18-21

Adversity, Competition, Faith and Community. Deuteronomy 20 begins with the fact that despite the adversity or the size and position of competition, the Lord will always be your equalizer. But in these circumstances, it is important to have the support and encouragement of the priests to ensure that your people recognize that the Lord is with them and that their job is to face adversity and competition with courage and faith.

When you go out to fight your enemies and you face horses and chariots and an army greater than your own, do not be afraid. The LORD your God, who brought you safely out of Egypt, is with you! Before you go into battle, the priest will come forward to speak with the troops. He will say, 'Listen to me, all you men of Israel! Do not be afraid as you go out to fight today! Do not lose heart or panic. For the LORD your God is going with you! He will fight for you against your enemies, and he will give you victory! Deut 20:1-4

When adversity looms, those participating in key roles must be fully committed and single-minded. Those who are immature, unprepared or wavering must be identified and used in rear-line support roles.

Then the officers will also say, 'Is anyone terrified? If you are, go home before you frighten anyone else.' Deut 20:8

When advancing in competitive situations, there should be opportunity given for those who are willing to make alliances with you as God's people. Those alliances will result in them serving your interests; without compromise. If the offer of alliances is refused, then they are to be conquered without mercy.

> *As you approach a town to attack it, first offer its*
> *people terms for peace. If they accept your terms*
> *and open the gates to you, then all the people inside*
> *will serve you in forced labor. But if they refuse to*
> *make peace and prepare to fight, you must attack the*
> *town.* Deut 20:10-12

Be wary of the practices of the entities that you take over and the customers you serve. Seek the Lord on the wisdom needed on decisions regarding their reorganization and thrust, so that all conforms to that which will be pleasing to the Lord.

> *This will keep the people of the land from teaching*
> *you their detestable customs in the worship of their*
> *gods, which would cause you to sin deeply against*
> *the LORD your God.* Deut 20:18

When you take over an area from competition, be wise not to destroy the elements needed for you to operate successfully.

> *When you are besieging a town and the war drags*
> *on, do not destroy the trees. Eat the fruit, but do not*
> *cut down the trees. They are not enemies that need to*
> *be attacked! But you may cut down trees that you*
> *know are not valuable for food. Use them to make*
> *the equipment you need to besiege the town until it*
> *falls.* Deut 20:19-20

Principles of Community and Business Relations. Deuteronomy 22 begins with the exhortation of treating those within the believing community as family, even those who may be competitors. If a competitor from the community has experienced a loss, be willing to help and extend yourself in aiding them.

> *If you see your neighbor's ox or sheep wandering*

away, don't pretend not to see it. Take it back to its owner. If it does not belong to someone nearby or you don't know who the owner is, keep it until the owner comes looking for it; then return it. Do the same if you find your neighbor's donkey, clothing, or anything else your neighbor loses. Don't pretend you did not see it. If you see your neighbor's ox or donkey lying on the road, do not look the other way. Go and help your neighbor get it to its feet! Deut 22:1-4

One should always operate with kindness. Greed should never be allowed to impact you so that your judgment is marred and you become so opportunistic that you overlook basic kindness.

If you find a bird's nest on the ground or in a tree and there are young ones or eggs in it with the mother sitting in the nest, do not take the mother with the young. You may take the young, but let the mother go, so you may prosper and enjoy a long life. Deut 22:6,7

The safety of those who work for you and community members must be a priority. Ensure you provide adequate measures to prevent injury.

Every house you build must have a barrier around the edge of its flat rooftop. That way you will not bring the guilt of bloodshed on your household if someone falls from the roof. Deut 22:8

Do not cut corners in order to increase your output; it may compromise the value of your primary business. Operate with balance in all that you do. Do not attempt expedient measures that are achieved by unequal yoking. Consistency and dependability are vital in all that you do. Maintain high standards and do not compromise these principles.

Do not plant any other crop between the rows of

your vineyard. If you do, you are forbidden to use
either the grapes from the vineyard or the produce of
the other crop. Do not plow with an ox and a donkey
harnessed together. Deut 22:9-11

Honorable and respectable behavior is expected in all relationships. Relationships are built upon trust. Especially covenant relationships. That trust and the associated covenants are not to be violated through lies, compromise, subterfuge or simply being selfish or self-serving.

Employee and Business Alliance Standards. The 23rd chapter of Deuteronomy begins by admonishing caution to be taken with those who are counterfeits; those who would infiltrate and pervert the principles and promises God intends for the enterprise. These are those who recognize the blessings promised to God's people. They are ones who have the ability to "talk the talk" of those called according to His purposes — but as infiltrators, they seek to undermine and utilize the power and promises of God for their own selfish purposes. Mark those so identified.

Avoid the infiltrators, distracters and those undermining God's purposes in the enterprises and communities incorporating His people.

No Ammonites or Moabites, or any of their descen-
dants for ten generations, may be included in the
assembly of the LORD. These nations did not
welcome you with food and water when you came
out of Egypt. Instead, they tried to hire Balaam son
of Beor from Pethor in Aram-naharaim to curse you.
(But the LORD your God would not listen to
Balaam. He turned the intended curse into a bless-
ing because the LORD your God loves you.) You
must never, as long as you live, try to help the
Ammonites or the Moabites in any way. Deut 23:3-6

There are however, outsiders with whom you may enter into alliances. Understanding the differences between those who can be trusted and those who cannot be trusted will rest on issues regarding honor, integrity and their response to the Lord.

> *Do not detest the Edomites or the Egyptians, because the Edomites are your relatives, and you lived as foreigners among the Egyptians. The third generation of Egyptians who came with you from Egypt may enter the assembly of the LORD.* Deut 23:7,8

Conducting your business must be done without compromise. You will provide an example in the marketplace that should set the standard in all that you do.

> *When you go to war against your enemies, stay away from everything impure.* Deut 23:9

Should employees from ungodly competitors come to you, because they recognize the difference in terms of your enterprise reflecting honor and integrity; be open to them serving you.

> *If slaves should escape from their masters and take refuge with you, do not force them to return. Let them live among you in whatever town they choose, and do not oppress them.* Deut 23:15,16

Within your own enterprise and community, be ready to help those who are members without trying to profit from it. Loaning money at interest is perfectly acceptable outside your own community and enterprise, but not among your own.

> *Do not charge interest on the loans you make to a fellow Israelite, whether it is money, food, or anything else that may be loaned with interest. You may charge interest to foreigners, but not to Israelites, so the LORD your God may bless you in everything you do in the land you are about to enter and occupy.* Deut 23:19,20

Do not hastily make a vow to the Lord or any within your community or enterprise. But when you do — take care to fulfill it completely and without delay. Honor your word.

> *When you make a vow to the LORD your God, be prompt in doing whatever you promised him. For the LORD your God demands that you promptly fulfill all your vows. If you don't, you will be guilty of sin. However, it is not a sin to refrain from making a vow. But once you have voluntarily made a vow, be careful to do as you have said, for you have made a vow to the LORD your God.* Deut 23:21-23

Don't take advantage of those in your community or enterprise.

> *You may eat your fill of grapes from your neighbor's vineyard, but do not take any away in a basket. And you may pluck a few heads of your neighbor's grain by hand, but you may not harvest it with a sickle.* Deut 23:24,25

Relationship Standards and Commitments. Deuteronomy 24 gives emphasis to relationships and commitments. There is no honor to be fickle in relationships. Stand firm in commitments and avoid pettiness and self-righteous judgments in order to serve your own purposes.

Family relationships are foundational and must be at the core of any organizational requirements — whether community or enterprise. Allowances should be made to strengthen and keep stable the family units reflected in the enterprise.

> *A newly married man must not be drafted into the army or given any other special responsibilities. He must be free to be at home for one year, bringing happiness to the wife he has married.* Deut 24:5

Never provide or require the foundation of an enterprise's

operation to serve as collateral.

> *It is wrong to take a pair of millstones, or even just*
> *the upper millstone, as a pledge, for the owner uses*
> *it to make a living.* Deut 24:6

There are standards of conduct and propriety governing lending among members of the believing community. They begin with consideration, love and respect.

> *If you lend anything to your neighbor, do not enter*
> *your neighbor's house to claim the security. Stand*
> *outside and the owner will bring it out to you. If*
> *your neighbor is poor and has only a cloak to give*
> *as security, do not keep the cloak overnight. Return*
> *the cloak to its owner by sunset so your neighbor*
> *can sleep in it and bless you. And the LORD your*
> *God will count it as a righteous act.* Deut 24:10-13

Be fair. Never take advantage of your employees — be they believers or non-believers. As a leader, you set the standard. Be timely in meeting your obligations and treat each employee in a way that honors the Lord.

> *Never take advantage of poor laborers, whether*
> *fellow Israelites or foreigners living in your towns.*
> *Pay them their wages each day before sunset*
> *because they are poor and are counting on it.*
> *Otherwise they might cry out to the LORD against*
> *you, and it would be counted against you as sin.*
> Deut 24:14,15

Responsibility is an individual thing. Fairness must be extended to all — believers and non-believers alike within your enterprise and community.

> *Parents must not be put to death for the sins of their*

children, nor the children for the sins of their parents. Those worthy of death must be executed for their own crimes. True justice must be given to foreigners living among you and to orphans, and you must never accept a widow's garment in pledge of her debt. Deut 24:16,17

Be merciful in your relationships with employees — and especially the poor, the orphans and widows in your community. Take care not to operate in a tight-fisted way, but be generous to those you employ with your heart always open to helping the poor and needy.

When you are harvesting your crops and forget to bring in a bundle of grain from your field, don't go back to get it. Leave it for the foreigners, orphans, and widows. Then the LORD your God will bless you in all you do. When you beat the olives from your olive trees, don't go over the boughs twice. Leave some of the olives for the foreigners, orphans, and widows. This also applies to the grapes in your vineyard. Do not glean the vines after they are picked, but leave any remaining grapes for the foreigners, orphans, and widows. Deut 24:19-21

Equity, Fairness and Conflict Resolution. Deuteronomy 25 begins with principles for dealing with disputes. It is important in disputes that there is always a way for your opponent to recover and move on. Taking an issue too far will create a backlash that will bear on the person in the right.

Suppose two people take a dispute to court, and the judges declare that one is right and the other is wrong. If the person in the wrong is sentenced to be flogged, the judge will command him to lie down and be beaten in his presence with the number of lashes appropriate to the crime. No more than forty lashes may ever be given; more than forty lashes would publicly humiliate your neighbor. Deut 25:1-3

A workman is worthy of his hire.

Do not keep an ox from eating as it treads out the grain. Deut 25:4

Honesty and fairness in business are foundational to receiving God's blessing and being a trusted member of the community.

You must use accurate scales when you weigh out merchandise, and you must use full and honest measures. Yes, use honest weights and measures, so that you will enjoy a long life in the land the LORD your God is giving you. Those who cheat with dishonest weights and measures are detestable to the LORD your God. Deut 25:13-16

There are those who simply cannot be trusted. Mark them and do no business with them; nor enter into alliances with them. Avoid them at all costs.

Never forget what the Amalekites did to you as you came from Egypt. They attacked you when you were exhausted and weary, and they struck down those who were lagging behind. They had no fear of God. Therefore, when the LORD your God has given you rest from all your enemies in the land he is giving you as a special possession, you are to destroy the Amalekites and erase their memory from under heaven. Never forget this! Deut 25:17-19

CHAPTER 15

THE COVENANTAL FOUNDATIONS FOR A GOD-CENTERED ECONOMIC COMMUNITY

With the change and disruptions coming into the world's economic sphere today, variant forms of economic systems are becoming increasingly evident. For generations past, underground economies, black markets and hidden power structures have impacted the status quo. But what has until recently been seen as an innocuous behind-the-scenes infrastructure operating in support of terrorist activities is taking on proportions that are seriously challenging, infiltrating and undermining what we might label as "business as usual."

In her book "*Modern Jihad, Tracing the Dollars Behind the Terror Networks,*" Loretta Napoleoni systematically traces the arteries of a $1.5 trillion international economic system. This 'new economy of terror' has infiltrated and become deeply imbedded in what have heretofore been considered above-board, acceptable, traditional global governmental and financial structures. There is no question of the destabilization this illegal economy's functions will have on the operation of legal businesses, stock exchanges, cartels and financial institutions across the globe.

Yet, amidst the penetration and undermining of the 21st century global economic system, there is quietly reemerging a back to basics.

In an infrastructure that supports economies without borders and untraceable mobile businesses, this "back to basics" business movement represents the untainted and biblical-based foundations of business. It is an economic system based on biblical, covenantal community-based entrepreneurial principles I refer to as God's economy. To better understand the dynamics of God's economy, a closer look at its biblical foundations is in order.

The first clear example of the operation of an entrepreneurial community is with Abraham. The scriptures tell us he was very rich in livestock, silver and gold. When his nephew Lot was captured by the kings that had routed the communities where Lot had settled, Abraham had sufficient employees to muster an armed band of 318 men to rescue him. Subsequently, Moses outlined the principles of operating a God-centered, covenantal economic-based community in the book of Deuteronomy.

Deuteronomy: Operating an Entrepreneurial Community

Deuteronomy comprehensively outlines the principles that undergird the smooth operation of an entrepreneurial community. It addresses business issues such as fairness and customer-service, unrighteous gain, God's intention in the ability to create wealth, principles for business loans, the use of collateral, parameters for eliminating poverty, accountability and stewardship, worker's rights, community support of one another, and the conditions for God's blessings.

These are principles that believers in business need to understand and be acquainted with. They reflect the wisdom needed to be the head and not the tail. They are foundational to operating in challenging times. They hold the keys to avoiding unnecessary economic reversals.

Throughout the Bible, God's Word is rich with principles, illustrations and promises which are foundational to operating an enterprise in an economy that supercedes those of the world. Deuteronomy is the starting point. It is the context and foundation that outline how God intends for His people to subdue the earth and succeed.

Deuteronomy speaks of the power given to God's people to get wealth:

> *Remember the Lord your God, for it is He who has given you the power to get wealth that He might establish His covenant.* Deut 8:18

Deuteronomy speaks of the results of the blessings of God upon His people that God's people shall rule over many nations, but those nations shall not rule over them. Deut 15:6

It speaks of how these blessings are tied to obedience:

> *All these blessings shall come upon you and over-take you because you obey the voice of the Lord your God.* Deut 28:2

But it makes clear a leadership role to be played by God's people in the financial and economic arena:

> *The Lord is making you the head and not the tail and you will always mount higher and not decline.* Deut 28:13

Deuteronomy outlines the elements involved in success and prosperity among God's people:

> *The Lord is making you abundantly prosperous in all the work of your hands, the Lord takes delight in prospering you because you take delight in obeying the voice of the Lord your God.* Deut 30:9

God's Promises: Multiplication, Wisdom, and Community. The first chapter of Deuteronomy provides a concise overview of how God's promises operate. They are interrelated to faith and multiplication; to wisdom, leadership and authority; and to community and unity.

*The Lord your God has multiplied you, and behold,
you are this day like the stars of heaven in number.
'May the Lord, the God of your fathers, increase you
a thousand-fold more than you are and bless you,
just as He has promised you!* Deut 1:10-11

From the historical relevance of what these opening verses
outline, they represent the principles of how God responds to faith
and those in covenant and right relationship with Him. Faith and
right relationship with Him are foundational to the examples and
principles of the Bible becoming the patterns and promises we can
count on.

The promises of God exceed anything we might accomplish on
our own. A thousand-fold! That's an enormous multiplication
factor that comes on the tail of having already been multiplied to
where God's people were already likened unto the stars of heaven
in number. From that foundation, the promise extended another
thousand-fold, which was tied to both the numbers and the level of
blessings that could be expected.

*'How can I alone bear the load and burden of you
and your strife? Choose wise and discerning and
experienced men from your tribes, and I will appoint
them as your heads.' "You answered me and said,
'The thing which you have said to do is good.'* Deut
1:12-14

The qualifiers for receiving these astronomical promises of
multiplication are the operation of wisdom and community. It is the
operation of community and wisdom that involves order, accountability, organization and cooperative efforts that serve not only the
families involved, but the good of the community. An order, organization and cooperative effort that results in a multiplication factor
that, because of God's involvement, will far exceed the expectation
that might come through any design of human effort.

God-Centered. Deuteronomy 12 gives focus to the foundational difference between free-enterprise or capitalism and God's

economy: in God's economy, God is at the center! Kingdom businesses are God-centered and community oriented. Free enterprise and capitalism have the foundations of many of their principles found in the principles of God's economy. But first, they have left God out. Second, with God being left out, they have a tendency to become perverse. In a word, God's economy is not some form of replicating the world's economy, but rather the other way around.

Kingdom businesses are an integral part of the community, which supports them — AND they honor the Lord in the way they operate and impact their communities.

> *" There you and your families will feast in the presence of the LORD your God, and you will rejoice in all you have accomplished because the LORD your God has blessed you."* Deut 12:7

As milestones are accomplished with the Lord at the center, the Lord will provide wisdom and power to bypass the cycles and downturns experienced by the worldly businesses displaced by Kingdom businesses.

> *You will soon cross the Jordan River and live in the land the LORD your God is giving you as a special possession, where he gives you rest and security from all your enemies.* Deut 12:10

This will be no accident. God's purpose is not only to bless those embarking in these God-centered businesses, but that they might provide a witness to the people around them. For this reason there will be times of celebration. These times of celebration are very revealing because they serve to strengthen and bless the community, honor its community and spiritual leaders and help those in need within the household of faith.

Those known by His name will be the ones with answers and solutions. By following the Lord and the principles outlined in His Word, His people will have both practical and spiritual answers and solutions, and will be an example to the people of the world around them of the reality of the Lord operating in their midst.

> *There you must bring everything I command you—*
> *your burnt offerings, your sacrifices, your tithes, your*
> *special gifts, and your offerings to fulfill a vow—to*
> *the place the LORD your God will choose for his*
> *name to be honored. You must celebrate there with*
> *your sons and daughters and all your servants in the*
> *presence of the LORD your God.* Deut 12:11-12

Generosity, Firstfruits and Community Celebrations. The first principle of tithing is tied to the enterprise's annual increase. The increase is reflected in the firstborn males of the flocks, in the wine produced from the vineyards, the olive oil from the olive harvest and the yield on grain. It is a principle that involves the enterprise (family or community) gathering to honor the Lord with a celebration in which they participate and partake of this increase. The celebration will involve those members of the enterprise and their families.

> *You must set aside a tithe of your crops—one-tenth*
> *of all the crops you harvest each year. Bring this*
> *tithe to the place the LORD your God chooses for*
> *his name to be honored, and eat it there in his pres-*
> *ence. This applies to your tithes of grain, new wine,*
> *olive oil, and the firstborn males of your flocks and*
> *herds. The purpose of tithing is to teach you always*
> *to fear the LORD your God. When you arrive, use*
> *the money to buy anything you want—an ox, a*
> *sheep, some wine, or beer. Then feast there in the*
> *presence of the LORD your God and celebrate with*
> *your household.* Deut 14:22-23, 26

Every third year, the tithe is to be used for support and blessing of those serving the local priestly function, as well as the widows, orphans and those "foreigners" who are not a part of the enterprise/community but in some way serve in its support. The principle of the third year tithe blessing the priesthood, the needy and those outsiders (extended part of the enterprise/community) will honor the Lord, bless the participants in the Name of the Lord, and bring forth God's pleasure and blessing upon the enterprise/community.

> *And do not forget the Levites in your community, for they have no inheritance as you do. At the end of every third year bring the tithe of all your crops and store it in the nearest town. Give it to the Levites, who have no inheritance among you, as well as to the foreigners living among you, the orphans, and the widows in your towns, so they can eat and be satisfied. Then the LORD your God will bless you in all your work.* Deut 14:27-29

Celebration: Honor the Lord, Your Calling and Heritage. The first ten verses of Deuteronomy 16 outline the significance of the festival of Passover. Operating in the world's system as Israel did during the days of Joseph represented a season of time that God sovereignly used that system for the redemption of his people.

But that time passed, and the world's system eventually closed itself around God's people and reduced them to slavery and bondage. That dynamic has happened again and again as God's people have sought to be like everyone else, rather than embracing the distinctive calling of being God's chosen.

The Passover was God's mighty deliverance from that bondage. It was the transition into establishing the independence needed for God's people to be all that the Lord intended for them to be.

For God's people to be the head and not the tail necessitates the independence reflected by enterprises that are directed by modern-day Abrahams, Issacs and Josephs.

The conclusion of this celebration, the Festival of Harvest, represents a time to honor the Lord and rejoice in the increase by gathering together and bringing a freewill offering proportional to the increase.

An important focus of the Jewish festivals, celebration gatherings is the freewill offerings — the giving. These gatherings are designed for all the participants in the enterprises — the families, employees, the priests and those representing the needy from within the circle of the enterprise community.

Grateful and Generous Hearts. There is a significant correlation between God's blessing — the increase — and a grateful and generous heart *that gives back* to both support the work of the Lord in the community, and to continually help employees and the needy within the community.

Fairness, Honor and Accountability. Fairness, right and honorable decisions, and accountability are an essential part of the operation of godly community enterprises. Everything should be above-board and honest. Each enterprise should have a godly board to which they are accountable.

> *Appoint judges and officials for each of your tribes in all the towns the LORD your God is giving you. They will judge the people fairly throughout the land. You must never twist justice or show partiality. Never accept a bribe, for bribes blind the eyes of the wise and corrupt the decisions of the godly. Let true justice prevail, so you may live and occupy the land that the LORD your God is giving you.* Deut 16:18-20

Honoring the Word, Priests and Prophets. The 18th chapter gives focus to the importance of God's Word in both businesses and the community, together with recognizing and honoring the role of those who minister as priests and prophets.

The local priesthood, who ministers to the people may have other sources of income, but still deserves the honor of receiving the firstfruits during the feasts and celebrations established to corporately gather to worship the Lord.

> *For the LORD your God chose the tribe of Levi out of all your tribes to minister in the Lord's name forever. Any Levite who so desires may come from any town in Israel, from wherever he is living, to the place the LORD chooses. He may minister there in*

*the name of the LORD his God, just like his fellow
Levites who are serving the LORD there. He may eat
his share of the sacrifices and offerings, even if he
has a private source of income.* Deut 18:5-8

Be sensitive and discerning regarding the enticements of the
occult practices of the world around you, like astrology. Be especially discerning not to be beguiled or seduced by the occult practices of non-believers.

*When you arrive in the land the LORD your God is
giving you, be very careful not to imitate the
detestable customs of the nations living there. For
example, never sacrifice your son or daughter as a
burnt offering. And do not let your people practice
fortune-telling or sorcery, or allow them to interpret
omens, or engage in witchcraft, or cast spells, or
function as mediums or psychics, or call forth the
spirits of the dead.* Deut 18:9-11

Be alert to recognize, among the believing community, those
with prophetic gifts. Do not confuse their counsel and insights with
those serving the kingdom of darkness.

*The people you are about to displace consult with
sorcerers and fortune-tellers, but the LORD your
God forbids you to do such things. The LORD your
God will raise up for you a prophet like me from
among your fellow Israelites, and you must listen to
that prophet.* Deut 18:14,15

While people have a natural tendency to fear the Word of the
Lord, the Word of the Lord must be honored; and any counterfeits
should be identified and banished.

*'I will raise up a prophet like you from among their
fellow Israelites. I will tell that prophet what to say,*

175

*and he will tell the people everything I command
him. I will personally deal with anyone who will not
listen to the messages the prophet proclaims on my
behalf. But any prophet who claims to give a
message from another god or who falsely claims to
speak for me must die.'* Deut 18:18-20

Those claiming to speak in the Name of the Lord will be recognized by the accuracy of their Words.

*You may wonder, 'How will we know whether the
prophecy is from the LORD or not?' If the prophet
predicts something in the Lord's name and it does
not happen, the LORD did not give the message.
That prophet has spoken on his own and need not be
feared.* Deut 18:21-22

Reciprocity and Spiritual Responsibility. When your enterprise begins to turn a profit; it will be time to honor the Lord with the firstfruits of that profit. Each enterprise should establish a means by which a portion of the profits is taken to the priest as an acknowledgement that the Lord has blessed your enterprise.

*When you arrive in the land the LORD your God is
giving you as a special possession and you have
conquered it and settled there, put some of the first
produce from each harvest into a basket and bring it
to the place the LORD your God chooses for his
name to be honored. Go to the priest in charge at
that time and say to him, 'With this gift I acknowledge that the LORD your God has brought me into
the land he swore to give our ancestors.' The priest
will then take the basket from your hand and set it
before the altar of the LORD your God.* Deut 26:1-4

It is important to be reminded, in conjunction with our worship, that the Lord is responsible for bringing us out of the bondage and oppression represented by the worldly system; and giving us freedom and blessing in Him.

> *You must then say in the presence of the LORD your God, 'My ancestor Jacob was a wandering Aramean who went to live in Egypt. His family was few in number, but in Egypt they became a mighty and numerous nation. When the Egyptians mistreated and humiliated us by making us their slaves, we cried out to the LORD, the God of our ancestors. He heard us and saw our hardship, toil, and oppression. So the LORD brought us out of Egypt with amazing power, overwhelming terror, and miraculous signs and wonders. He brought us to this place and gave us this land flowing with milk and honey!* Deut 26:5-9

The token of the profits (firstfruits) should include a celebration gathering; that should include the priests and the employees participating in your community enterprise.

> *'And now, O LORD, I have brought you a token of the first crops you have given me from the ground.' Then place the produce before the LORD your God and worship him. Afterward go and celebrate because of all the good things the LORD your God has given to you and your household. Remember to include the Levites and the foreigners living among you in the celebration.* Deut 26:10,11

Every third year, you should prepare a tithe of your revenues for that year — that will be as a gift to be distributed to the priests, the employees, and the poor and needy to insure there is no hunger or poverty within the believing community. When this is done, the Lord will bring forth special blessings upon your operation and its future.

> *Every third year you must offer a special tithe of your crops. You must give these tithes to the Levites,*

foreigners, orphans, and widows so that they will have enough to eat in your towns. Then you must declare in the presence of the LORD your God, 'I have taken the sacred gift from my house and have given it to the Levites, foreigners, orphans, and widows, just as you commanded me. I have not violated or forgotten any of your commands. Deut 26:12,13*

This principle of "noblesse oblige" is an opportunity to demonstrate not only gratefulness to the Lord; but the principle of His mercy which operates through his people. Being the people of God, gratefulness for what He has done should always extend in generosity to others who serve the enterprise and to those in the believing community.

The LORD has declared today that you are his people, his own special treasure, just as he promised, and that you must obey all his commands. And if you do, he will make you greater than any other nation. Then you will receive praise, honor, and renown. You will be a nation that is holy to the LORD your God, just as he promised. Deut 26:16-19*

Standards and Principles for God's Blessings. The 27th and 28th chapters of Deuteronomy summarize the blessings and curses associated with the covenant tied being God's people. Deuteronomy 27:14-26 clearly establishes that violations of the Lord's principles will bring a curse upon the people. Compromise of His principles in family, community, or business relationships will undermine the blessings the Lord has promised to His covenant people. They deal with issues of idolatry, respect for familial authority, theft, mercy and kindness, sexual deviation and perversion, and murder.

But adherence to God's principles will bring blessings to every dimension of your life: individually, family, business and community. In whatever way you turn, obedience to his principles will result in an overflow of increase in all that you do.

> *If you fully obey the LORD your God by keeping all
> the commands I am giving you today, the LORD your
> God will exalt you above all the nations of the world.
> You will experience all these blessings if you obey the
> LORD your God: You will be blessed in your towns
> and in the country. You will be blessed with many
> children and productive fields. You will be blessed
> with fertile herds and flocks. You will be blessed with
> baskets overflowing with fruit, and with kneading
> bowls filled with bread. You will be blessed wherever
> you go, both in coming and in going.* Deut. 28:1-6

You will be protected from those who try to overcome you.
Regardless of their strategy or power, their efforts will be fruitless
and they will eventually scatter.

> *The LORD will conquer your enemies when they
> attack you. They will attack you from one direction,
> but they will scatter from you in seven!* Deut 28:7

Everything you put your hand to will prosper; and you will reap
incredible increase. Your enterprise will be fruitful and blessed.

> *The LORD will bless everything you do and will fill
> your storehouses with grain. The LORD your God
> will bless you in the land he is giving you.* Deut 28:8

You will be a testimony to those who don't know the Lord;
because they will recognize your success as being a result of you
being the obedient, covenant people of God. The land and the
weather will serve you in all that you do. Your timing on decisions
and growth will always be in sync with the blessings required to
make you prosper.

> *If you obey the commands of the LORD your God*

*and walk in his ways, the LORD will establish you
as his holy people as he solemnly promised to do.
Then all the nations of the world will see that you
are a people claimed by the LORD, and they will
stand in awe of you. The LORD will give you an
abundance of good things in the land he swore to
give your ancestors—many children, numerous livestock, and abundant crops. The LORD will send rain
at the proper time from his rich treasury in the heavens to bless all the work you do.* Deut 28:9-12

By adhering closely to God's principles, He will make your
efforts shine in darkness; and will always bring you through with
success.

*If you listen to these commands of the LORD your
God and carefully obey them, the LORD will make
you the head and not the tail, and you will always
have the upper hand. You must not turn away from
any of the commands I am giving you today to follow
after other gods and worship them.* Deut 28:13,14

If you become stubborn, prideful, disobedient and arrogant; you
will begin to see these blessings flee as fast as they came.

*But if you refuse to listen to the LORD your God and
do not obey all the commands and laws I am giving
you today, all these curses will come and overwhelm
you: You will be cursed in your towns and in the
country. You will be cursed with baskets empty of
fruit, and with kneading bowls empty of bread. You
will be cursed with few children and barren fields.
You will be cursed with infertile herds and flocks.
You will be cursed wherever you go, both in coming
and in going.* Deut 28:15-19

Disobedience and arrogance will result in the Lord withdrawing

His presence, which is tied to His blessings. The consequence will be curses, confusion and disillusionment in all you do. Disobedience to the Lord will reverse every blessing He intends for you and will bring destruction into all you put your hand to.

> *The LORD himself will send against you curses, confusion, and disillusionment in everything you do, until at last you are completely destroyed for doing evil and forsaking him.* Deut 28:20-22

Principles of God's Covenant Relationships. Deuteronomy 29 summarizes the principles of God's covenant relationship with His people. God's blessings and provisions are an integral part of the relational covenant. He will, if we will: obey the provisions He has outlined in His Word. It is a covenant that allows those who genuinely seek him to know the alternatives between life and death; and blessing and cursing.

God's covenant relationship begins with a demonstration of his power; but then evolves into simple steps in following him that we must take. It is a step by step growth in understanding and operating in his principles — principles that reflect the fact that God is Spirit and those that are in relationship with Him must approach and relate to Him "in Spirit" and "in truth." We are not to despise the small beginnings; because even in the small beginnings there will always be the evidence of his love, direction and provision.

> *These are the terms of the covenant the LORD commanded Moses to make with the Israelites while they were in the land of Moab, in addition to the covenant he had made with them at Mount Sinai. Moses summoned all the Israelites and said to them, "You have seen with your own eyes everything the LORD did in Egypt to Pharaoh and all his servants and his whole country—all the great tests of strength, the miraculous signs, and the amazing wonders. But to this day the LORD has not given you minds that understand, nor eyes that see, nor*

ears that hear! For forty years I led you through the
wilderness, yet your clothes and sandals did not
wear out. Deut 29:1-5

God will meet our every need along the way. When challenges
arise; He will cause us to overcome and conquer regardless of our
ability, when we trust in Him.

You had no bread or wine or other strong drink, but
he gave you food so you would know that he is the
LORD your God. When we came here, King Sihon of
Heshbon and King Og of Bashan came out to fight
against us, but we defeated them. Deut. 29:6,7

Adherence to the principles of his covenant relationship will,
step by step, bring increase and success in what we do in our enterprise and community development.

We took their land and gave it to the tribes of
Reuben and Gad and to the half-tribe of Manasseh
as their inheritance. Therefore, obey the terms of this
covenant so that you will prosper in everything you
do. Deut. 29:8,9

A covenant with the Lord will extend and have overflow for not
only those who make the covenant; but for those associated with
those in covenant relationship with Him; and with their heirs and
future generations.

The LORD is making this covenant with you today,
and he has sealed it with an oath. He wants to
confirm you today as his people and to confirm that
he is your God, just as he promised you, and as he
swore to your ancestors Abraham, Isaac, and Jacob.
But you are not the only ones with whom the LORD
is making this covenant with its obligations. The
LORD your God is making this covenant with you

> *who stand in his presence today and also with all*
> *future generations of Israel.* Deut 29:10-15

There are pitfalls that may not appear as such to the natural eye; but with obedience and a right heart, they will be overcome and result in God's covenant people prospering. The issue involves trust; that we recognize that God's ways are higher than our ways; and that His plans for His people are for good and not for evil. We must trust in His ways if we expect not to be seduced into the destruction associated with the ways promoted by the world. For step by step will we possess the land — if we trust Him with all our heart and are faithful in our obedience to His principles — designed to protect and prosper us.

> *Let none of those who hear the warnings of this*
> *curse consider themselves immune, thinking, 'I am*
> *safe, even though I am walking in my own stubborn*
> *way.' This would lead to utter ruin!* Deut 29:19

> *The surrounding nations will ask, 'Why has the*
> *LORD done this to his land? Why was he so angry?'*
> *And they will be told, 'This happened because the*
> *people of the land broke the covenant they made*
> *with the LORD, the God of their ancestors, when he*
> *brought them out of the land of Egypt.* Deut 29:24,25

As we grow in Him and His ways; we will begin understanding His secrets. It is a building process — that the more we obey, the more will be revealed — as we adhere to his principles, trust in Him and are obedient.

> *There are secret things that belong to the LORD our*
> *God, but the revealed things belong to us and our*
> *descendants forever, so that we may obey these*
> *Words of the law.* Deut 29:29

Success, Holiness and Community. The final two chapters in

Deuteronomy address the correlation between success, holiness and our role in not only the community, but among the nations. Those who come to the Lord and begin meditating on and practicing His principles will be seeing success come forth in their business activities. They will also begin to be gathered together and connected — as a part of God's global purposes and agendas.

> *Suppose all these things happen to you—the blessings and the curses I have listed—and you meditate on them as you are living among the nations to which the LORD your God has exiled you. If at that time you return to the LORD your God, and you and your children begin wholeheartedly to obey all the commands I have given you today, then the LORD your God will restore your fortunes. He will have mercy on you and gather you back from all the nations where he has scattered you. Though you are at the ends of the earth, the LORD your God will go and find you and bring you back again.* Deut 30:1-4

There will be the restoration of His promises to Israel/Jacob and you will be a participant in it.

> *He will return you to the land that belonged to your ancestors, and you will possess that land again. He will make you even more prosperous and numerous than your ancestors!* Deut 30:5

When you turn to Him, Lord will draw you and yours closer. He will cleanse you and bring you into a relationship of holiness in Him — which will innoculate you against those who would persecute you and undermine your activities and purposes.

> *The LORD your God will cleanse your heart and the hearts of all your descendants so that you will love him with all your heart and soul, and so you may live! The LORD your God will inflict all these curses*

on your enemies and persecutors. Then you will again obey the LORD and keep all the commands I am giving you today. Deut 30:6-8

The Lord then will make you successful in all that you put your hand to — you will prosper and experience steady growth as the Lord delights in you as you delight in Him.

The LORD your God will make you successful in everything you do. He will give you many children and numerous livestock, and your fields will produce abundant harvests, for the LORD will delight in being good to you as he was to your ancestors. The LORD your God will delight in you if you obey his voice and keep the commands and laws written in this Book of the Law, and if you turn to the LORD your God with all your heart and soul. This command I am giving you today is not too difficult for you to understand or perform. Deut 30:9-11

It will not be a difficult thing. But the choice is ours. Having made this choice, you will be blessed personally, family-wise, corporately and as a community in all that you do.

The message is very close at hand; it is on your lips and in your heart so that you can obey it. Now listen! Today I am giving you a choice between prosperity and disaster, between life and death. I have commanded you today to love the LORD your God and to keep his commands, laws, and regulations by walking in his ways. If you do this, you will live and become a great nation, and the LORD your God will bless you and the land you are about to enter and occupy. Deut 30:14-16

The choice is yours — to serve and follow the Lord with a complete heart — or to follow after the enticements of the world.

The way of the Lord will bring life and blessing. The way of the world will bring death and destruction.

> *But if your heart turns away and you refuse to listen, and if you are drawn away to serve and worship other gods, then I warn you now that you will certainly be destroyed. You will not live a long, good life in the land you are crossing the Jordan to occupy. Today I have given you the choice between life and death, between blessings and curses. I call on heaven and earth to witness the choice you make. Oh, that you would choose life, that you and your descendants might live! Choose to love the LORD your God and to obey him and commit yourself to him, for he is your life. Then you will live long in the land the LORD swore to give your ancestors Abraham, Isaac, and Jacob.* Deut 30:17-20

There will be changes in God's leaders. Recognize that it is the Lord you are following — and He, Himself will go before you regardless of who the leaders are. You are His — and when changes come, He will be in the change. He will protect you and enable you to anticipate the tactics of those who want your destruction. So be bold and confident; knowing that the Lord is with you. Do not be afraid, for the Lord is true to His Word and utterly and completely reliable and dependable.

> *When Moses had finished saying these things to all the people of Israel, he said, "I am now 120 years old and am no longer able to lead you. The LORD has told me that I will not cross the Jordan River. But the LORD your God himself will cross over ahead of you. He will destroy the nations living there, and you will take possession of their land. Joshua is your new leader, and he will go with you, just as the LORD promised. The LORD will destroy the nations living in the land, just as he destroyed*

Sihon and Og, the kings of the Amorites. The LORD will hand over to you the people who live there, and you will deal with them as I have commanded you. Be strong and courageous! Do not be afraid of them! The LORD your God will go ahead of you. He will neither fail you nor forsake you. Deut 31:1-6

Those called to lead will be empowered to do so; and will be strong, courageous and decisive in leading and providing the direction your enterprise and community require.

Then Moses called for Joshua, and as all Israel watched he said to him, "Be strong and courageous! For you will lead these people into the land that the LORD swore to give their ancestors. You are the one who will deliver it to them as their inheritance. Do not be afraid or discouraged, for the LORD is the one who goes before you. He will be with you; he will neither fail you nor forsake you. Deut 31:7,8

Gather the people together whenever major changes are pending; ensure that the priests are grounded in the Word and supporting those called as leaders of the enterprise.

So Moses wrote down this law and gave it to the priests, who carried the Ark of the Lord's covenant, and to the leaders of Israel. Then Moses gave them this command: "At the end of every seventh year, the Year of Release, during the Festival of Shelters, you must read this law to all the people of Israel when they assemble before the LORD your God at the place he chooses. Call them all together—men, women, children, and the foreigners living in your towns—so they may listen and learn to fear the LORD your God and carefully obey all the terms of this law. Do this so that your children who have not known these laws will hear them and will learn to

*fear the LORD your God. Do this as long as you live
in the land you are crossing the Jordan to occupy.*
Deut 31:9-13

Provide the people with the means to always keep their focus on
the Lord. As prosperity and growth come, there is the temptation to
forget that it is the Lord that has blessed and prospered them. Let
them never forget.

*Now write down the words of this song, and teach it
to the people of Israel. Teach them to sing it, so it
may serve as a witness against them. For I will bring
them into the land I swore to give their ancestors—a
land flowing with milk and honey.* Deut 31:19,20

We will now look more closely at the principles of business and
entrepreneurialism found outlined in other segments of both the
Old and New Covenants.

CHAPTER 16

BIBLICAL PRINCIPLES OF BUSINESS

The biblical principles of business extend beyond those found in Deuteronomy. But Deuteronomy concludes its comprehensive principles on operating an entrepreneurial community by addressing the choice tied to the most essential element involved in entering God's economy.

The Choice

> *"God has set before you life and death, blessing and cursing."* Deut 30:19

Without God, the choice will always be curses and death. Therefore choose life and blessing! To do that, whether in business or whatever you endeavor you face in life, you need to operate according to the principles in God's Word.

I have outlined three levels of biblical business principles that undergird the operation of God's economy. The first level is the foundational level. The second is the basic biblical principles of business. The third consists of biblical success principles.

Foundational Principles to Enter God's Economy

Trust in the Lord. Operating in God's economy has its foundation in Proverbs 3:5,6 that we *"trust in the Lord with all our heart, we lean not unto our own understanding; in all our ways we acknowledge Him, and He WILL direct our paths."*

Operating in God's economy, as with the book of Deuteronomy can be summed up with the expression of "THE REALITY OF THE LORD OPERATING IN OUR MIDST." The reality of the Lord operating in our midst — for the enterprise, the community and the family; but also as a testimony and example to those of the world.

The Priestly Role. Whether a one-employee entrepreneur or the owner of a large corporation, the prototypes for establishing and leading Kingdom enterprises were the patriarchs such as Abraham, Isaac, Joseph and David. These forebearers of God-centered entrepreneurial communities each served as "kings" in their domains. God was central to their purposes and roles over their operations. They served as God's emissaries.

In that capacity, they carried a priestly responsibility to ensure the Lord was at the center of their activities and that His guidance was sought in the decisions and direction of their operations. Deuteronomy 17 describes the priestly responsibility and role of kingly leaders — which carried the requirement of being soundly grounded in God's Word.

That same priestly responsibility for the spiritual dimension is an essential requirement for those called to lead Kingdom enterprises. Incumbent upon Kingdom entrepreneurs and executives is the need to clearly understand the principles in God's Word that govern His Kingdom and the applications of those principles to the enterprises they operate.

Kingdom Principles. Operating in God's economy has its foundation in God's Kingdom principles. The Kingdom of God operates by principles that are quite often contrary to those of the world. Thus, it's important to understand them if you are going to operate a Kingdom business and enter into the world of God's economy. I highly recommend Pat Robertson's book *The Secret Kingdom*, which outlines in detail key laws that govern the operation of God's Kingdom.

In introducing His earthly ministry, over and over, Jesus used the Words *"the Kingdom of God is at hand."* Jesus' earthly ministry was uniquely focused on opening the eyes of those who could see the Kingdom of God and showing them how it worked.

In Matthew 6:33, Jesus tells us to *"seek first His Kingdom and righteousness and all these other things will be added to you."* This statement followed a teaching our Lord gave on food, clothing, shelter and all the "things" needed for life.

The principles of God's Kingdom are based on the fact that the material world around us is controlled by an invisible world — the world of the spirit. The world of the spirit and the Kingdom of God are unlimited, unrestricted and infinite.

But most of us are like the servant of the prophet Elisha who went outside one morning and saw that his city was surrounded by Syrian troops, ready to close in. But Elisha very calmly asked the Lord to open his servant eyes — to the invisible world — and He did. There, surrounding and protecting Elisha and God's people were the heavenly hosts in chariots of fire. The prophet's words were that *"they that are with us are more than they that are with them."*

The reality is that spirit controls matter. That's why we pray first before ever acting. It's the reason we constantly spend time in God's Word, because God's Word is filled with the principles that undergird this invisible world, the Kingdom of God.

The Kingdom of God rules the affairs of men and nations. While there is indeed a kingdom of darkness out there, God is greater, if His people would just rise up and begin operating according to the principles He has outlined in His Word. That begins by recognizing that God is unlimited in His power and provision. It also means recognizing that He has called us as instruments of His purpose — and for those who can hear His voice (who seek first His Kingdom and His righteousness), He entrusts us with an authority to be His ambassadors. And with that authority, we learn to exercise the dominion that has been His all along.

In Luke 10:19 Jesus said, *"Behold, I have given you authority to tread on serpents and scorpions, and over all the power of the enemy, and nothing will injure you."*

While the evil one has power, he has no authority — WE are the ones with authority. But to use it, we need to recognize first that we have it! To use it, we can't be walking in sin. But once we have dealt with sin, we can walk boldly into His presence.

Dominion. Authority, faith and dominion go hand in hand. Dominion involves the creative process required to subdue the earth. Dominion is foundational to operating in God's economy. When God created man, He made man to have dominion over the work of His hands. In Genesis 1 it states, *"And God said, let us make man in our image, after our likeness and let them have dominion...."*

Deuteronomy 28:13 tells us that *"The Lord is making you the head and not the tail and you will always mount higher and not decline."* In business, it takes faith to establish and build an operation that will offer something of value at a profit, and then work at it so that it grows and prospers and provides the means to support a family and over time, many families. This process is based on the principle of dominion, or *"ruling over the work of His hands"*.

But too often God's people don't grasp this. They live in fear and defeat. Not all, but far too many live in a bondage shrouded by the false security of being tied to a meaningless nine-to-five job-existence. That is not to discount that sometimes you have to do what is needed to find that place of purpose in God. For many, finding that place in God will involve the need to exercise dominion by establishing their own small business.

Establishing a successful business means that God's people must exercise their faith and authority — and the principle of dominion in order to embrace God's purposes and blessings, which are tied to this entrepreneurial principle of "subduing the earth."

Small Beginnings. Zechariah 4:10 admonishes us NOT to despise small beginnings. However, far too many new business owners have visions of grandeur rather than being willing to start small and build.

Starting small allows for the ability to manage things while you learn. In my original business, it was a walk of faith for me. I didn't have a business background. While our start was painfully slow, we began growing until we hit a period of time in which we experienced some very fast growth. But after this growth brought us some wonderful successes, the bottom dropped out of the primary market we were serving.

God had clearly initiated the steps that birthed my original business. I was obedient in seeking Him first. But when it exploded with growth, it was almost overwhelming. Since I assumed this fast growth was all God's blessing, I pushed the growth and failed to prepare for a slowdown. An abrupt market slowdown came and we created hurdles I wasn't prepared for — and it cratered. Yet I learned more about the principles of business during this time of failure than I did during all the wonderful successful years.

Beginning small allows for the opportunity to gain a good grasp of the techniques required to operate a business. It will also enable learning to operate by Kingdom principles — which begins by not despising small beginnings.

Stewardship, Faith and Multiplication. Business involves risk. But when risk is faced with faith and wisely managed, a process of multiplication will begin taking place.

In Matthew 25, Jesus illustrated the Kingdom of God with this story. *"For it is just like a man about to go on a journey, who called together his servants and entrusted his possessions to them. And to one he gave five talents, to another two, and to another one, each according to his own ability, and then he went on his journey."*

The first two servants in this parable MADE THEIR ASSETS WORK FOR THEM. They were rewarded for their efforts. But the third servant did nothing. He simply hid the talent away. He didn't lose anything. But he was strongly rebuked by his master upon his return. His master called him a wicked servant and took what he had away from him. His words were *"You wicked, lazy servant, you knew that I reap where I did not sow and gather where I scattered no seed."* The man was considered wicked, sinful, because he refused to take what his master had given him and put it to work, improving upon it. The principles of faith and multiplication assume good stewardship or use of what we've been entrusted with.

Proper use gives entry into the place of joy. The principle is that *"to everyone who has shall more be given and he shall have an abundance; but from the one who does not have, even what he does have shall be taken away."* It's not an issue of social justice: it is God's principle of USE that governs the ultimate distribution of wealth.

George Washington Carver was a man of God. The story goes that in zeal he once prayed, "Lord, show me the secrets of the universe!" The Lord responded by saying: "Little man, I'll show you the secret of the peanut." And with those evolving insights, George Washington Carver invented three hundred uses for peanuts and hundreds more for soybeans, pecans and sweet potatoes. He invented peanut butter and countless products. While only three patents were ever issued to him, among his listed discoveries are: adhesives, axle grease, bleach, buttermilk, chili sauce, fuel briquettes, instant coffee, linoleum, mayonnaise, meat tenderizer, metal polish, shaving cream, shoe polish, synthetic rubber, talcum powder and wood stain. George Washington Carver exercised his faith with what God showed him and his stewardship resulted in a multiplication factor that far exceeded what he might have accomplished in the natural.

We've already outlined the principle of multiplication of a "thousand times more" noted in the first chapter of Deuteronomy. A seed planted produces a multiple of itself. Our faith works in the same way when combined with hard work, diligence and prudence. In almost every instance, the beginnings are small and humble. When operating according to God's economic principles, growth results and multiplies and eventually begins to exceed our expectations. It's why we are admonished in Zechariah not to despise small beginnings.

Perseverance. Proverbs spells it out very plainly: *"The hand of the diligent shall rule."* Diligence is tied to perseverance. That means you keep on "keeping on." It means you don't give up in the face of adversity. Subduing the earth and dominion involves tough work, ingenuity and sticking with it.

In Matthew 7, Jesus illustrated this principle with the Words, *"Ask and it shall be given to you; seek and you shall find, knock and the door will be opened."* Understanding the Greek words helps us to understand this principle more — because the Greek implies "Keep on asking and it shall be given to you; keep on seeking and you shall find; keep on knocking and the door will be opened.

In Matthew 11 the Lord taught that *"the Kingdom of heaven*

suffers violence and the violent take it by force." There is a struggle involved in the faith required when we believe for something — but persistence will reap its reward. Remember the story of the woman who kept bringing her request to the unrighteous judge in Luke 18. Basically, she wore him out with her persistence! Keep on asking. Keep on seeking. Keep on knocking.

Perseverance also implies **patience**.

"Those who wait upon the Lord shall renew their strength." I've long recognized that nine-tenths of faith is patience. God's economy operates on the type of patience that will not give up.

Thomas Edison conducted thousands of experiments that failed before achieving success with his transforming invention of the incandescent light bulb. Edison was quoted as saying, "Genius is one percent inspiration and 99 percent perspiration."

Having served in the Illinois legislature Abraham Lincoln experienced failure but never gave up. In 1858 he ran against Stephen Douglas for Senator. He lost the election, but in debating with Douglas he gained a national reputation that won him the Republican nomination for President in 1860.

John Maxwell has written a book entitled *"Failing Forward."* The premise on which his book is based is that the difference between everyday people who achieve their goals is their perception of and response to failure. Success and accomplishment are the result of diligence and refusing to give up. Again, as Solomon wrote in Proverbs, *"The hand of the diligent will rule."*

Unity. This principle is foundational to achieving success in the business world. Companies flounder when they don't have a clear-cut mission and goals. It is tied not only to having a clear vision, but in operating in a manner that reflects teamwork and singleness of purpose. A double-minded man is unstable in all his ways and so is a double-minded business.

Unity and power reflects a truth outlined by Jesus in Matthew 18:19-20, that *"If two of you AGREE on earth about anything that they may ask, it shall be done for them by My Father who is in heaven. For where two or three have gathered together in My name, there I am in their midst."* Whenever you meet together to discuss and pray about business decisions, first ensure that that the Lord is central to the gathering. Opening with prayer is a potent way to insure His presence in the gathering. As things proceed, ensure every one is on the same page. Identify the common goals and strategies to achieve them and allow unity to flow.

God's power flows when there is unity among the brethren. This is just as true in a Kingdom business as it is in the midst of a congregation or fellowship of believers.

There is likewise a multiplication factor that operates with unity. It can be seen in the law of Moses spoken to all Israel at the end of his life. *"One would chase a thousand and two would put ten thousand to flight."* Unity does not just cause a mere doubling or tripling of power. It multiplies it.

The early Church exploded with the power of God. Acts 1 says that *"they were all of one mind and one accord."* The potential within an organization will be multiplied when it works in unity. When there is contention and division then God's power is undermined. Unity must begin on an individual basis. It's why we immerse ourselves in the truths of God's Word. It's why James pointed out that a *"double-minded man is unstable in all his ways ... and will not receive anything from the Lord."* Likewise, Jesus taught in Matthew 12 that *"any Kingdom divided against itself is laid waste; and any city or house divided against itself shall not stand."*

Basic Biblical Business Principles

- **Learn the art of diligence**.
  The hand of the diligent will rule. Proverbs. 12:24

- **Become excellent at something you do**. Prosperity and economic freedom result from excellence. This involves becoming financially literate.
  Do you see a man who excels in his work, he will stand before kings. Proverbs 22:29

- **Assume responsibility and manages detail**.
  Be diligent TO KNOW the state of your flocks and attend to your herds. Proverbs 27:23

- **Strive for trustworthiness and dependability**.
  He who walks with integrity and works righteousness and speaks truth in his heart ... who swears to his own hurt and does not change. Psalm 15:2-4

- **Discipline yourself to view things from long-term perspective**.
  Little by little I will drive them out from before you, until you have increased and are numerous enough to take possession of the land. Exodus 23:30 and Deuteronomy 7:22

  A long-term perspective means patience in doing the right thing. It may mean sacrifice and selecting the priorities that will ensure stability; but stability with a long-term future.
  Prepare your outside work, make it fit for yourself in the field; and afterward build your house. Proverbs 24:27

- **Be alert for opportunities for ownership**.
  Ownership provides opportunity, freedom and influence. Private ownership is foundational to the principles outlined in Deuteronomy. It is an important part of what Proverbs refers to as an "excellent woman."

  Who can find an excellent wife? For her worth is far above jewels. She is like the merchant ships bringing her food from afar. She considers a field and buys it, out of her earnings she plants a vineyard. She sets about her work vigorously. She sees that her trading is profitable and her lamp does not go out at night. Proverbs 31:10,14-18

- **Learn to manage risk**.
  Ownership involves risk. Risk requires faith and faith requires risk. Learn to seek the Lord on matters of this type AND to manage risk.
  Against all hope, Abraham believed God. Romans 4:18

- **Make your assets work for you**.
  Learn to handle money wisely and make it multiply. In Scripture, those who multiplied their money not only gained the Lord's approval, but entered into a place of greater blessings and responsibility.
  Well done good and faithful servant, you were faithful over a few things, I will make you ruler over many things. Enter into the joy of your Lord. Matthew 25:18

- **Treat your customers like family**.
  Customer relationships are covenant relationships. They involve trust and honor. Honesty, fairness and generosity will reap the rewards of riches and honor and life.
  A good name is to be chosen over great riches, loving favor more than silver and gold. By humility and the fear of the LORD are riches and honor and life. He who sows iniquity will reap sorrow, and the rod of his anger will fail. He who has a generous eye will be blessed. Proverbs 22:1,4,8,9

- **Surround yourself with wise counselors**
  In the multitude of counselors there is safety. Proverbs 11:14; 24:6

- **Make decisions based on the right thing to do**
  Let not mercy and truth forsake you. Proverbs 3:3

  And what does the Lord require of you but to do justly, and to love kindness and mercy, and to humble yourself and walk humbly with your God? Micah 6:8

- **Make the Lord your senior Partner**
  Trust in the Lord with all your heart, lean not unto your own understanding. In all your ways acknowledge Him and He will direct your paths. Proverbs 3:5,6

  Seek first His Kingdom and righteousness and all these other things will be added unto you. Matthew 6:33

A partnership is a covenant. We enter into a covenant relationship with the Lord when we believe and make Him our Lord and our God. But the principle of covenant extends into the work of our hands:

Let your work appear to servants and your glory to their children; and establish the work of our hands for, yes establish the work of our hands. Psalm 90:16

Partnership with God means business owners who can approach their businesses first in their prayer closets — with faith and with a generous eye. When God is given first priority, this partnership will begin incorporating the kingly anointing reflected by Abraham, Isaac and Jacob. It involves all the scriptural dimensions reflected by the entrepreneurial community principles in Deuteronomy and Proverbs. Tithing/giving. Taking care of your employees. Operating with fairness. And most important, trusting in the Lord at each step reflected in an interactive and practical prayer life that bears uniquely on the decisions of the business.

Inquiring of the Lord on decisions. When we enter into that covenant relationship that establishes the Lord as our senior partner — we need to make it our practice to inquire of the Lord on the decisions we have before us.

Scripture tells us that again and again King David "*inquired of the Lord.*" David's life operated on much more than following principles of the Torah. He sought God's presence and guidance, believed in His goodness and entered an ongoing trust relationship that guided him in his decisions.

God's economy involves the merging of the sacred and secular in a way that interlinks business and ministry into a Kingdom enterprise. When business and ministry are operating the way God intended, the supernatural will result.

Biblical Success Principles
The Edge: the Supernatural. God is not bound by the laws governing His own creation. Because of the desperate condition of the world today, we need miracles. Jesus operated with miracles as

a normal part of His ministry and then introduced a new order at Pentecost. He expected His followers to do GREATER things than He did, and sent the Holy Spirit to facilitate this.

He rebuked His disciples for their lack of faith for miracles and healing and casting out of demons — but He praised an outsider, a Roman centurion, who understood Jesus' spiritual authority and discerned the relationship between the spiritual and the natural worlds. The centurion declared to Jesus, *"just say the Word and my servant will be healed."* And Jesus marveled at the Roman's understanding of this principle of faith.

For miracles to happen, we have to have faith in God. We have to know that He is and that He diligently rewards those who seek Him. We have to have a revelation of His sovereignty over His creation. In Mark 11, Jesus said, *"have faith in God."* Without faith it is impossible to please Him.

Caleb and Joshua are a clear example of the result of operating in faith. When they went into the Promised Land with the other Israelites sent to spy out the land, they saw things through the eyes of faith. They had the spiritual vision to see things from God's perspective.

While their counterparts responded with fear by announcing they were like grasshoppers compared to the people occupying the Promised Land, Joshua and Caleb gave a good report of what they knew God would do on their behalf.

Interlinking Business with Ministry. In Luke 5 we have a very apt illustration of this connection between business, ministry and the supernatural. The story begins when Jesus noticed Simon had just come back from plying his trade of fishing. He had come back empty-handed.

> *"He noticed two empty boats at the water's edge, for the fishermen had left them and were washing their nets. Stepping into one of the boats, Jesus asked Simon, its owner, to push it out into the water. So he sat in the boat and taught the crowds from there."*
> Luke 5:2-3

The Lord will use vessels of business. It is where the people will be. The Lord will be very innovative in establishing business platforms for ministry.

> *"When he had finished speaking, He said to Simon,*
> *"Now go out where it is deeper and let down your*
> *nets, and you will catch many fish."* Luke 5:4

There will be a blessing for those who utilize their enterprises for God's purposes. When the Lord has used an enterprise for His own purposes, the command is to push out further "where it is deep." Extend your faith. And expect more in less time with less effort than before.

> *"Master,"* Simon replied, *"we worked hard all last*
> *night and didn't catch a thing. But if you say so,*
> *we'll try again."* Luke 5:5

Peter demonstrates that until the Lord shows up on the scene that toil in doing things in the natural may not avail much. But it is important to recognize when the Lord gives the command; and then to respond in obedience regardless of whether it seems realistic or not.

> *"And this time their nets were so full they began to*
> *tear! A shout for help brought their partners in the*
> *other boat, and soon both boats were filled with fish*
> *and on the verge of sinking."* Luke 5:6,7

When your enterprise is genuinely used as a platform for God's purposes; and the Lord then gives the command — the result will not only be miraculous, but it will provide a positive impact on other members of your business community who support you as well.

> *"When Simon Peter realized what had happened, he*
> *fell to his knees before Jesus and said, 'Oh, Lord,*
> *please leave me—I'm too much of a sinner to be*
> *around you.' For he was awestruck by the size of*

their catch, as were the others with him." Luke 5:8,9

The Lord is going to bypass natural patterns and expectations and begin blessing His people with awe-inspiring miracles.

Charity and Reciprocity. In Luke 6, Jesus made a simple, but very powerful statement. He said, *"give and it will be given unto you."* He told us, *"just as you want people to treat you, treat them in the same way."* He also told us to bless those who curse us! Love your neighbor as yourself.

> *He who has a generous eye will be blessed.* Proverbs 22:9

> *The generous soul will be made rich, and he who waters will also be watered.* Proverbs 11:29

The principle of reciprocity tells us that the standard of measure we operate with will determine the standard with which we will receive in return. If you are critical of everyone, you can expect to receive critical judgments from others. It is the principle behind tithes and offerings. It is the principle that undergirds operating with a generous and kind spirit.

Community Responsibility. In Luke 12, Jesus taught that *"unto him that much is given, much is required, and to whom men have committed much, of him they will ask the more."* Whatever level of opportunity is given to us, both God and man will expect us to operate with a certain standard of performance. Favor carries with it responsibility. As favor increases, so does the responsibility.

Not only is this made very clear in Deuteronomy, but Isaiah 58 ties the blessings of God to how we treat the poor, the widow and the stranger.

Faith and good stewardship will bring success, especially if it is used together with the principle of perseverance. But the rewards of those two principles demand observation of the principles of **responsibility** — principles clearly spelled out in Deuteronomy.

This is illustrated in the book of James where it says, *"Let not many of you become teachers, my brethren, knowing that as such we shall incur stricter judgment.*" At the heart of this principle are two words, "Noblesse oblige." Nobility obligates. But humility and purity have to be coupled with this principle for it to operate according to God's standards. Responsibility is tied to a generous and benevolent spirit.

The principle of responsibility is behind the admonition in Isaiah 58 to reach out to the hungry and oppressed, to the needy and orphans.

Servant Leadership. You've heard the story of the Jewish mother walking down the street with her two young sons. A passerby asks how old the boys are. Her response is "*the doctor is three, and the lawyer is two.*" Everyone aspires to greatness! If not for themselves, then for their children.

In Matthew 18, the disciples asked Jesus, "Who then is the greatest in the Kingdom of heaven?" In response, Jesus called a child to Himself, and said, "*Truly I say to you, unless you are converted and become like children, you shall not enter the Kingdom of heaven. Whoever then humbles himself as this child, he is the greatest in the Kingdom of heaven.*"

"*God is my strength and power, and He makes my way perfect. He makes my feet like the feet of deer, and sets me on high places. He teaches my hands to make war, so that my arms can bend a bow of bronze. You have also given me the shield of Your salvation; Your gentleness has made me great.*" 2 Samuel 22:33 This is an amazing contrast. After using all these terms of war and power to describe the pathway God has enabled on behalf of David, David ties the greatness he has achieved to gentleness. Something very different from the way of power of the world.

> "*What is desired in a man is kindness.*" Proverbs 19:23

In another instance, the disciples were in a dispute about which of them were the greatest. Even within circles of believers, people get concerned about their status. But the Lord's response was this. "*The king of the gentiles lords it over them; and those who have authority over them are called "benefactors." But not so with you.*

Let him who is the greatest become as the youngest, and the leader as the servant. For who is greater — the one who reclines at the table or the one who serves. But I am among you as the one who serves." Luke 22:25-27

Greatness is tied to the qualities of being trusting, teachable and humble. Greatness is tied to service and servanthood.

A major department store chain was birthed in the States when JC Penney sought to give a square deal to everyone — honest merchandise at an honest price. The deeper the sacrifice and the broader the scope of the service, the greater the individual. We need to DARE to live the Beatitudes at this level.

Work yourself out of a job. Make yourself dispensable. Starting a business often means having to be willing to do anything and everything. I've known some business owners who joke about being president and chief bottle washer. They did what was required to get the job done. But there comes a point in the life cycle of a business when the owner periodically replaces himself. As an organization grows, the functions of its founders evolve and change. They learn how to train others in the things they do. They learn how to turn responsibilities over to others.

Biblical principles of business work. They defy the odds and adversities that define the economic systems of this world!

CHAPTER 17

KINGDOM ENTREPRENEUR— LEADERS AND THE PROPHETIC

"Now concerning spiritual gifts, brethren, I do not want you to be ignorant. But the manifestation of the Spirit is given to each one for the profit of all." (1 Corinthians 12:1, 7)

The most pivotal and strategic initiatives facing the Church, the Messianic Jewish community and Israel can probably be accurately described in the natural as "against all odds."

They are situations bound for failure — unless God shows up. Historically, the way the Lord has "shown" up in instance after instance described in His Word has been through His people — who have learned to hear His voice. The role of God's economy in the course of world events today involves a particular group of leaders whose callings follow after that of the patriarchs.

Throughout Scripture are examples of economic-based communities founded on faith in God and the principles of His Word. Economic-based covenant communities led by prophetically-gifted entrepreneur-leaders.

Entrepreneur-leaders who reflect a merging of the creative wisdom needed to harness opportunity, with the leadership required to make it happen and the ability to discern the Lord's leading in its planning and execution.

The Lord has always had as His intention to be central to the goals, plans and everyday lives of those who are called by His Name. That necessitates the practical dimensions comprising the dynamics of community and economics. It necessitates the spiritual, which not only rightly interprets the Word of truth, but provides the contemporaneous relevance of hearing His voice. Hearing and discerning the voice of the Lord is encompassed in what has become known as the prophetic.

The Practicalities of the Prophetic

Most dictionary definitions of "prophetic" target two dimensions. One is the prediction of future events. The other is that which is revelatory. While the prediction of future events is a central role of those who hold the office of the prophet, revelation and guidance from the Holy Spirit is much broader and should be central to those called according to His purposes.

God's people have always been guided by His voice. While Scripture has recorded the Lord thundering before God's enemies, in most instances His guidance has been through that "*still, small voice.*" Before the outpouring of the Holy Spirit described in Acts 4, the voice of the Lord was recorded through numerous gifted and anointed leaders. God spoke to Abraham. Abraham believed God and acted on the guidance he received from the Lord. This interaction between hearing the truths and direction God gives is foundational to what we refer to as biblical faith. It is the aligning of the human heart with God's heart: and the reason King David was referred to as a man after God's own heart.

Many of the patriarchs possessed gifts that when combined with the dimension of being Spirit-led, resulted in them being astute business leaders. They built small kingdoms that were economic, God-centered communities. The examples of Abraham, Isaac and David are rich examples of God's Kingdom intentions for His people. Each were in reality Kingdom entrepreneur-leaders, whose hunger for the Almighty was such that it became the primary factor in establishing who they were and what they were to do. This hunger for Him in each instance would open the way for their communication and interactions with Him and would shape their calling and destiny.

God spoke. They responded. These interactions unleashed the blessings of God not only for His chosen, but those they would align themselves with.

But let's look at the dynamic operating in God's prophetic entrepreneur-leaders with the example of Joseph the patriarch. Joseph is significant to us because of the parallel of our times to the times he lived in. They were times of uncertainty, crisis and reversals.

Joseph is also significant because of the unique way God used him. God used him to harness the resources of a pagan nation and bless that nation in the process; as he accomplished God's redemptive purpose for His covenant people.

Joseph was clearly prophetic. While Joseph heard God's voice, this wasn't just a casual matter. Joseph's orientation was always centrally focused on being about God's business. That fervency defined the depth at which he discerned the voice of the Lord. It encompassed a righteousness that was reflected in the excellence and caliber of work he did regardless of the position he held during his tenure in Egypt.

Joseph's prophetic role merged the practical with the eternal. As he facilitated the survival needs for the nation he served and his own people, Joseph was put in a position to establish the continuity that ensured God's covenant purposes being accomplished for and through His people Israel.

Joseph's role was also as a nation-changer. He created an economic bypass strategy to avert the disaster faced by the world of that day. But the Word of the Lord — the prophetic Words of wisdom spoken by Joseph — were embraced by the people of the world around him as being from God AND they were acted on. That's the basis of faith and that is the basis on which nations are changed.

Joseph was an entrepreneur-leader whose prophetic gift positioned him to be a nation-changer. He was an entrepreneur-leader whose gifts merged the creative wisdom needed to harness opportunity, with the leadership required to make it happen and the ability to discern the Lord's leading in its planning and execution. Let's take a closer look at these elements marking Kingdom entrepreneur-leaders

— creative wisdom, leadership and the prophetic — as they operated in Joseph.

Creative Wisdom

> *"The LORD was with Joseph, and he was a successful man; and he was in the house of his master the Egyptian. And his master saw that the LORD was with him and that the LORD made all he did to prosper in his hand. So Joseph found favor in his sight, and served him. Then he made him overseer of his house, and all that he had he put under his authority. So it was, from the time that he had made him overseer of his house and all that he had, that the LORD blessed the Egyptian's house for Joseph's sake; and the blessing of the LORD was on all that he had in the house and in the field. Thus he left all that he had in Joseph's hand."* Genesis 39: 2-6

In each phase of Joseph's tenure in Egypt, he was a problem solver. He possessed the ability to grasp the big picture and to know what to do about it. Joseph possessed the creative type of wisdom needed to see the opportunity in the midst of problems and disorganization — and the operation of this creative wisdom made him prosper in what he did. This is the mark of an entrepreneur.

Entrepreneurs are those who spot opportunity and then are able to organize, promote and manage the risk and hurdles to create something new in a way that it becomes self-sustaining and makes a profit. It is a creative gift that sees that which is not and knows how to make it happen. Joseph's wisdom and creative gift as an entrepreneur operated in such a way that it had to be exceptional — because at whatever level he operated in, his excellence and results-orientation gained him the favor, trust and promotion.

Leadership

> *"And Joseph was there in the prison. But the LORD*

> *was with Joseph and showed him mercy, and He gave him favor in the sight of the keeper of the prison. And the keeper of the prison committed to Joseph's hand all the prisoners who were in the prison; whatever they did there, it was his doing. The keeper of the prison did not look into anything that was under Joseph's authority, because the LORD was with him; and whatever he did, the LORD made it prosper."* Genesis 39:20-23

Joseph's creative, problem-solving wisdom was coupled with a gift of leadership. True leadership inspires confidence as it accomplishes results and creates order out of disorder and chaos. True leadership exercises authority and dominion without being either controlling or dominating. True leaders trust, delegate and supervise, whereas micro-managers and those who crave control tend to operate on the premise that their own abilities are second to none. Joseph's leadership was of the type that motivated, inspired, nurtured and trusted. Joseph's leadership abilities gained him recognition — then the confidence, trust and promotion first from Potipher, then the keeper of the prison and then Pharaoh.

The Prophetic

> *"And Pharaoh said to his servants, 'Can we find such a one as this, a man in whom is the Spirit of God?' Then Pharaoh said to Joseph, 'Inasmuch as God has shown you all this, there is no one as discerning and wise as you. You shall be over my house, and all my people shall be ruled according to your word; only in regard to the throne will I be greater than you.'"* Genesis 41:38-41

First Joseph interpreted Pharaoh's dreams; but then he gave Pharaoh a clear plan of action to take. Pharaoh recognized the importance of Joseph's gifts in the area of problem-solving wisdom and leadership, but saw his real value in his prophetic gift with his statement: *"Can we find such a man as this in whom is the Spirit of God."* Joseph's promotion hinged not on the wise plan of action he outlined, but on his ability to hear from God. Otherwise, Pharaoh could have simply taken the plan and dismissed Joseph.

Joseph was a clear witness to the Egyptians of how the Lord desired to operate through His people. God was with Joseph. His interactions with the Lord filled him with prophetic wisdom. And the blessings of God followed Joseph. But these blessings were extended to his Egyptian masters because of Joseph; and his Egyptian masters clearly recognized the blessing of God they received because of Joseph.

With His promotion to sit alongside Pharaoh, an alliance was created that served to redeem God's people from the coming disaster and to bless their hosts in the process.

The Significance of These Gifts

So why is this so significant? It is because over the centuries, Kingdom entrepreneur-leaders with the ability to discern the voice of the Lord have been at the forefront of the change brought about by the Spirit of the Lord. It is very clear in the lives of Abraham, Isaac, Joseph and David. But let's view how this has been operating since World War II.

Priestly entrepreneur-leaders were at the forefront of the parachurch movement that began emerging in the late '60s. These priestly entrepreneur-leaders both heard from God and recognized the Kingdom opportunity reflected by the mass media. Their efforts changed the thrust and role of the traditional church. Their efforts have impacted countless millions with the relevance of putting God at the center of our lives.

Many of these Kingdom innovators began paving the way for a current emerging move of God, which is penetrating the infrastructures and seats of power in business and government.

So, today as the parachurch leadership of the late '60s is transitioning from the entrepreneurial to the corporate, still another group of Kingdom entrepreneur-leaders is emerging. This new group will advance the Kingdom into the fabric of society — into the spheres of business and government.

These twenty-first century Kingdom entrepreneurs will be those Jesus spoke of in Luke 11:12 (NIV): *"The Kingdom of heaven has been forcefully advancing, and forceful men lay hold of it."* They will be ones like the patriarchs of old who operate with creative abilities to build and seize opportunity — but with the distinction that they will be God's community builders and nation-changers for the pivotal times we are entering.

There are some interesting steps leading up to this present move of God.

We've previously noted that at the conclusion of World War II and the defeat of Japan, General Douglas MacArthur called for missionaries to come. Missionaries who would infuse the basics of biblical faith and values into the Japanese culture.

Four showed up. Western society had just emerged from the death throes of everyday people praying their way through the horrors of the potential of losing their freedom — and yet the traditional church simply wasn't prepared for MacArthur's call to help change a nation.

Then in the late 40s, two very significant things unfolded. The first was the birth of the state of Israel. During that same time frame, there were something like 250 healing revival ministries that were birthed. And the traditional church was NOT quite sure about all these unusual large meetings and tent revivals and miracles taking place.

In the late '60s, 1967 to be exact, two more very significant things took place. First, the Jews regained control over Jerusalem. The second was the birth of what became known as the Charismatic Renewal or the Jesus Movement. There was more — it also marked the time of the rise of Messianic Jewish movement. Along with the Charismatic Revival and Messianic Jewish movement came the rise of radio and television ministries — and the Parachurch movement.

Two Paradigm Shifts

Now these events represent two paradigm shifts — paradigm shifts impacting the order and thrust of the traditional church. The first paradigm shift was the rise of miracle-working ministries in the late '40s. The second, in the late '60s, was the Charismatic Renewal and rise of the Messianic Jewish movement — with a massive change happening as people became hungry for more of God and His Word — and people began getting acquainted with the ministry of the Holy Spirit on a very large scale. Along with that, people began realizing that the God of all creation spoke to people and not only had a plan and purpose for their lives, but was intimately involved in directing the course of world events — through His people.

Within each of these two paradigm shifts are the operation of three elements. First, something significant was happening in the restoration of ISRAEL. The second was REVIVAL. The third was major CHANGE in the traditions of how the church operated.

So, in 1948: the nation of **Israel** was birthed; an event which coincided with the rise of miracle ministries and **revivals** of healing. The **change** at that time was a major break from the traditions that resulted in only four missionaries showing up when General MacArthur called for missionaries to come play a role in changing a nation.

As the Jews regained control of Jerusalem in 1967, simultaneously the Charismatic **renewal** and Messianic Jewish movement were getting underway. These events initiated major **change** — as the traditional church began receiving an influx of not only new believers, but also those who were having life transforming experiences with the Holy Spirit. Simultaneously, Christians began seizing the initiative with the medium of television and radio which was reaching countless numbers of people both within and beyond the scope of the traditional church!

That brings us to the present — as we are facing another paradigm shift. My book, *"The Joseph-Daniel Calling,"* targets this paradigm shift — the penetration of the business and governmental arenas with God's anointed and chosen. These will be God's anointed and chosen who hear His voice.

Like the other two paradigm shifts, this current move of God is going to involve CHANGE in the way the church has operated. It will challenge the "traditions of men" and outdated modes of operation.

The dynamic of what is happening regarding the restoration of ISRAEL has yet to emerge. But it will and it will be led by Kingdom entrepreneur-leaders. Before us will be a major influx of on-fire

Messianic Jewish believers to Israel. The return of the Jews to the land of Israel is known as Aliyah. What we have before us, as business and governmental spheres are being penetrated by Spirit-led entrepreneur-leaders is a major wave of Messianic Jewish Aliyah.

What has been happening behind the scenes since 1967, is that more Jews have come to embrace Jesus as their Messiah than in all the years since our Lord walked the face of the earth. This behind-the-scenes revival will be the catalyst for REVIVAL in Israel. So, as we witness the influx of God's anointed into the infrastructures and seats of power of business and government; and we witness the return of Spirit-led, God-fearing Jews to Israel; we can also expect the overflow to extend into lands of persecution; into Jewish communities and deep within the fabric of society where the religious traditions of men are being challenged and God embraced.

Kingdom Entrepreneur-Leaders

The penetration of the seats of power and infrastructures of the world today is being led by Kingdom entrepreneur-leaders. Entrepreneur-leaders who reflect a merging of the creative, faith-oriented wisdom needed to harness opportunity, with the leadership required to make it happen and the ability to discern the Lord's leading in its planning and execution. Kingdom entrepreneur-leaders who, like Joseph the patriarch, will be seen as bearing the blessings and wisdom of God. Men and women of God with the calling and gifts to build communities and change nations.

Jill Mitchell of Kingdom Connections International is a clear example of a Kingdom leader, whose keen prophetic gift discerns strategic opportunity long before others recognize it. Then by a combination of her creative, faith-oriented wisdom and a gift of leadership again and again, she has mobilized others to seize opportunities that release God's purposes to impact nations.

Jill is a modern-day Josephina. Her response to the invitation from the President of a developing African nation was to organize a unique business-ministry team that would bring release to God's purposes for this nation. She has served a role as a catalyst to not only those in seats of power, but her efforts have also resulted in fueling indigenous believing business communities with vision and direction from Israel to the nations. Her prophetic foresight and wisdom has influenced the roles and callings of many, many Christian business, governmental and ministry leaders over the years, while changing the course of nations.

Barbara Wentroble is another prophetic entrepreneur-leader called to speak into the lives of governmental kings and leaders and in so doing to impact the course of nations. I recall in early 2002, when Carol and I were a part of a Christian disaster response team in Afghanistan, that Barbara spoke the Word of the Lord to a high-level Islamic Afghan governmental official. The Word she spoke was insightful, pertinent and delivered with grace and authority. It was received as a Word from the Lord — one that not only encouraged and helped this government official, but served to open unique doors of opportunity on subsequent Afghan Kingdom initiatives of which Barbara was a part.

The parachurch movement, which began penetrating the sphere of the mass media in the late '60s, has set the stage for today's penetration of the marketplace and seats of government. The leaders who initiated the parachurch movement as a rule were entrepreneur-leaders with a priestly anointing. The leaders of the marketplace movement will be those who combine a kingly and prophetic anointing. A kingly anointing like that of Abraham, Joseph and David. When the traditional church and the leadership in the parachurch movement begin collaborating with the leaders of the marketplace movement, the result will be a mighty impact for the Kingdom of God.

The Worldly Point of View and the Prophetic

> *"So from now on we regard no one from a worldly point of view. We are therefore Christ's ambassadors."* 2 Cor 5:16, 20 NIV

Kingdom entrepreneur-leaders view both opportunity and their relationships from God's point of view, which is a Kingdom perspective. Kingdom entrepreneur-leaders are Kingdom ambassadors. Jesus outlined the principles to operate from a Kingdom perspective. With His resurrection, He sent the Holy Spirit and made available the gifts needed to mobilize those who would advance His Kingdom.

With today's advancements in technology and communications, we have entered an era unlike any the past has ever held.

With the Internet we live in a world of instantaneous communications. It is a world that has begun operating outside the box — a "box" previously constrained by the infrastructures of national and regional economies and the power of the governments that controlled them. But we have entered an era with economies without borders. It is an era where 53 of the largest economies in the world are corporations. It is an era in which the "world's view" of seats of power falls far short.

It is a time in which the developments in technology, communications and the changes emerging in the world of commerce are coinciding with a vibrantly potent infrastructure tied to the Kingdom of God: A Kingdom infrastructure that holds the potential of building communities and changing nations in the midst of chaos, reversals and distress. It is a time in which those with a Kingdom perspective will see the opportunity and move to build.

As already noted, the Church at the end of WWII was in essence largely disconnected and anemic. Largely disconnected and anemic, at least in terms of being able to answer General McArthur's prescient call to the Church to change a nation. But since that time, we have experienced strategically sovereign moves of God. Moves of God that in essence have begun awakening and preparing the Body, while simultaneously preparing God's covenant people for such a time as this.

So, as we endeavor to respond as the sons of Issachar to understand the times and know what to do, we can no longer regard our roles from a worldly point of view. We are no longer a part of an anemic, disjointed Body. We are entering a season in which those with eyes to see and ears to hear are recognizing the signs of the times and the significance of the roles reflected by this emerging move of God. The roles of those called as ambassadors and entrepreneur-leaders who see *that which is not as though it were* — and then do something about it.

Ambassadors and entrepreneur-leaders who hear God's voice and will embrace opportunity and their relationships from God's point of view. Ambassadors and entrepreneur-leaders who possess the gifts, anointing and calling to penetrate the fabric of society in business and government and speak God's Words of wisdom into the dilemmas and crises in order to build God's Kingdom. Ambassadors and entrepreneur-leaders who will be marked by the creative wisdom, leadership and prophetic gifting needed to build communities and change nations.

CHAPTER 18

AGAINST ALL ODDS: GOD'S ECONOMY ENTREPRENEURIAL PROGRAM

Understanding how the Kingdom of God can operate against all odds was brought home to me during our first trip to Minsk, Belarus.

The devastation at the hands of the Nazis compounded by the hopelessness and controls of the communist system have marred individuals and families across generations in Belarus.

So it was into this hopeless environment that I led a team to put on a business startup workshop — based on Kingdom principles and God's economy. Our hosts Stewart and Chantal Winograd lead a Messianic Jewish congregation in Minsk. From their congregation, they selected 30 members to attend our workshop. From those attending, 20 realistic business plans were submitted.

Background

But first, I need to describe some background. Minsk comes from an old Slavic word that means EXCHANGE. Minsk was birthed as a place of trade. Very fitting for the business startup workshop we put on.

Yet Belarus is functionally a dictatorship. Within its policies and infrastructure is much carry-over from the oppression and control from its 70 years of communism. In ways that seem to parallel the operation of the Three Self Church in China, the Russian Orthodox Church has been designated as the "official state church" of Belarus. Similar again to the Chinese "state" church, the Belarusian Russian Orthodox Church is not in anyway receptive to the born-again community. This "official" church has run series of TV ads designed to scare the people away from any involvement with believers. They have proactively attempted to establish policies that hinder, discourage and drive out believers from this land.

Despite their concerted efforts to stamp out the born-again community, unusual things have been taking place. God is sovereignly at work in Belarus. Revival is in the air. Baptists, Pentecostals, Charismatics and Messianic Jews are praying for and supporting each other. The day of my arrival marked the first city-wide gathering of believers to pray for the economy of Belarus.

Prayer for the economy is no small matter. The average salary in Minsk is $80 to $100 a month. Ninety percent of the population live in overcrowded government housing. During our visit, 450 businessmen were rounded up and put in prison. The official reason was corruption. The word on the street was that these businessmen represented a power structure that was a threat to certain sectors of the government.

Our friends, the Winograds, have been in Belarus since 1994. They have established themselves on several levels as good citizens and contributors to the welfare and positive thrust of this nation. They have come to consider Belarus as their home. They treat not only the members of their congregation, but their friends in the community, as family. Because of that, they are embraced and treated as family. They have become genuine community builders and as Messianic Jewish believers, they have become an integral part of the Jewish community across Belarus.

When the Winograds first arrived in Belarus — partly because of the oppressive controls of the Belarusian system and partly because of the aim of the "official church" to stamp out the credibility and work of the born-again community — they were advised by seasoned local Christian friends to be very cautious. They were advised to remain hidden and secretive in their aims and activities.

But God spoke a very clear Word to this couple to be open and up front concerning their aims and activities. They refused to respond in fear or with guile. They refused to hide or to operate in the shadows. They have been bold, but also wise and discrete. Because of their honest and sincere approach, the Winograds have come to have unusual favor not only within the community, but in some very high government circles. They operate as modern-day Josephs and Daniels within the sphere of their calling.

Shortly after their arrival was a time when other congregations were losing their meeting halls. Yet the Winograds obtained an approved facility in the center of Minsk. Keep in mind that most buildings suitable for meeting on any level are owned by the government. Most businesses rent their facilities from the government.

And so, Stewart and Chantal proceeded to build a congregation from scratch. And now, their leaders and members are committed and very soundly grounded in God's Word. They are people of the Spirit who know how to pray. Not one person I met is playing church — they are a people serious about growing in the Lord, with a vision of being used by Him.

Since their early days in Belarus, the Winograd's strong, credible, trust-centered approach to their relationships has become pivotal to what they have been doing within the believing community, as well as within the Belarusian community. They have likewise become a respected, loved and integral part of the Jewish community in Belarus.

Belarus as a Pivot Point

While in prayer prior to our arrival, the Lord spoke a very clear Word to me that Belarus was spiritually a pivot point in this region of the world — and very much at a crossroads. I was discerning that spiritually speaking, in terms of God's purposes for this land, this nation is at a point at which it could go one way or another. There is a spiritual battle underway for the soul of Belarus. But what I also heard from the Lord was that the outcome of this battle was in the hands of the believers in this land. And that the outcome of this battle will impact what is played out in other key regions of the

Former Soviet Union.

After my arrival, I shared this perception with Stewart. He then gave me a tape with a message he gave his people over three years ago — based on the same Word I received from the Lord. Stewart is raising up his people to be leaders in the midst of this spiritual battle. Leaders who will go out and take up the mantle of addressing this issue of spiritual dominion — and make a difference in this land. Just not to make a difference — but to determine the difference of seeing God's agendas birthed in this land that for years and years has been oppressed and controlled and devastated.

Raising Up Leaders

Stewart shared with me that when he and Chantal first came to Belarus, it was to raise up a leader and then to go. Instead, they have raised up LEADERS who are the ones to go. They are going with a calling. Seasoned leaders who understand the realities and dynamics of spiritual warfare. Some have left to minister in other parts of Belarus, but most are leaving to minister to the very large Russian-speaking community in Israel.

As a former combat officer, I recognize that in a battle you plan and you move strategically and with wisdom. You understand who your real enemy is. You then simultaneously seek to win the hearts and minds of the people, while engaging the enemy. The Winograds are people of faith. They will not be intimidated. They have not succumbed to the fear or paranoia or awe of the enemy before them. They have proactively been advancing the Kingdom of God, strategically and with wisdom.

They have gone to leaders in the system — as God has anointed and directed them — and said, this is who we are and this is what we want to do. They have found favor and respect — and with this approach, assistance has come from some of the most unlikely places.

Against all odds, they have gained access to open doors that counter the intentions of the policies and direction of this system, as well as that of the anti-born-again movement operating in this land.

This is a land that historically has been a bastion of anti-Semitism, devastation and anti-God movements and initiatives. It is still referred to as the "land of great controls." But God is and has always been in the redemption business. Our Lord has always penetrated the seats of the world's power with His own, who have been anointed, bold and wise in their stance for Him. Our friends, Stewart and Chantal indeed have the Lord's heart and mind for this nation. They truly operate as the biblical Joseph and Daniel did, as faithful and effectual ambassadors and instruments of God's purposes. They are like spearheads in determining THAT difference that God intends for the wonderful people in this land of Belarus.

Chantal's part of the Winograd ministry is focused on the admonition in Isaiah 58 — to reach out to the poor and the needy; to the afflicted and oppressed; and to the widows and the orphans. Her efforts have touched leaders and influenced policies that have had a stranglehold on this system. It has all been done in the Name of the Lord. Whether with orphans or in hospitals or in the Jewish community, this couple has earned not only the love and respect of those with whom they work, but they have become an integral, positive force in the changes that are opening hearts for the Lord.

Stewart leads the congregation. He serves like a father not only to the members of his congregation, but to the members of the community that he and Chantal serve. Stewart is a genuine community-builder who is making a positive impact on the nation he has been called to serve.

His efforts have not been unlike those of Joseph the patriarch. Joseph created an economic bypass strategy to turn crisis into opportunity for the nation he served, as he spoke God's wisdom and created solutions for dilemmas being faced by the world during his time. It was Stewart's "father's heart" that resulted in the invitation for us to put on our God's Economy Entrepreneurial program.

Global Initiatives Foundation's God's Economy Entrepreneurial Program offers a biblical-based entrepreneurial, small business development program that will provide employment, strengthen the community and build the Kingdom of God. This program is based on biblical principles and pivots on the truth from Genesis 26 that with God as our partner, Kingdom entrepreneurs can expect to defy the odds.

Belarus represents a business environment not very conducive to private business ownership. Yet, against all odds the principles of God's economy are giving birth to a new dimension operating through the believers in this land. The business environment of Belarus is a modern day test of how God's economy can operate.

With wise spiritual oversight from Stewart, leaders were established from the participants in the workshop who demonstrated the expertise and calling to be Kingdom entrepreneurs. These are committed, praying entrepreneurs with a vision to be used for God's purposes as they have planned, launched and developed their businesses.

The basic structure of this program is worth noting because of the special application it has for surmounting the hurdles tied to the practicalities of reaching out and building communities in the Former Soviet Union and in Israel. Israel and the Former Soviet Union each represent challenging environments for operating small businesses — which emphasizes the significance of operating according to God's principles of business.

The Seedbeds for God's Economic Principles

Israel was already a costly place to live, with nothing coming cheaply or easily. But since the launch of the intifada, challenges have multiplied against our Jewish brethren living within the Israeli economy.

Studies indicate that poverty in Israel appears to be spreading to the middle class. Each day ordinary people — ranging from the self-employed to teachers, lawyers, tour guides, artists and construction workers, the older as well as the younger, — are facing mounting obstacles in their attempts to pay their bills and feed their families. Many who were self-sufficient are now seeking assistance. Unemployment is rising. Unemployment, of course, causes a ripple-effect.

With different types of economic challenges from Israel, the situation across the Former Soviet Union reflects disjointed adjustments to entering the world's economy. In many locations, primary industries from former communist days were bequeathed to corrupt political cronies or fell prey to Mafia-type control or both. In essence, most FSU states have little by way of a middle class.

Poverty in these regions is a reality for a broad cross-section of the populace.

I've already noted the Orthodox Jewish community's response to unemployment and poverty is a high biblical community standard of Tz'dakah or charity. The Messianic Jewish community also embraces the biblical standards of community and Tz'dakah.

One of the primary objectives of our ministry, Global Initiatives Foundation, is to partner with local leaders to take a stand against the impact of the intifada, anti-Semitism, corruption and poverty. *Small business development* is a very biblical solution and goal. Global Initiatives Foundation's God's Economy Entrepreneurial Program provides the tools for small business development and a tangible counter-balance to both anti-business and poverty problems.

God's Economy Entrepreneurial Workshops

In a previous chapter I mentioned a similar entrepreneurial program put on by a UK business-owner group led by Mike Bundock; in which by simply utilizing standard principles of business, 50 new businesses were launched. Over their first four years, there was only one failure.

The key was in the support group that brought these new business owners together regularly to pray and to seek the Lord and to pool their wisdom. These support groups were tied to local congregations.

The program was put on for believers: to build up the believing community in regions experiencing tough economic challenges. Once a business started cash-flowing, the owners agreed to help their neighbors as mentors in doing what had been done for them, which provides opportunity for the believing community to bless those outside the believing community by sharing the practical principles of God's economy.

Globally, economic foundations have become increasingly unstable and subject to the ups and downs of regional economic cycles. Yet, in the midst of all the change and reversals and uncertainty, God indeed has an economy — one that is impervious to the fluctuations of the world's economic system. Scripture outlines the role, the need, the principles and the purposes of God for those gifted in business and entrepreneurialism.

Developing entrepreneurial communities has as its initial proto-types the patriarchs Abraham, Isaac and Jacob. The biblical principles of operating an entrepreneurial community are tied to the biblical truth of dominion when the Lord gave His people authority to rule over the work of His hands. It is time for the believing community to mobilize and become the head and not the tail and extend these biblical truths in practical terms into the economic sphere. It is time for the believing community to become an extension of God's love for His people with these practical and spiritual answers and solutions that defy the evil and destruction coming against the Jewish community.

The Distinctives

Our God's economy entrepreneurial program and workshops being presented in the Former Soviet Union and Israel provide:

- biblical principles from both the Old and New Covenant on operating a business;
- a very practical teaching on how to put a business plan together; and
- practical insights into the character qualities comprising an entrepreneur.

Of course, we adapt the program to fit laws, regulations, taxes and business climate for each locale.

Not everyone is an entrepreneur. In some cases we recommend combining various managerial and business talents to create an entrepreneurial team. We have testing soon to be introduced that will enable us to enhance this dimension of our program: which plays into increasing the chances of success of those that take this leap of faith into business ownership.

The program is tied to local congregations: which presumes a select number of congregations are willing to get behind the program. That's where the support groups will be most effective. Those overseeing the support groups need to include both business and spiritual acumen. In environments such as the FSU and Israel, the function of these support groups is key to the success ratios achieved for the small businesses launched.

The size of new businesses birthed needs to be limited as the program is first instituted. The focus is on micro-businesses. Many are the kind that people can operate out of the home or can take advantage of skills that the individual can commercialize. While there undoubtedly will be those who have the capabilities for larger sized businesses, the program targets the goal of starting small and growing. This premise enables more new businesses to be started and improves the chances of their success. Having stated this focus, we are exploring a complementary program that targets those capable of launching and operating mid-sized businesses.

The instruction we provide on putting together business plans is foundational and very practical. Typically support is raised to fund a limited number of the workshop participants. This provides a positive motivation for putting together realistic business plans when the group realizes only a limited number will be funded. We stress ingenuity for starting businesses from scratch. Many businesses have the potential of starting and succeeding without the need for outside funding.

Funding could be given as grants, but it is for the benefit of the new entrepreneur to learn how to keep records and become successful by yielding to standard practices of business by paying their loans back. Business involves risk. There may be failures. But there will also be successes that will bless the entrepreneurs, provide spiritual growth within the business community and add a fresh, biblically-based acumen within the congregations; with opportunity that will bless and attract the community at large.

We've previously outlined the three dimensions of God's "riches:" spiritual, community (social) and economic. These "riches," in essence connect the dots to the operation of the Kingdom of God. The God's Economy Entrepreneurial Program will empower local congregations with the economic dimension of God's "riches."

The Purpose and Impact

The God's Economy Entrepreneurial Program will serve to:

- Awaken, mobilize and unify the talents of potential entrepreneurs and business owners by recognizing the gifts and call of God on business people to build God's Kingdom
- Harness the talents of the believing business community to build a bridge between their businesses, congregations and local communities
- Release entrepreneurs to be a blessing to their families, congregation and local community through the biblical principles of spiritual, community (social) and economic wealth and riches
- Equip believers with vision, principles, opportunity and support groups to birth and nurture community businesses to provide income, employment and community-building inertia for congregations to be a blessing to their local communities

Our efforts not only with the workshops, but in setting up the program to follow have been very well received. Not only have new businesses been birthed, but new entrepreneurs and those planning to become entrepreneurs are committing themselves to regularly meet together — to seek the Lord and to pray regarding the role of their Kingdom businesses in support of their community.

The principles of God's economy and programs like ours and those of Mike Bundock's serve to overcome hurdles presented by less-than-favorable business environments and bondage represented by poverty. As programs like these develop and mature, they provide the launch-pad for God's people to reach out and build communities. It is foundational to the advancement of God's Kingdom.

CHAPTER 19

ENTREPRENEURS AND KINGDOM WEALTH

"But you shall remember the Lord your God, for it is He who is giving you power to make wealth, that He may confirm His covenant." Deut 8:18

Jesus was the catalyst for the release of the greatest power shift the world has ever seen. Again and again, Israel's Messiah introduced His earthly ministry with the Words, *"the Kingdom of God is at hand.* In a matter of three short years, Jesus entrusted those who could see it with a power that would change the world. Some have described it as a clash of kingdoms. Wheter viewed from the practical or the strategic dimension, Jesus' earthly mission released restoration and redemption that would shake the nations.

The restoration and redemption Jesus set in motion involved an incredible groundswell of change. It was change creating an extraordinary confrontation of power. In the fourth chapter of Acts, the response of the brethren after Peter and John's release from jail gives insight into this confrontation of power. *"They raised their voice to God with one accord and said, 'Lord, You are God, who made heaven and earth and all that is in them; who by the mouth of Your servant David has said, 'Why do the nations rage, and the peoples plot vain things? The kings of the earth took their stand,*

and the rulers were gathered together against the Lord and His Anointed.'" (Acts 4:24-26)

Why indeed do the nations rage? It is because Jesus set in motion the conflict of all ages, which will result in the greatest power shift of all ages, as God's sovereignty over His creation is restored, His covenant confirmed and His people become the head and not the tail. This conflict encompasses everyday life and extends from the spiritual to the community (social and governmental) to the economic. It involves the principle that is clearly outlined in Genesis and then is seen throughout the rest of the Bible — dominion. God made His people to rule over the works of His hands. That rule involves principles governing what Jesus referred to as the Kingdom of God.

So, to grasp the significance of this issue of Kingdom wealth, it is essential to understand the dynamic of the power shift underway. It is a power shift that will restore Almighty God to the central role in the everyday life of people. It will involve a central role for His emissaries. It will dispel the non-biblical myth of the separation between the sacred and secular — because He is central to ALL. It is a power shift that is mobilizing a mature Body with God's Kingdom perspective and purposes guiding their steps. It will reorient the perverse and the godless orientations of our age with the result that interlinks secular enterprises with overriding Kingdom objectives.

It will be this interlinking of secular enterprises with Kingdom objectives that will be the gateway for the release of the flow of Kingdom wealth.

At the focal point of the purposes for "Kingdom wealth" will be God's end-time agendas for Israel, the Body, and the peoples and nations. The *"power to get wealth to establish his covenant"* and the wealth transfer is about God's Kingdom. It's about restoration, redemption, dominion and authority. As ambassadors and emissaries endowed with His power and authority, the Body of Christ is tasked with establishing beachheads and aligning things for the return of Jesus the Messiah. Before us lies a time of Kingdom restoration which will release hope and redemption to all peoples and nations.

Kingdom Wealth and God's Economy

Kingdom wealth and God's economy work hand-in-hand. Like all dimensions of God's Kingdom as explained by Jesus, it starts like a grain of mustard seed: small, innocuous, but potent and unstoppable in its growth.

"God's economy" defies the principles and assumed power structures commonly accepted by this world as the foundations of wealth. The odds-defying potential of "God's economy" is illustrated by the results of God's guidance to Isaac during a time of extreme economic distress:

> *"There was famine in the land and the LORD appeared to Isaac and said: 'Dwell in this land, and I will be with you and bless you and perform the oath which I swore to Abraham your father.' So Isaac sowed in that land, and reaped in the same year a hundred-fold; and the LORD blessed him. So he began to prosper, and continued prospering until he became very prosperous."* (Genesis 26:1-3, 12, 13)

"The power to get wealth, that He might establish His covenant." Against all odds and prevailing wisdom, Isaac sowed during a famine, because God told him to do so. The result was he prospered. Operating in covenant with Almighty God is foundational to the operation of God's economy. In God's economy, not only is God involved and at the center of the activity; but the expectation for the outcome exceeds what might ever be hoped for or accomplished in the natural.

The Micro and the Macro-Levels of God's Economy

In God's economy, micro-enterprises represent an important foundation to God's economic system, because they are linked to building up not only God's people who operate the small business ventures, but to the community of which they are a part. Micro-businesses are like the grain of mustard seed with their potential. Today, entrepreneurial Kingdom ventures are appearing in distressed areas not unlike that faced by Isaac and bypassing the economic down-cycles of those regions. Like the astounding result of Isaac reaping a *hundred-fold* during a time of famine, they are serving as a witness to the goodness and blessings that God has for his people. Kingdom micro-enterprise development is already impacting entire communities around the world for the Lord.

While there is a pronounced growth of entrepreneurial, small business-development Kingdom activity emerging in areas of poverty and distress around the globe, God's economy is by no means limited to the micro-level. Mid-sized and larger successful Kingdom businesses bring even greater impact. Simultaneously, Kingdom business coalitions are sponsoring and working together to establish community-based initiatives for God's purposes. Likewise, believer-directed business start-up incubator programs are creating businesses that will flourish while competitors struggle and lose ground.

In God's economy there will also be believers who establish special venture funds, as well as operations that acquire failing businesses and turn them around. Businesses are already being set up specifically with Kingdom agendas in mind. Businesses incorporating business-ministry alliances. Regardless of the size of the initiative, Kingdom entrepreneurs will be at the forefront of these activities.

Kingdom Entrepreneurs

Kingdom entrepreneurs should be distinguished from believers who otherwise might simply be described as successful business persons. A Kingdom entrepreneur is Kingdom-directed and motivated. Kingdom entrepreneurs build. They innovate. They create. They innovate, create and build in a manner that advances the community around them and the Kingdom of God. Kingdom entrepreneurs represent the essence of Jesus' teaching on the parable of the talents.

Likewise, the ability to make money is not the same as the *"power to get wealth that He might establish His covenant."* Our standards for success often are shaded by a worldly mind-set focused on the superficial dimensions. It's the reason Jesus made the distinction the positive and negative uses of money with his referral to *"filthy lucre."* There's a significant difference between the ability to make money and the anointing to get wealth. It's a question of motivation, purpose and control. It's a difference tied to how the "power" of wealth is used: for personal gain or to advance God's Kingdom. It's why generosity has been such a pivotal factor in the operation of community as clearly outlined in both the Old and New Covenants.

In example after example, the Word of God illustrates what happens when we become controlled by the world's system. It results in bondage. It results in slavery. Far too many of God's people have tried to venture into the arena of God's economy — but without the principles or perspective required, they have believed the same lie which the Israelite spies believed upon their return from their initial scouting trip of the promised land: that they were like grasshoppers in a land of giants.

God's economy operates on faith: a faith that believes God is a good God who diligently rewards those who seek Him. But the unbelief reflected by the Hebrew spies who viewed themselves as grasshoppers in a land of giants shuts the door to "Kingdom" opportunity. Unbelief and fear are deadly. Unbelief undermines operating in faith and avoids calculated risks of faith. Risk-taking is always foundational to the entrepreneurial premise of opportunity. But the "grasshopper" mind-set releases a venomous spirit of timidity and fear that avoids God's Kingdom potential and sets the stage for failure. The "grasshopper" avoidance of risk results in God's people who are not building, creating and innovating; but rather are stuck in the mediocre that boxes in the potential of what God might do through them.

Kingdom entrepreneurs are not defined by the size of their business enterprise, but rather by their approach to the enterprise. Kingdom entrepreneurs innovate, create and build. They are faith-oriented risk-takers who keenly discern opportunity and know how to take the calculated risks needed to believe and act on the premise of turning that which is not into something tangible.

Kingdom entrepreneurs are the ones who embrace and exercise the truth of God's Word that says that He has given us the power to get wealth, that He might establish His covenant.

The Strategic Dimensions of Kingdom Wealth
Kingdom wealth will evolve from the dimensions of Kingdom

riches previously discussed: spiritual riches, community riches and economic riches. The Word of God is rich with a balance between all three. We have entered a time in which these three dimensions will operate in concert with one another as Kingdom entrepreneurs who have specialties in each begin working together. These Kingdom entrepreneurs will change the world as we know it today.

The five-fold ministry of apostle, prophet, pastor, teacher and evangelist will always be with us. But the needs for the coming harvest are such that functionally the five-fold gifts can be expected to manifest more strongly in the community and economic arenas, as the Body begins operating with a greater unity and singleness of purpose. What that will mean is that the ministries making the biggest impact in the days before us will be those that touch not just lives, but entire communities. Ministries that understand the dynamics of the interactions between the spiritual, the community and the economic dimensions of "God's Kingdom riches" — and know how to apply them toward the advancement of His Kingdom.

The ministries poised for the coming power shift will recognize the very significant role of the emerging group of nation-changers patterned after the biblical Joseph and Daniel, and that of the enterprises they direct. Modern-day Josephs will serve key roles as anointed kingly leaders in the accomplishment of God's purposes. "Leaders" modeled after Old Testament "entrepreneurial kings," like Abraham, Isaac, Joseph and King David, who time and again served God's purposes of redemption and restoration for His people.

Similarly, alliances between these modern-day nation-changers and anointed, chosen non-believers patterned after the Joseph-Pharaoh alliance will take the kingly paradigm a step further. It is an apt parallel to the unique opportunities associated with God's initiatives that will be brought forth for the critical times we are entering. The fact is the Joseph-Pharaoh model was outside the box of the traditional religious mind-set God's people had in Joseph's era which was not inclined to associations with those outside their community. It was an unusual, unconventional alliance to the religious standards embraced by Joseph's family. But it was the divine strategy God chose to circumnavigate the famine coming to the earth at that time.

Today's Josephs will address the power shift and upheavals of our day by anticipating change and facilitating initiatives beyond the scope or vision of traditional ministries. At the forefront of their key functions will be the spearheading of the wealth transfer. This role of releasing Kingdom riches will facilitate the restoration and redemption needed to build communities and impact nations. Restoration and redemption facilitated by coalitions and strategies targeting the restoration of Israel and the command in Isaiah 58:10 of reaching out to help the oppressed, the poor, the hungry, and afflicted.

As this wealth transfer begins unfolding, there will be a shift from the ministry model of recent decades. Most established parachurch organizations are the result of entrepreneurial exploits that have built medium-sized to worldwide organizations based on a high profile, personality-based, fund-raising model. There is no question that this God-given model has served an essential role for its time in connecting and building up the Body spiritually.

But the times are changing. The parachurch model that arose in the '50s and '60s will give way to models more suited to the needs of the era we have entered: models incorporating not only the spiritual, but the community and economic dimensions of God's riches. These models will birth a mix of both micro and macro-level entrepreneurial Kingdom initiatives.

These models will operate on the basis of God's economy, and be driven by cooperative, community and inter-organizational efforts. They will exemplify the principle of the power to get wealth that He might establish His covenant. As the establishment of God's covenant paradigm reemerges, it will be coupled to the restoration of God's economic model.

God's economy will release redemption and restoration that will build communities and change nations. The old paradigm will shift to one with Kingdom entrepreneurs and modern-day Josephs and Daniels advancing cooperative initiatives encompassing the spiritual, community and economic dimensions of God's riches.

Kingdom entrepreneurs who will operate with a gift for spotting opportunity and translating that opportunity into community-building and nation-changing agendas that advance the Kingdom of God.

Kingdom Opportunity

The parable of the sower makes a spiritual point by using a known economic principle of Jesus' day, that of sowing in fertile ground. It parallels the parable of the talents: of making your assets work for you, again using an economic principle to make a spiritual point. Each parable deals with how we are to respond to opportunity. Yet, how many tend to overlook giving genuine focus to the economic dimensions of these two parables?

In embracing the economic truths of these two parables, we have to face the dimension of opportunity. With opportunity, we have to look hard at the issue of risk. Just like faith is in constant tension with unbelief, so opportunity cannot be embraced without surmounting the hurdle of risk. Addressing risk enters the practical realm of where we live. Isaac took steps that went against all odds when he sowed in famine. The result was he reaped a hundred-fold return.

The economic side of the issue posed by these parables raises the question of how faithfully we invest our time and economic talents into fertile ground that will yield the hundred-fold return in the advancement of God's Kingdom.

Identifying that fertile ground, along with what it takes to do the sowing, is the foundation of opportunity and the area that Kingdom entrepreneurs, big and small, will exploit. That ability to spot opportunity and maximize it is the basis on which entrepreneurs innovate, create and build. But as we enter a time with evil being multiplied on every hand, it will become a primary basis on which God's Kingdom advances. It's the new paradigm.

Kingdom entrepreneurs are not new to Christendom. From their ranks have come the pioneers and change-artists who recognize the need and opportunity of the times and then do something about it. During the '50s and '60s the Lord raised up a unique breed of Kingdom entrepreneurs. They were "spiritual" entrepreneurs and pioneers. These pioneers began seizing the opportunity represented in the mass media, which in effect extended the reach and complemented the role served by the local church infrastructure. With the development of technology and the pervasive role radio and television began playing spiritually in lives across the globe, these "spiritual entrepreneurs" paved the way for changing the paradigm of how the Church operated.

These changes that seized the opportunity and transformed the game rules advancing God's Kingdom were anticipatory responses which the Spirit of the Lord was unfolding to enable the Body to meet the challenges of the times. At the time, the emerging challenges were simply not seen by many, and some of the heaviest opposition came from Church leaders who resisted the change. So it is today. We have entered a time in which the days are evil and becoming increasing more so. Along with that is the fact that the paradigm is shifting.

The companion to risk and resistance has always been the propensity to interpret future development based on the constraints of past models. The parachurch movement brought in a new order and dimension to the way the Church operated.

Recognizing and Responding to the Change and Opportunity

In similar fashion, the restoration of God's economy and the wealth transfer will usher in changes that dramatically impact priorities, perspectives and methodologics. Many of these now-familiar ministry models have been refined and reached satisfying comfort levels. But rather than having arrived, much work remains. Much of it incorporates new challenges. And recent days have realized many experiencing turbulence tied to the old models.

God's Kingdom is advancing. The scope of both the risk and the opportunity are demanding change. The shaking and resistance underway is to spur us on. For those who begin embracing the new paradigm, the shaking and resistance will be met with sovereign responses of the Holy Spirit and a fresh release of signs and wonders and miracles. In this process, the Spirit of the Lord is preparing us for a timely and more strategic-level impact, as the paradigm in both approach and perspective shifts.

Since the inception of the parachurch movement, the pace of change within the Body and the way the Church operates has been gradual and steady. But the accelerated pace of events and the ease and speed with which the world interacts today is demanding much more. The change required is not an end in itself, but a part of the process of establishing new beachheads that will mobilize the Body in ways relevant to the times and seasons. It is the change required to advance the Kingdom of God victoriously. Opportunity seized in the arena of the mass media since the '50s has more recently been combined with inroads made by Kingdom pioneers through the medium of the Internet. The result has been a quantum leap impacting the means by which this generation of the Body is informed, connected and matured.

Catalysts for the Wealth Transfer

As the Body has been awakened, matured, informed and connected, there has been a convergence tied to a fresh and major move of redemption and restoration. This convergence will actuate the Deuteronomy 8 principle of the *"power to get wealth that He might establish His covenant"* as a transfer of wealth tied to the power shift in process emerges. This dynamic will serve as a catalyst for unfolding a level of redemption and Kingdom restoration that will be unlike anything seen in recent times.

There are two other key scriptures which together with Deuteronomy 8:18 form the broader perspective encompassing the transfer of wealth. The first is the Proverbs 13 principle that the *"wealth of the wicked is stored up for the just."* The second is from Isaiah 60 and marks the expectation of what will unfold with the restoration of Israel.

We have entered an era in which numerous end-time conditions are being aligned. This alignment includes four key emerging factors tied to the wealth transfer.

When they mature and converge, they will be significant catalysts to the release of enormous wealth and resources into the hands of those at the forefront of strategically advancing the Kingdom of God. These four dimensions include:

- the restoration of God's economy;
- a new outworking of Body-unity whereby community initiatives become Kingdom initiatives;
- strategic partnerships between spiritual, community and economic Kingdom entrepreneurs, and
- the restoration of Israel.

Restoration of God's Economy. Because of the nature of these times the restoration of God's economy will be as a light shining in the deepening darkness coming upon the earth. These are times described in Scripture as times of earthquakes and famines; of wars and rumors of wars. They are described as evil days.

The principles in Deuteronomy that govern entrepreneurial communities work in the face of adversity. The awakening and calling of Kingdom entrepreneurs will globally penetrate bastions of poverty and destruction with hope. The restoration of God's economy will become foundational to the groundswell of "repossessing the land" that is tied to the release of the wealth transfer described in Proverbs 13.

Body Unity Whereby Community Initiatives Become Kingdom Initiatives. There are numerous models operating today, like in the days of Issac, by which God's economy operates against all odds. Each of them, in some significant way, is tied to community. Each involves community-directed unity that supersedes the Western mind-set of the self-contained, rugged individualist-type that we tend to associate with pioneers and entrepreneurs. The Kingdom entrepreneurs of this day will not fit the superstar mold often seen in high profile corporate settings, but rather a servant-leader model. Joseph was a servant-leader whose strategies bypassed the destruction of the famine and strengthened his nation while accomplishing God's redemptive purposes.

Kingdom entrepreneurs will be facilitators of setting others in motion as they serve as catalysts in community activities that in turn impact and bless the regions and nations of which they are a part, in the advancement of the Kingdom of God. As the world views those who have been given the "power to get wealth" and those who sow in famine and reap a hundred-fold; they will see the tangible result of how God Almighty establishes His covenant among His people.

Strategic Partnerships between Spiritual, Community and Economic Kingdom Entrepreneurs. As we enter a time when the clash of kingdoms is intensifying and the struggle over dominion begins reaching vicious levels, we will also see a convergence of the roles of the various types of Kingdom entrepreneurs. Spiritual Kingdom entrepreneurs. Community Kingdom entrepreneurs. And economic Kingdom entrepreneurs. With this convergence will arise partnerships flowing in the principle of *"God giving us the power to get wealth that He might establish His covenant."*

These partnerships will build communities, change nations and advance and align the Kingdom of God. In the process, there will be a monumental "Proverbs 13" power shift, that will result in an incredible release of resources into very timely, strategic and effective Kingdom initiatives: Kingdom initiatives that merge the functions served by spiritual, community and economic Kingdom entrepreneurs.

As the paradigm shifts, the focus and importance God has always placed on Israel is moving center-stage.

The Restoration of Israel. Restoration and redemption has always included Israel, the apple of God's eye. The Throne Room perspective to God giving us the power to get wealth that He might establish His covenant comes from Isaiah 60. It speaks of the restoration of Israel. It points to the truth that in the overall scheme of what the Lord is releasing for the days before us: Israel and Jewish revival is the pivot point.

> *"For the wealth of the seas will be brought to you and the riches of the nations will come. Your gates will stand open continually, so that men may bring to you the wealth of the nations. You are the Lord. You will do this swiftly and they will be called ministers of our God and they will feed on the wealth of nations."* (Isaiah 60:5,11)

The restoration of the land and the people Israel is already in process. With more Jews having met their Messiah since 1967 than in all the years since Jesus' earthly ministry, the momentum and impact of the Messianic Jewish movement is very much on the increase. The nation of Israel has become the number-two center for venture capital projects in the world. Israel's Technology Incubator program produces a high ratio of new business enterprises entering the world market in a matter of a handful of years.

Despite more than 50 years of war and the impact of the most recent intifada designed to destroy Israel, the desert blooms there and against all odds, it thrives. But the pressures against Israel have never been greater and they mark the steps toward the time Scripture points to as when "all Israel is saved." As the spiritual "restoration of Israel" unfolds, the initiatives that merge the efforts of spiritual, community and economic Kingdom entrepreneurs will serve as catalysts for the macro-level releases of the wealth transfer. An Israel-directed wealth-transfer is described by these verses of Isaiah 60 as "the riches of the nations" and the "wealth of the nations."

The Power Shift

Centuries and centuries ago, seats of power rested with those with the military might. Then there was a time when those who reigned and conquered were those controlling the organizational religious establishments. Most recent centuries have seen rule and authority controlled by national governments. But during the most recent decade or so, the real seats of power have been tied to economic power. That's why so much of the focus today, in terms of God's agendas and the building of His Kingdom, involves the mobilization of economic Kingdom entrepreneurs.

There is an awesome alignment in process. It is an alignment that will release the greatest move of redemption and restoration the world has ever seen. Restoration and redemption tied to a massive power shift: the power shift of all ages. God's sovereignty over His creation is being restored, His covenant confirmed and His covenant people becoming the head and not the tail. This alignment and power shift coincide with the preparation of the gatekeepers and administrators who understand the times and the dynamics of this divine orchestration of restoration and redemption that is unfolding. It is a shift in dominion. A power shift that will incorporate new venues of resources and wealth that will be entrusted to the hands of prepared and chosen vessels like Joseph the Patriarch, who understand the times and will administrate them in the accomplishment of God's purposes for this strategic hour.

CHAPTER 20

KINGDOM WEALTH AND GATEKEEPERS

...whose hand I have held, to subdue nations and loose the armor of kings, to open the double doors, so that the gates will not be shut. I will give you the treasures of darkness and hidden riches of secret places. Isaiah 45:1,3

Isaiah 45 speaks of gates and gatekeepers with roles tied to financial initiatives established long before their time. It reveals truths regarding not only Israel's return from captivity hundreds of years ago, but it also points to dynamics that can be expected as we approach the time of the restoration of Israel.

The implication from Isaiah's prophetic words is that these treasures of darkness and hidden riches have been reserved for appointed times — and will be released by chosen gatekeepers. Similarly, it will be the uncovering and unveiling of these current-day gates to hidden riches that will mark a transition into a whole new era in the operation of God's Kingdom.

While there is much to be revealed about the function of these gates; it is the emerging role and calling of an unusual group of gatekeepers that needs to be clearly discerned. These are the ones to be released into these pivotal functions. Clearly the gates are a means of access and a means to control access, but the gatekeepers are the ones entrusted with the keys.

In Matthew 16:19 Jesus said *"I will give you the keys of the Kingdom of God. Whatever you lock on earth will be locked in heaven, and whatever you open on earth will be opened in heaven."*

The gates of hell will not prevail against the gatekeepers entrusted with the keys.

The operative word for gatekeepers is entrusted. They are entrusted and they are chosen. Joseph was not a committee appointee. Nor did he set up a committee to make his decisions. His role in sitting alongside of Pharaoh was his unchallenged calling. It was a calling not recognized by those closest to him until he had entered the fullness of that calling.

Gatekeepers are mature, seasoned servants of the Lord. Like Joseph, their eye is single, with their hearts fixed on the Lord's agendas. Tested by fire, from a human stance they are broken; but spiritually they are as a fortified wall of bronze. They are steadfast, stable and utterly reliable. They serve and support with dependability those they are called to stand alongside. Their prophetic giftings and insights are always balanced with wisdom and compassion. Gatekeepers operate with a razor-sharp discernment that sees deeply into situations and people. They are men and women of God endued with great authority. These are people of faith who are decisive and know what to do to advance the Kingdom of God.

Since the time the Lord spoke to Peter and entrusted him with the keys to launch the building of the Church, there have been gates and gatekeepers. Yet, what we have emerging will be significant, previously unseen, untapped, strategic-level gates; and a chosen group of gatekeepers, proven in their spheres and entrusted with the keys to the gates.

These are the gates and the gatekeepers connected to the power shift in process that will initiate the release of Kingdom wealth — what Isaiah prophesied long ago as hidden riches and treasures of darkness.

Identifying the Gates

There is an anointing and calling to unlock enemy gates.

Heretofore, when God's people have come anywhere near the enemy's gates, the typical encounter has involved a flurry of smokescreens, entanglements, distractions and diversions. This has especially been the case when the gates have involved believers penetrating seats of power in business and government. Misplaced zeal too often has resulted in a tendency to give primary focus to doing battle with the enemy's minions, while too often missing the gates. Similarly, there has been a preoccupation with attempts to employ outmoded or misplaced approaches to confront these targets without the anointing and calling of those with the keys. Deeply embedded, high-level gateways and domains will only give way to those with the calling to unlock these gates.

As the Body matures into what Ephesians 4 refers to as the knowledge of the Lord and of unity — the masking of the enemy-guarded gates is being dispersed. As the masks are dispersed, God's anointed, chosen gatekeepers will serve uniquely in identifying and penetrating these gates of access to these hidden riches and treasures of darkness.

The Gatekeepers and Their Spheres

The primary gatekeepers for the uncovering and release of these riches will be found among the Josephs and Daniels of our day. These are spiritually seasoned and prepared-ones whose callings are in the heart of the world's systems of business and government, technologies and economies — the gateways into the resources and seats of power of this world.

Operating within the spheres of their callings is essential for these gatekeepers. The cost of their callings, like that of Joseph, will be found to be extremely high. Similarly, operating outside their sphere, or for those who presume to attempt entrance to gates for which they don't have the calling, the cost can be deadly. Uzzah paid with his life for touching the ark (II Samuel 6:7). Jude (v. 11 Amplified Bible) emphasizes this truth: *"Woe to them! For they have run riotously in the way of Cain, and have abandoned themselves for the sake of gain [it offers them, following] the error of Balaam, and have perished in rebellion [like that] of Korah!"*

Those who are called as gatekeepers will KNOW it. Those not

genuinely called will be wise not to touch it.

In days past, individual gatekeepers called by God have periodically gained access into the arena encompassed by what rightfully belongs to God — into the resources and seats of power of this world. Yet, it's been sporadic and the exception. That will change. In the time approaching us, companies of Kingdom gatekeepers will operate in concert to open gates into seats of power previously deemed beyond the scope of the possible for the people of God. It will be a time of extraordinary exploits as God's anointed gatekeepers push past the impossibilities to accomplish feats that operate against all odds. In the process, God's end-time purpose of redemption and restoration will begin unfolding.

Gateways to Seats of Power

Historically, gates served not only as a means of access, but as a place where people in authority gathered with those within their spheres or boundaries. The city-gates and gates to dwellings-for-refuge and business have traditionally been centers of authority, rule and economic power. Places where decisions and judgment occur. Places for in-gatherings to advance the mutual benefit of those with common community and business purposes. These are seats of power.

Today, the world's marketplaces embody a significant proportion of its seats of power. Cities contain the pulse of these marketplaces. It is largely through the marketplace mechanisms of commerce, economies, technology, government, and the media that the nature and order of the course of world events is determined. Within the marketplace are the gateways into the seats of power that control the destinies of communities, economies and nations.

Seats of power determine whether the resources under their control are used for good or for evil. It was at the city of Babel that the Lord undermined the potential dominion and power being assembled, by confusing their language. Revelation 17 speaks of the great city that rules over the kings of the earth. But it was also Joseph, as administrator over Egypt, who redirected the use of the available resources in his sphere. In the process Joseph reached out to the hungry and afflicted, while averting disaster and providing for the protection and continuation of the destiny of God's covenant people.

Kingdom Gates and Strongholds

Gates serve not only as access to power and resources, they provide protection, strength and a place of observation. So, as high-level enemy-guarded gates are identified and penetrated, there will also come a greater fortification and strategic functioning of Kingdom gates.

II Samuel 18:33 speaks of the *"chambers over the gates."* The chambers over the gates are where those in authority meet, plan, strategize and make decisions. The chambers over the gates provide a place of safety for its decision-makers with a view of distant things approaching. Today within the Body, there are strong alliances emerging through chambers of commerce and coalitions where decision-makers assemble — spiritually fortified places that serve as centers for planning, deal-making and decision-making. These spiritually fortified places are Kingdom strongholds.

Yet, far too many within the Body tend to view strongholds as only something that the enemy has. That is only partially true. The dictionary defines a "stronghold" as: 1. A fortified place or a fortress. 2.a. A place of survival or refuge. b. An area dominated or occupied by a special group or distinguished by a special quality: such as a stronghold of democracy.

We need a fresh perspective to give us greater clarity in defining both Kingdom strongholds and what we may consider as enemy strongholds. There are many "non-Kingdom" strongholds that are foundationally neutral. A stronghold is something worth conquering. Strategically, we need to view strongholds as seats of power, with the potential to serve the Lord's purposes, once they are penetrated. In the manner that the Lord used Joseph to penetrate Egypt to create a cooperative alliance, so there will be strongholds today with non-believing kings, rulers and leaders who have been uniquely prepared by the Lord for the accomplishment of His purposes.

The enemy of our souls is feverishly working to extend his control over the seats of power of this world. His underlings and gatekeepers work hard to misdirect the efforts of God's people and keep them separated from the seats of power of this world. Yet God always has a plan and a purpose that usurps the enemy's intentions that ultimately seek the destruction of God's people. Joseph's entrance into Egypt was far from glorious. He came in as a slave and then found himself in prison before he was elevated to his position to administrate Pharaoh's kingdom. But in the process, he learned the system, established his credentials by the results he achieved — which he ascribed to God and was positioned to enter the gates to operate alongside Pharaoh. When he entered those gates, what unfolded was against all odds. It worked that way because Joseph was the chosen gatekeeper — and he was prepared, as was Pharaoh.

What we often view as enemy strongholds and seats of power may be masks — that unrighteously cover what in reality belongs to the Lord. Mammon, for example, is a high-level demonic gatekeeper whose designs are to protect the strongholds of wealth and power. But as long as the focus of the battle is with mammon, we'll never recognize the Pharaohs or the means to gain access to the Pharaohs.

In a word, God's strongholds are places where His people partake. The enemy's strongholds are places where God's people plunder and gain dominion.

God's gatekeepers guard and control entrance into His strongholds. God's gatekeepers also identify, open the gateways and provide access to gain dominion of enemy-held strongholds. Those holding the keys will strengthen and protect the access to Kingdom strongholds, while gaining access to plunder enemy seats of power to:

- release God's initiatives
- bring restoration and
- facilitate the building of God's Kingdom.

Seats of Power and Strategic Alliances

As God releases His Joseph and Daniel gatekeepers, what will soon follow will be their connections with the Cyrus-type gatekeepers. These modern-day Cyrus gatekeepers are those positioned to enable the Josephs' and Daniels' entrance into the seats of power needed in the accomplishment of God's purposes. The results will be unusual strategic alliances.

Cyrus was a non-believing king, who the Lord used mightily in opening gateways for His people. Isaiah 45 outlines the Lord's perspective about Cyrus:

> *Cyrus, His anointed one, whose right hand He will empower. Before him, mighty kings will be paralyzed with fear. Their fortress gates will be opened, never again to shut against him. This is what the LORD says: "I will go before you, Cyrus, and level the mountains. I will smash down gates of bronze and cut through bars of iron. I will give you the treasures of darkness and hidden riches of secret places, that you may know that I, the LORD, am the God of Israel. For Jacob My servant's sake, and Israel My elect, I have even called you by your name; I have named you, though you have not known Me. I am the LORD, and there is no other; there is no God besides Me. I will gird you, though you have not known Me.*

Cyrus was a gatekeeper with access to the resources needed to bring about restoration and empowerment for God's people. What is significant about today's Cyruses is that they will recognize, welcome and work together with God's anointed in releasing the hidden riches and treasures of darkness toward the accomplishment of God's Throne Room initiatives.

No doubt there will be battles as the Kingdom of God advances and the violent take it by force. But there are also times when the enemy's designs to keep us away from the gates can simply be bypassed by Kingdom gatekeepers — because they already hold the keys. Bypass strategies will often accelerate the accomplishment of the Lord's purposes. There are other instances in which the Lord will have prepared gatekeepers in what may appear as the enemy's camp, who like King Cyrus, will serve as strategic facilitators for God's purposes.

Multiplication Through Coalitions and Partnerships

Gates are places of authority where great decisions are made. We live in a time of unusual change and opportunity. It is a time in which God's thrust in penetrating the seats of power of this world will involve Kingdom gatekeepers who need to maximize the opportunity and the impact. It is a time when as Kingdom gatekeepers encounter the gates yielding these hidden riches and treasures of darkness, they need to "know what to do." The Amplified Version of Matthew 16 outlines the Kingdom dynamic operating for genuinely-called gatekeepers: *"the powers of the infernal region shall not overpower it — or be strong to its detriment, or hold out against it."*

There are different types of gatekeepers with different levels of authority. There is unquestionably a need to avoid presumption, to operate within the boundaries of our appointed spheres — and to maximize the potential for success. Jude 1 speaks of the angels who did not stay within the limits of the authority God gave them, but left the place where they belonged — and now await in outer darkness for their judgment. With that in mind, the wisdom drawn from the Word of God (Leviticus 26:8) illustrates the principle of Kingdom multiplication which results from the combined unified efforts of those operating under God's anointing and calling.

> *"Five of you shall chase a hundred, and a hundred of you shall put ten thousand to flight; your enemies shall fall before you by the sword."*

The potential and the impact of individual spheres of authority are multiplied through alliances and cooperative efforts. The significance and magnitude of the initiatives before us necessitate coalitions and partnerships in efforts to build communities, change nations and advance the Kingdom of God.

As the Lord reveals the gates to the hidden riches and treasures of darkness, priority access will be given to Kingdom ventures that foster not only the spiritual, but the economic and community dimensions of God's Kingdom rule. The enormity of the potential is requiring a casting down of personal crowns, as appropriate gatekeeper-entities implement combined strategies with results that far exceed the sum of what might have been accomplished by their individual independent efforts.

We have entered a time of restoration. However, obtaining this restoration will be at a cost. There will be confrontations, battles and power shifts. Yet there will also be the operation of the supernatural with miracles in the midst of these encounters. It will not be unlike the time when Elijah had his face-off with the prophets of Baal — with the fire of the Lord falling. The pathway to restoration will involve the conflict of all ages — the conflict between good and evil; the conflict over dominion and power.

As we enter these turbulent, but dynamic times, there is a need to embrace new mind-sets in assessing the status quo, along with the goals and strategies needed to seize emerging Kingdom opportunity. It is a time to reevaluate the big picture and make the needed changes to fulfill the Words of Jesus (Matthew 11, Amplified Bible) when He said: "*From the days of John the Baptist until the present time, the kingdom of heaven has endured violent assault; and violent men seize it by force [as a precious prize—a share in the heavenly kingdom is sought with most ardent zeal and intense exertion].*"

Hidden Riches and Treasures of Darkness

Many of the gates to these hidden riches and treasures of darkness will be found amid existing governmental and business systems. But it is going to take Kingdom gatekeepers to recognize them. Key words to their unveiling will be discovery and development. Just as in the days of Joseph, the Lord is raising up Kingdom gatekeepers with prophetic insights to unveil, penetrate and administrate these sources of hidden riches and treasures of darkness. In some cases, access will come through alliances with secular gatekeepers supportive of the agendas entrusted to these Kingdom gatekeepers. In ways paralleling Joseph's role alongside Pharaoh, these Kingdom gatekeepers will serve a role that challenges the myopic religious perspective that defines those called into the marketplace as the "laity."

Other gates to these hidden riches and treasures of darkness will be found in the very heart of darkness. Underground economies that extend from mafias to drug lords to terrorist networks control a level of wealth sufficient to challenge the equilibrium of major national economies. But Proverbs 13 is not only a principle, it is a promise, that *"the wealth of the wicked is stored up for the just."* Individuals and groups with unusual callings, employing unusual strategies, will be found boldly operating in these settings with favor, wisdom and signs and wonders and miracles. These strategic gatekeepers will be facilitators whose roles will realize the transfer of "filthy lucre" into "kingdom riches."

Whether amid existing government and business systems or in penetrating underground economies, Kingdom gatekeepers will be those who operate in the very heart of the marketplace — in businesses, communities, nations, economies and technologies — in spheres of influence heretofore considered as and relegated to the enemy's camp.

Four primary catalysts to release this wealth spoken of in Scripture have previously been identified. They include:

- the restoration of God's economy;
- a new outworking of Body-unity whereby community initiatives become Kingdom initiatives;
- strategic partnerships between spiritual, community and economic Kingdom entrepreneurs, and
- the restoration of Israel.

Kingdom Wealth Gatekeeper Initiatives

The Kingdom wealth gatekeepers will be defined by the strategic initiatives tied to their callings. These strategic initiatives will uniquely embody the catalysts to release this Kingdom wealth. As these catalysts for the release of Kingdom wealth unfold and develop, there will be a merging into initiatives that give focus to:

- Kingdom entrepreneurial efforts that offer God's hope to the impoverished and oppressed;
- Christian/Messianic Jewish coalitions in support of Israel;
- Kingdom community building and nation-changing agendas; and

- Support of Messianic Jewish aliyah and Jewish revival.

The focus in Scripture is clear: first Israel and then the nations. With the same priority expressed by Jesus that He was *"sent first to the lost sheep of the house of Israel,"* so it is with the unfolding agendas in the era before us. There is a wonderful infrastructure of believers that God has prepared throughout the nations — and today these believers from Asia to Africa to the West are poised in preparation and expectancy for what the Lord is doing in Israel—the land, and in Israel—His covenant people.

Israel is the pivot point. It is as Paul wrote to the Romans (11:15) about the Jewish people: *"For if their rejection is the reconciliation of the world, what will their acceptance be but life from the dead?"*

We are likewise closing in on a time that will see the fulfillment of what is referred to in Ephesians 4 as the Body coming into the full knowledge of the Lord, as it comes into unity. The Body is indeed coming together in unity. As it does, there will be a diffusion of the enemy's webs of distraction — tactics targeting Kingdom gatekeepers. Infiltrators, counterfeits, phonies, the foolish, the self-serving and those otherwise operating under delusions of grandeur are being exposed and removed. The Body is rapidly transitioning into an offensive posture and gaining strength, as the Lord releases the strategies to possess gates heretofore under the control of the enemy — to release the hidden riches and treasures of darkness and advance His Kingdom.

As the Lord brings His Body together, His dominion will penetrate and utilize the systems of this world for His purposes. As in the days of Joseph and Daniel, the Lord God Almighty, the King of Kings and Lord of Lords is today sending forth His trusted Kingdom pioneers and gatekeepers. Kingdom gatekeepers who are paving new ground to work alongside the Pharaohs, Cyruses and Dariuses of our day, to open the gates, execute judgment, restore dominion and bring forth God's redemptive purposes and agendas for this hour.

This is the generation of those who seek You, who seek Your face — even Jacob. Lift up your heads, O gates, and be lifted up, O ancient doors, that the King of glory may come in! Who is the King of glory? The Lord strong and mighty, the Lord mighty in battle. Lift up your heads, O gates, and lift them up, O ancient doors, that the King of glory may come in! Who is the King of glory? The Lord of hosts, You are the King of glory. Psalm 24:6-10

In the time of the end, many shall be purified and refined, but the wicked shall do wickedly and none of the wicked shall understand; but the wise shall understand. And those who are wise shall shine like the brightness of the sky, and those who lead many to righteousness, like the stars forever and ever. Daniel 12:3, 10

CHAPTER 21

NATION-BUILDING, MIRACLES AND SET TIMES

"And He sent a man before them, Joseph, who was sold as a slave; and they hurt his feet in fetters and laid him in irons; until his word came to pass, the Word of the Lord tested him." Psalm 105

"*The Word of the Lord tested him.*" When Joseph shared his dreams with his father and brothers; because these dreams were prophetic, they HAD to be proclaimed. But from that point on — from the time of "proclaiming" what God had shown him, a process was begun whereby the Word of the Lord tested Joseph.

There was never a time when the Word of the Lord testing Joseph must have been harder on him than when he correctly interpreted the dreams of the baker and cup-bearer, after which for two years NOTHING happened. After all those years of faithfully waiting and operating as God's discerning witness, Joseph must have known the potential involved: with his plea to the cup-bearer to "remember him." But there was a set time involved in the fullness of Joseph's calling.

During a recent time in prayer I was uniquely reminded of Joseph's final two years in prison. I pondered his many long years of slavery and then prison; then the potential and the expectation represented by the cup-bearer pleading Joseph's cause. Time passed and nothing happened. A situation in the natural that must have been far beyond a human ability to bear.

Beyond a Human Ability to Bear

This dynamic of operating "beyond a human ability to bear" is a truth the Lord has been revealing to me. Specifically, there are some of us who are called as "burden bearers." Ones who carry the burden for a God-given initiative that oftentimes will be tied to a dimension of their own calling.

Like Joseph, many of us called as burden-bearers will experience a testing tied to the God-given burden and our calling; with pressures beyond a human ability to bear. If we stay the course, we will play a role in giving birth to significant changes or initiatives that the Lord has for "set times." There are many of us who as burden-bearers are in that very critical last stage before the promotion represented by being called into the presence of Pharaoh.

This dynamic of operating "beyond a human ability to bear," also represents the very foundation for what will emerge as a release of operating in a new level of the supernatural. A release into a supernatural flow of miracles that will break through bondages and constraints hindering the emergence of vital and fresh initiatives tied to God's sovereignty in this critical hour of the global clash between good and evil.

Many of the burden-bearers of this hour are pioneers. Most have been misunderstood and more than a few have been persecuted. Individually not all these modern-day pioneers will serve a role quite as dramatic or significant as that of Joseph — although some will. But there will be significance in the combined birthing of parallel individual efforts — being orchestrated for a set time by the hand of God.

The Dynamic

There exists a link between the burden, the timing, the waiting, the birthing and the pressure that goes beyond the "human ability to bear," and the supernatural faith required to birth what God has put in these burden bearer's hearts.

There are many "burden bearers" today who are faithfully waiting in harness. "Burden bearers" who have had expectations flounder and entered that final stage akin to the time Joseph watched the cup-bearer return to Pharaoh and then entered what became the hardest, but also the most miraculous of the time in which "the Word of the Lord tested him."

What will be required for the birthing of these "burdens" into the divine initiatives they were destined to be will involve the very thing these burden-bearers will be released into: a flow of miracles. At the set time before us, what will be birthed will be a global-impacting paradigm shift.

In terms of understanding the times, the world is in the midst of a massive "build-up". A build-up reflecting an amassing of the forces of good against the forces of evil. We are fast approaching a time reflected by the words of the psalmist when he wrote: *"the nations raged and kingdoms were moved; He uttered His voice and the earth melted."*

When Joseph began operating alongside of Pharaoh, the significance was not in his arrival at that position; but in how he then began using that position.

With his new position, everything fit. Everything was aligned. Joseph had entered into the level of resource and authority required for him to serve as the instrument of God's purpose that he was called to be. Joseph's position enabled him to set in motion the initiatives and strategies of God needed to circumvent the enemy's destructive intentions and bring about God's redemptive purposes for His people. As he served in that position, Joseph uniquely understood the divine partnership involved in "establishing the work of His hands."

The Work of His Hands
The Psalmist eloquently speaks of the work of His hands. *"Satisfy us early with Your mercy, that we may rejoice and be glad all our days! Let Your work appear to Your servants, and Your glory to their children. And let the beauty of the LORD our God be upon us, and establish the work of our hands for us; yes, establish the work of our hands."* Psalm 90:14-17

"Let Your work appear to Your servants ... and establish the work of our hands." For the burden-bearer, it is a divine partnership between "HIS work" manifesting for us; as simultaneously the Lord "establishes the work of OUR hands for us."

Psalm 103:22 says: *"Bless the LORD, all you His works, in all places of His dominion."*

This verse comes after we are admonished to *"bless the Lord, O my soul."* It follows the focus to *"bless the Lord you His angels,"* and then to *"bless the Lord all you His hosts."* *"Bless the Lord all you His WORKS, in all places of His dominion."* The Lord's "works" will manifest in blessing back to Him. His "works" become an integral part of the essence of Who He is.

God's "works" are centered around His dominion and the alignment required for the accomplishment of His purposes and will. King David understood this when before all Israel, he blessed the Lord and prayed his famous prayer: *"Yours, O Lord, is the greatness and the power and the glory and the victory and the majesty; indeed everything that is in the heavens and the earth is Yours; Yours is the dominion, O Lord, and You do exalt Yourself as head over all. Both riches and honor come from You, and You do rule over all, and in Your hand is power and might; and it lies in Your hand to make great and to strengthen everyone."* (1 Chronicles 29:11,12)

So what is it that the scripture is speaking of in terms of the "work of His hands?"

The *"work of His hands"* begins with an understanding of His heart. But it goes beyond that to a grasp of His purposes. Throughout the history of God's people, we see the stories of lives that come into such a level of harmony and oneness with His purposes: that in the priorities, passions and purposes reflected by these people of God, there was not one vestige of variation between God's will and what their life purpose was accomplishing. Through their faith and the authority tied to their callings, these burden-bearers have played significant roles in divine alignments for set times. They were establishing the works of HIS hands through what they had embraced and what had been entrusted to them: which became the work of THEIR hands.

The work of His hands involves the redemption and restoration from the death and destruction wrought by the evil one over the centuries. It is the place to where the pivot point is the spiritual dimension in which God is the center. Jesus proclaimed that He came that we might have "life:" which interpreted is "zoe" or the "life of God." He also announced that He came to destroy the "works of the devil."

Over the centuries, despite the unruly and unrighteous caretakers who have perverted their power and deceived themselves and others, the fact is that the earth is the Lord's. Despite the devil's best intentions, dominion belongs to the Lord. And as His people who are called by His Name are humbling themselves and praying; the work of His hands is being manifested, as His Body is being strengthened and mobilized, and His choice of caretakers is factored into the equation.

The Divine Partnership and Faith

Burden-bearers operate in a divine partnership. It is a divine cooperation. It is a mark of that *"high calling"* described by Paul in Philippians 3. AND there comes a time: a time in which faith connects and gives birth.

Faith has phases. Faith is needed to grasp the reality of that which is not as though it were. Depending on the significance of what faith is tied to, faith then is needed to hang on during the times when there is no evidence of its manifestation other than what exists in our hearts. Then it is faith that eventually takes dominion, and is the facilitator of the birth of the promise.

Boom! It is where that which was hoped for gives birth to the reality. Faith will be an integral factor in determining the set time when God's purposes regarding the burden carried will be birthed.

The Gateway

For the burden-bearers, there exists a place in God BEYOND the "human ability to bear." Getting beyond that place involves serious struggle and pressure.

But entering that place in-God involves a choice. That choice involves NOT giving up. That choice involves not giving into despair or fear or unbelief or religious spirits of distortion. It is a choice involving a passage into that place in God in which you "*love not your life unto the death*," as referred to in Revelation.

It is a place of unwavering faith. It was exhibited by Shadrach, Meshach, and Abednego, when as they faced being thrown into Nebuchadnezzar's burning fiery furnace they boldly declared: "*Our God, Whom we serve is able to deliver us from the burning fiery furnace, and He will deliver us out of your hand, O king. But even if He does not, let it be known to you, O king, that we will not serve your gods or worship the golden image which you have set up!*" (Daniel 3:17,18)

Passing beyond the "human ability to bear" involves a level of faith reflected by the principle that "you can't hurt a dead man." That's the premise behind Galatians 2:20, that in the Lord, it is no longer our lives we live. For those called to be burden-bearers who WALK BEYOND a human ability to bear, there is a place of transition.

More often than not, this passageway involves a face-off with death; and will include a victory over what the psalmist refers to as "the throne of destruction." It is a place beyond which the "*accuser of the brethren*" no longer has power over the burden-bearer.

Passage beyond the "human ability to bear" involves a choice beyond just staying the course. The "human ability to bear" is based on a sensory level. Pure faith is based on the supernatural.

Over and over Proverbs points to the choice to move beyond the limiting constraints of the sensory-level, as the decision to choose wisdom. The decision to choose wisdom is based on the choice to rule your own spirit.

> "*A fool has no delight in understanding, but in expressing his own heart.*" Proverbs 18:2

> "*A fool vents all his feelings, but a wise man holds them back.*" Proverbs 29:11

> "*He who is slow to anger is better than the mighty and he who rules his own spirit than he who takes a city.*" Proverbs 16:32

I know of no genuine burden-bearers who knowingly walk in sin. There may be slippages along the way. There may be character imperfections, but not conscious sin. Religious spirits can create stumbling blocks for burden bearers with a preoccupation of flaw-seeking and perfectionism, which are far different than walking in sin.

The Entrance

Having bypassed the snares of the sensory, of religious spirits, unbelief, fear, offenses and the entanglements of mixed priorities; there is a place to where faith then surmounts the level that is "beyond a human ability to bear" and the connection is made to the supernatural acquisition of that which was first seen by faith. It is then that the birthing takes place.

It is a place of entering His supernatural rest; a place to where doubt and fear and unbelief no longer can take root. It is a place in His presence, to where HIS peace reflected by YOUR presence becomes your most lethal weapon in the assaults of the evil one. It is the place seen by Job where you "*will laugh at destruction and famine and not be afraid.*" It is a place marked by a cloak of humility, but simultaneously with an authority that consistently imparts the wisdom and purposes of God; and establishes the work of His hands.

It is place "in Him" to where "no weapon formed against you will prosper." A place to where the priorities of the world are but mere shadows because of the oneness of the heart of the burden-bearer with the One who called them. A place to where the connection is made that results in entering a flow of the supernatural.

In the midst of the build-up underway in our day are many faithful burden-bearers. Waiting. Faithfully waiting. Operating with burdens that are "beyond a human ability to bear." Ones who are enduring the pressures of carrying burdens that will tie together and release and give birth to initiatives and strategies of God for an appointed, set time.

Burdens that when birthed will be as dramatic as when Joseph the slave and prison inmate was promoted to rule over Egypt. Burdens that will result in birthing a significant paradigm shift tied to what the Lord is doing in this hour regarding revival, Israel and the response of His Body to the issues of dominion and establishing the work of His hands.

Our Role with Set Times

Set times have to do with an alignment of things. More often than not it involves a supernatural convergence of a number of independently operating factors; that in coming together creates the release of a strategic divine initiative. While the Lord always knows the end from the beginning, there is a role played by the burden-bearer or burden-bearers that will bear significantly on WHEN that set or appointed time will be.

In the case of Joseph, the set time involved his release from slavery and prison. But his encounter with the cup-bearer no doubt created the impetus whereby Joseph sought the Lord for the illumination needed to understand the elements involved when his release would manifest.

Because of the psalms he wrote, we know much more about the prayers of King David, who like Joseph played a strategic role as a burden-bearer in advancing God's Kingdom. David's prayers took him through years in which everything seemed to operate in reverse for him. But David had learned as a young shepherd what it meant to spend time in the presence of the Lord. He was a worshipper and one described by Scripture as a man after God's own heart.

David's years on the run were years as a burden-bearer. This was the time that followed Samuel anointing David to be king. They involved a process and an alignment of his prayers and his grasp of what his calling was designed to serve. Being described as a man after God's own heart clearly exhibited the oneness in vision and purpose with which David grasped his calling; and which played a significant role in birthing that calling. The birthing came when there was established a oneness of David's spiritual comprehension of his purpose in God with what God called him to do as king. The birthing also involved the alignment of factors involved that needed to come together for his promotion.

Also implied in this convergence that established the "set time" for both David and Joseph was the fact that the release from the "burden" was not the end in itself, but rather the gateway into the role God had for each of them for the rest of their days. The timing issues of Pharaoh's troubled dreams and when the clock began for the good years versus the years of famine hinged on Joseph's grasp of his role and the purpose for his life. It hinged on his grasp of why the scripture describing "the Word of the Lord tested him" also explains that "the Lord sent a man before them."

Understanding the Times: The Birthing

We live in an amazing generation!

Within this generation exists a committed and selfless remnant. A remnant of burden-bearers who will be promoted and serve as sparks to ignite the birthing of an age defined by the Lord as establishing the work of His hands. A remnant with leaders who will emerge as God's ambassadors; with the vision, wisdom and anointing to penetrate the seats of power of the world's infrastructures within their spheres. A remnant which will have among its midst those who will serve as community builders and nation-changers. A remnant which will be strong and do exploits; which will not be marked by human effort, but rather a flow of supernatural wisdom and the miraculous.

This IS an amazing generation. Over the last few decades we have witnessed an incredible transformation underway within the Body. It has been a transformation marked by the supernatural; a transformation marked by an alignment of those whose callings have grasped the heart of God and His initiatives and strategies regarding the land and people of Israel. It is a transformation that has involved the alignment needed for the release of a vibrant, mobilized Body equipped to go into every man's world. It is the transformation and alignment needed to release the greatest revival the world has ever seen.

There is a psalm that gives a picture of these times, that represents not only the heart-cry of David as the burden-bearer and burden-birther for his day; but its words were also prophetic in targeting the times being aligned before us. A time that for many burden-bearers within the Body today will represent a time of promotion: *"This is the generation of those who seek You, who seek Your face; even Jacob."*

CHAPTER 22

CONVERGENCE AND FULLNESS

Despite having passed my 60th birthday in 2003, my story is far from complete. But there is clearly a convergence and fullness that have come center-stage. It began as a walk of faith. It continues as a walk of faith. And after these many years, it seems as though the doors before us are becoming more and more strategic and meaningful.

I'm honored to be a part of a significant move of God in which what I refer to as "my story" is in reality the story of many, many others with like-callings. It is a move of God with a momentum that is just now getting fully underway. It is a move of God that will impact communities, shake nations and build His Kingdom.

In 2001, Carol and I incorporated our ministry Global Initiatives Foundation, to formalize the business-ministry thrust and role of proclaiming God's economy and mobilizing those called as Josephs and Daniels, those called to make an impact for God's Kingdom in the marketplaces of the world. The dreams and visions of my younger days are stronger today than they ever were before.

Many of the dreams I knew only from my prayer closet are emerging as bona fide agendas being directed from God's Throne Room. What I am today walking in is a direct result from the time I've spent with Him. The very pivotal prophetic word brought to me by my friend and co-laborer Barbara Fox, of being called to "map out, build up and bring wealth into Israel," is clearly in the process of being manifested.

While the focus of this book has targeted my own calling and the business-ministry equation, my wife Carol is a wonderful example of what the Lord is doing among those we label as the professional community: doctors, therapists, attorneys, accountants and the like. While Carol is a business woman who owns her own medical rehabilitation consulting firm, she is a psychotherapist-and certified EMDR trauma counselor by training.

At a time when most couples are making retirement plans, we each are finding the Lord's anointing is energizing us with Kingdom-focused opportunities that far exceed anything we have ever dreamed possible. As the opportunities to serve as a catalyst in implementing our "God's Economy Entrepreneurial Program" have increased in areas of persecution and distress, so have the opportunities for Carol's trauma-therapy ministry. During our business startup initiative in Belarus, she had therapy sessions lasting from early morning to midnight.

For us, it's about making a difference for the Lord in areas of distress and persecution, with a special focus on Israel and the Messianic Jewish community. There is also a mobilization factor involved in this calling.

I'm reminded of my good friend and co-laborer Peter Yesner. Peter is a CPA/CFO. He's been a business owner and currently is playing a central role in the growth of a $60 million operation. Peter also been involved in facilitating his wife Faith's anointed music ministry, as well as being the sound-man for the remarkable singing group Kol Simcha. Kol Simcha is an integral part of the FSU outreach festivals put on by Jonathan Bernis and Jewish Voice Ministries. Jonathan's efforts as a pioneer community builder have mobilized and strengthened the Messianic Jewish community across the Former Soviet Union.

Despite all that, Peter sensed there was something more to the fulfillment he sought as a committed believing businessman. Not long ago, during an interim crisis, Peter was given a copy of one of my unpublished manuscripts. The impact of what he read was such that he called and asked if we could spend some time together. So, he flew out for a weekend visit. During that time we shared and prayed together. The result was that the Lord touched Peter in a special way — and has added a completely new dimension to the focus of Peter's activities. Peter now travels with me, playing a key role in the God's economy business startup programs we put on.

The fact is that there is a unique dimension operating in what I've been called to do. Over the years, in instance after instance, I've been involved in bringing about unusual results in areas that I neither have the training nor the qualifications to do. What brings these results is the anointing of God operating within me. This operation of the anointing is tied to the fact that I've been willing to pay the cost: to pay the cost of spending time with Him. My sleep patterns are bizarre from a natural stance, but my passion is Him and spending time with Him.

What that also means is that I've been willing to pay the cost from an offensive rather than defensive standpoint. Spending time with Him includes spending time in His Word — and to embrace the truths of His Word, I set aside time each year to memorize significant portions of His Word. I know how to repent and I know how to forgive. But I also know how to stand in faith and be bold and unwavering — and God has given me the grace to know the difference in applying these truths. What I'm expressing is that my story is not about my talents or capabilities, although I may have a few, but the reality is that the life I am living is one that reflects a partnership I have with Almighty God.

My friend Bill Reese is a respected communications expert. Over the years, his firm has been a sought-after entity in high-profile complex court cases. His unique approach has become the premier means of communicating extremely complex cases to juries by means of understandable graphic summaries.

Bill does not fall short when it comes to being talented and capable. Yet he came to me recently and announced that "if Morris can do these things for the Kingdom, so can we!" He's right! Not only is he right, but that is the bottom line of my story. My story is about yielding ourselves to God and then entering into an adventure with Him, that becomes a cooperative effort. In so doing, we enter a fullness that is tied to walking into our real destiny.

When Paul wrote Timothy (II Tim 1) and admonished him to "stir up the gifts within him," he wasn't speaking to someone at the starting gate of his career. Timothy was the head of a congregation of 50,000 at the time Paul wrote him. Timothy, mentored by Paul was no slouch. Yet in the face of the incredible persecution of that day, Paul recognized there was something more for Timothy than the place at which he had arrived. He needed to grab hold of the big picture of what God was doing in that day — and DARE to press more into God in his quest to impact His community and build the Kingdom of God.

So, today we continue to seek God for the big picture and our role as instruments of His purpose. These marketplace activities are very much a part of the paradigm that can be expected for the days we have entered: with God's people providing answers and solutions during times of disruptions and upset.

The Lord indeed has His people positioned, networked and prepared.

As I ponder what lies ahead, I can't help but recall the specific time the Lord spoke to me about starting my own business. We were attending an Economics Club dinner. I recall the ride to that dinner. For no reason I could relate in the natural, I felt under extreme pressure. Something was brewing. Something was astir. As I shared this with Carol, she and I prayed before getting out of the car. Our conclusion was that there was a significant reason God had for us to be at that dinner. In retrospect, if I only knew!

The speaker was Otis Winters. At the time, Otis was the Executive Vice President of the fast-growth Williams Companies, as well as a respected believer in our community. As he spoke, the Lord simultaneously imparted to me something I was not expecting. Afterwards, I wrote this man of God who I had previously not met. That letter tells it all:

January 12, 1977

Mr. J. Otis Winters
Executive Vice President
The Williams Companies
320 South Boston
Tulsa, OK 74103

Dear Mr. Winters:

Due to obligations at home, my wife and I were unable to take the time after your talk at the Tulsa Economics Club dinner to thank you for your presentation.

Prior to our arrival last night, I had a real sense of expectancy that the Lord was going to use you to speak to me in a very special way. Through your talk He did just that.

Let me share briefly the Word I received. You used the analogy of a minnow swallowing a whale to illustrate what took place when Williams Brothers took over Great Lake Pipeline. The Lord said to me: "Attempt something so big that unless I (God) intervene, it is bound to fail." Then you noted the extraordinary timing associated with each of the moves made by Joe Williams. The Lord then said: "Be sensitive to Me and then obedient by responding to the initial promptings of my Holy Spirit." You then noted how the Williams Company had recently streamlined itself to focus its goals and how it has gone through a growth cycle to where it is totally different in function from which it was being reorganized to do only 10 years ago. The Lord spoke and said: "You are an instrument of my purpose. Keep your eyes on Me and I will mold you, shape you, and streamline you for what I have chosen you to do. I will do this in such a way that there will be a time when you will hardly recognize the former things. Because of that, I will receive the glory."

Thank you also for being a man of God who lets it be known that he is a man of God. Most of all let me thank you for being led by the Spirit of God in what you had to say. It was personally very meaningful to me.

Yours in Christ,

Morris E. Ruddick

That's how it started.

But then God is no respecter of persons. What He has done for me, He can — and maybe already has begun doing for you!

Believe God by attempting something bigger than you might undertake on your own. Stay close to the Lord — listen to Him, and don't hesitate in being obedient. Likewise, don't expect the latter end of your calling to be as it was in the beginning.

These are indeed strategic times for God's purposes. There is much change in the wind. We, like other key persons called into the marketplace as God's emissaries and ambassadors, will be serving to make a difference in terms of God's agendas, while we are here.

We are going to make a difference not necessarily because of our talents and abilities — although we might have a few; but we are going to make a difference because He has put His Spirit within us. He has prepared us and enabled us in ways that insure that we are not limited by the parameters of our own minds and abilities and experiences. Rather, as we work in oneness with Him, we will be entrusted with incredible opportunities and ventures — and will be used mightily in the accomplishment of His eternal purposes.

No doubt many of us with this calling are approaching the time when God's years of molding, shaping and streamlining will result in us hardly recognizing the format of our earlier days. For my calling in the marketplace, it is as a modern-day Joseph-Daniel Calling.

For others, their marketplace calling may be an entrepreneurial calling like Abraham, Isaac or Jacob. Or a Nehemiah calling to rebuild. Whatever the calling or however it is defined, it is about extending His Kingdom rule into the marketplace in order to bring forth His redemptive purposes.

It's about the reality of the Lord operating in our midst. It's about yielding ourselves to be used as instruments of His purpose — to impact communities, change nations and build His Kingdom.

Oftentimes as we proceed in this walk of faith, we simply have to take it a day at a time. But God, who is always faithful, will connect the dots. He will bring things together in a way that is always *"far exceedingly abundantly above all that we might ask, think or even imagine."*

So, as we move into these times of discontinuities — and opportunities, it is a time to rejoice. In this move in the marketplace, the Lord is releasing plans formed long ago and moving us onto the offensive!

As we enter these most challenging and unprecedented times, the Lord God Almighty is going to release and entrust us with new Kingdom opportunities — and use us mightily in the accomplishment of His purposes. It will be as outlined in Malachi 3:18: *Then you shall again discern between the righteous and the wicked, between the one who serves God and the one who does not serve Him.*

Just like Joseph and Daniel, Nehemiah, and Abraham, Isaac and Jacob of old, God's marketplace emissaries for this day will be in the direct center of the discontinuities — with solutions. Chosen and prepared men and women of God, who will impact nations and offer practical solutions that minister to the people of the world in the Name of the Lord.

God's economy, Israel and the nations: it will be as it was foretold in Zechariah 8:13: *So I will save you, and you shall be a blessing. Do not fear, let your hands be strong.*

AUTHOR

Morris E. Ruddick

A long-time ministry associate described Morris Ruddick with these words: "He heads several organizations and corporate entities, including Global Initiatives Foundation, The Ruddick Int'l Group, and a global intercession network. He has led development of entrepreneurial activities in critical needy areas and brought together business and ministry initiatives in several nations, with a focus impacting the Jewish community in Israel, Ethiopia and the Former Soviet Union."

Mr. Ruddick's Kingdom agendas reflect a unique merging of the secular and the spiritual with initiatives based on biblical principles of business. Since 1995, he has been at the forefront of encouraging and mobilizing spiritually-minded business leaders to step out in faith in employing their talents to build communities and impact their nations. He has been a national speaker and workshop leader for the National Religious Broadcasters, the GCOWE Missions Conference, the Marketplace Ministry Leader's Summit; and is a member of the editorial advisory board of the *Journal of Ministry Marketing and Management.* Mr. Ruddick has authored *The Joseph-Daniel Calling and Wealth Transfer*, as well as numerous articles on spiritual warfare, God's move in the marketplace, and the dynamics of markets undergoing change.

His Kingdom business initiatives have included workshops, plans and the birthing of business startups designed to help persecuted believers across the globe. He has also helped organize and launch a consortium of humanitarian aid for persecuted Jews immigrating to Israel. Mr. Ruddick is co-founder of two internet ministries, one networking believers and the other a distance learning school on prayer. He is a member of the Messianic Jewish Alliance and has been on the board of Marilyn Hickey Ministries and Orchard Road Christian Center since 1991. He served as Corporate Secretary of the International Christian Chamber of Commerce-USA and is a board member of Love Botswana Outreach Mission. He is the Executive Director/Co-Founder of the Strategic Intercession Global Network, an internet intercession ministry designed to address strategic level issues impacting the Church globally.

Over the years, he has served executive suite management with his planning and strategy development talents in a diversity of progressive mid-sized operations, ministry groups, and Fortune 500 companies. He has been at the helm of designing and implementing two successful corporate turnarounds, one being for a $1.4 billion firm. His specialty for both the business and ministry spheres is in evaluating *the dynamics impacting changing and emerging markets*. Mr. Ruddick has contributed to the development of a number of venture capital agendas. Clients served include names such as: Xerox Corporation; The US Postal Service; Smith International; CBN; Israel's Technology Incubator Program, Derek Prince Ministries; Brown & Root; TRW; Telecommunications Inc.; The Inspirational Network; FirsTier Banks; Far East Livingston Shipyard; Callidus, PAX TV; Goodyear; Nippon Kokan; Southwestern Bell; and many others.

His time as a US Marine Corps officer included missions behind enemy lines, as well as serving as a senior battalion advisor with the Vietnamese Marine Corps during the height of the Vietnamese conflict. He headed up the mobile training team/program that prepared parachute- scuba-qualified Marines (Force Recon) for reconnaissance and special operations in enemy territory. Mr. Ruddick was awarded the Silver Star, two Bronze Stars, the Navy Commendation Medal and the Vietnamese Medal of Honor for his actions in combat. He holds ordination papers from the United Christian Ministerial Association, a BS from Northwestern University; and an MS in communications and doctoral work in statistics. He has completed Southern Methodist University's Senior Management Program; as well as a year of biblical studies at a leading Christian University.

CONTACT INFORMATION

To contact the author
to speak at your conference or gathering of marketplace ministers,
please write

Morris Ruddick
Global Initiatives Foundation
P.O. Box 370291
Denver, CO 80237 USA

or email:

info@strategic-initiatives.org

or call 303.741.9000 and leave a message

You may wish to visit the Global Initiatives Foundation website. It
contains additional articles and information.
The website address is :

http://www.strategic-initiatives.org

Printed in the United States
87256LV00004B/109-501/A

9 781594 679032